Reforming Protestantism

Reforming Protestantism

Christian Commitment in Today's World

DOUGLAS F. OTTATI

Westminster John Knox Press
Louisville, Kentucky

Book and cover design by Alec Bartsch

First edition

Published by Westminster John Knox Press
Louisville, Kentucky

This book is printed on acid-free paper that meets the American National Standards Institute. Z39.48 standard. ∞

PRINTED IN THE UNITED STATES OF AMERICA

95 96 97 98 99 00 01 02 03 04 — 10 9 8 7 6 5 4 3 2 1

Library of Congress Cataloging-in-Publication Data

Ottati, Douglas F.
    Reforming Protestantism : Christian commitment in today's world /
Douglas F. Ottati. — 1st ed.
      p.   cm.
    Includes bibliographical references and index.
    ISBN 0-664-25604-X
    1. Liberalism (Religion)—United States—History. 2. Liberalism (Religion)—Protestant churches—History. 3. Christianity and culture. 4. United States—Church history. I. Title.
BR515.088 1995
280'.4'0973—dc20   95-10454

For
F.C.O.

Contents

Preface

M y purpose in this book is to explicate, promote, deepen, and extend the dynamic spirit of a particular Christian movement. The movement is what I call reforming Protestantism in America. Historically, it has extended from various Puritans through evangelicals, progressives, and realists. It has developed representative ecclesiastical associations where laypeople exercise significant powers and also are equipped and encouraged to participate in every aspect of the wider society. At different times and in different circumstances, the reforming movement has spawned Bible commonwealths, revivals, mission societies, Sunday schools, public schools, colleges, universities, journals, ecumenical organizations, and more. Indeed, a disproportionately large share of American business and political leadership has been drawn from its ranks. By reforming Protestantism, then, I mean a religious movement in America that long has enjoyed an aspect of cultural hegemony or "quasi-establishment"; I mean the living religious heritage of what some sociologists now call "old-stream" or "old-line" Protestantism in America.

The word *spirit* points toward something a bit more difficult to grasp. By it I mean a socially formed and transmitted wisdom or way of negotiating life that is rooted in a particular historical movement. I mean a matter of devotion but not only devotion, belief but not only belief, and activity but not only activity. As I understand it, the spirit of reforming Protestantism is a historically particular and characteristic formation of affect, imagination, and responsibility that disposes persons and communities to interpret, engage, and order their environments in a certain way. It is a particular temper or cast of mind, a practical attitude, stance, or posture.

More specifically, the spirit endemic to the reforming movement is a

theocentric (God-centered) and Christ-formed attitude of faithful participation in the world. It is a manner of living reordered and reformed by
a radical devotion to God and God's transformative purpose in Jesus
Christ; by an imaginative vision of God's all-inclusive reign, commonwealth, or city; and by an active tendency or disposition of responsibility
to all things in their appropriate interrelations with God and one another.
It is a critical temper or cast of mind rooted in the conviction that all persons, communities, and institutions are infected by sin's corruption. It is
an optimistic and generous spirit, uplifted by the sense that, despite sin's
corruption, grace abounds. The spirit of reforming Protestantism consists
of a faithfulness at home in the midst of things that is marked by a responsibly realistic effort to restrain evil and a creatively responsible attempt
to pursue good. It contains a practical wisdom borne by churches caught
up in dynamic interrelationships with other communities and institutions.
It is an active stance that comes to expression when we try both to sanctify the ordinary and to discipline the spiritual by holding together the
calling to be a Christian and our many other mundane callings and vocations.

Any attempt to further this distinctive spirit must come to grips with
the fact that, too often, the activities of reforming Protestants have been
unfaithful. The reforming movement in America has displayed troubling
tendencies toward the accommodation of predominant ethnic, class, regional, and political interests. It too often has contributed to racist, anti-
Catholic, anti-Semitic, and sexist attitudes and actions. A theology for reforming Protestantism must therefore exhibit a thoroughly self-critical
dimension. It must help equip and encourage reforming Protestants and
their communities in the discipline of repentance and the confession of
sin. Indeed, it should insist that without this discipline there can be no
faithfulness, no genuine renewal.

I am also aware that my own attempt to further the distinctive spirit of
reforming Protestantism comes during a time of significant transition, realignment, and restructuring in American religion. A spate of recent
books, articles, and denominational reports points toward something
called "mainstream Protestant decline," or what I prefer to regard as an
important shift in the cultural location of reforming Protestantism in
America. Many argue that, in effect, the reforming movement now has
been decisively disestablished and de-centered. It certainly has become
culturally less prominent.

I see little reason either to mourn or to celebrate this development. I
do not mourn it because I think that the prerogatives of mainline status
have not always brought out the best in reforming Protestants and because
our displacement may correlate with a realistic and potentially healthy rec-

ognition of the pluralism of American society. I do not celebrate it because I am enough a child of the reforming movement to believe that
some of its past achievements have been both faithful and considerable,
and because I do not see that our current recognition of cultural displacement, by itself, must be either purifying or invigorating. It may, after all, become the occasion for a new defensiveness or even a new otherworldliness.

My primary concern is for the continuing dynamism and integrity of
the reforming movement and its distinctive spirit. Will we retreat from
our participatory commitment now that we no longer occupy the center
of American culture? Will we relinquish our faithful activism, our distinctive quality of Christian commitment *in* the world, now that we no
longer are in control? I believe that during the present rather awkward period of transition, reforming Protestants are especially vulnerable to attitudes and currents that neither appreciate nor advance their distinctive and
living heritage. Indeed, we seem chronically to underappreciate the present prospects for a timely reformation and retrieval of our own particular
spirit of faithful participation.

That, essentially, is why I have written this book. I know that a somewhat scholarly theological volume cannot precipitate a widespread renewal of reforming piety and commitment, but I hope it can make a contribution. I hope it will suggest how a genuinely theocentric and faithfully
participatory stance can continue to make a vital witness.

I also hope that, although it is directed toward the self-understanding
of a particular Christian movement, my book will claim wider interest and
attention. This partially reflects the reforming movement's characteristic
ecumenical and dialogical commitments. Any attempt to explicate and
promote its distinctive spirit necessarily enters into conversation with diverse figures and traditions. A theology for reforming Protestantism is always also a Christian theology that tries to remain open to truthful insights
wherever they may be found as it seeks to illumine our human condition
in relation to God.

However, there also is a sense in which an appreciation for the distinctive spirit of reforming Protestantism remains important in order to
understand American society and culture at large. Within a secular and
post-Christian European community, after all, there is a sense in which
one may argue that to understand Sweden one must also understand
Lutheranism and to understand France one must also understand Roman
Catholicism. Even a post-Protestant America will not be adequately understood apart from the spirit of reforming Protestantism. Although we
are no longer Puritan-centered, we remain at least Puritan-haunted.

These purposes, suppositions, and hopes inform the chapters that follow. Chapters 1 and 2 set out the faithfully participatory spirit of reforming Protestantism in relation to the movement's history and present challenges. Chapter 3 gives a preliminary account of reforming theology as a mode of reflection in the service of that spirit or interactive orientation. Chapter 4 shows how the dynamic of sin and grace combines attitudes of pessimism and optimism in a way that lends to the stance of faithful participation the twin qualities of responsible realism and creative responsibility. Chapter 5, "The Church In, With, Against, and For the World," argues that, in a reforming perspective, the relationship between church and world is multivalent and dynamic. Indeed, I claim that only such a church truly bears the spirit of faithful participation and is able to help equip and form persons as faithful participants. Chapter 6 shows how the theme of calling and vocation points to both the sanctification of the ordinary and the mundane disciplining of the spiritual as complementary dimensions of the spirit of reforming Protestantism.

I have many people and institutions to thank as I bring this project to completion. During the summer of 1991, my work was supported by a stipend from the Louisville Institute for the Study of Protestantism and American Culture. I am also grateful to the Institute's Executive Director, James W. Lewis, for continuing opportunities to be in conversations with sociologists and historians about the changing shape of religion in America. T. Hartley Hall IV, the recently retired president of Union Theological Seminary in Virginia, worked together with an able dean, board of trustees, administration, staff, and faculty to sustain a supportive context for learning, teaching, and writing.

A study group called Presbyterian Theological Work Group, funded by a grant from the Lilly Endowment, and organized by Merwyn Johnson, patiently read and discussed two essays that eventually made their way into this volume. David Klemm, Terence Martin, Richard Miller, and Charles Wilson read and commented on significant parts of the manuscript, as have my colleagues at Union, Charles E. Brown, William P. Brown, Donald G. Dawe, H. McKennie Goodpasture, James M. Smylie, Charles M. Swezey, and Rebecca Harden Weaver. So have James Calvin Davis, John W. Ehman, Jeremy M. Grant, Martha L. Moore-Keish, William Stewart Rawson, Robert T. Snell, and Timothy Allen Verhey—all of them students at Union while this book was being written. Max L. Stackhouse and David Tracy read and commented on all of it. And no one would have read any of it had Kathy Davis not "word processed" and Millie Burks not copied a seemingly endless series of drafts.

Portions of chapters 1 and 2 were published in *The Christian Century* as "The Spirit of Reforming Protestantism" (December 16, 1992) and "Conservatives, Progressives, and the Spirit of Reforming Protestantism"

(July 28–August 4, 1993). A version of chapter 5 was presented as a Francis Youngker Vosburgh Lecture at the Theological School of Drew University in October of 1993, and I should like especially to thank Robin W. Lovin (then dean of the Theological School) for his helpful counsel and good hospitality on that and other occasions.

This is an appropriate place to say that I have learned a great deal from Stanley Hauerwas (who also read and commented on my entire manuscript), at first through his writings, then also in engaging conversations. The reader may note that we differ significantly, but not entirely. I am also particularly grateful for the regular theological discussions I have had about this book and much more with Paul E. Capetz, J. Frederick Holper, Douglas Schuurman, and William Schweiker.

Things are different, however, with my wife Pamela and my children, Katherine and Albert. They have made no direct contribution to this project at all, thus ensuring that many of my most significant debts remain entirely unacademic. Finally, and very important to me, although not many books about Protestant theology in America have been dedicated to a Brazilian father and the joys of *jogo bonito,* this one is. Take it as another sign of the restructuring of American religion.

1

The Spirit of Reforming Protestantism

A many-sided debate about Christianity and American culture is being carried on by camps whose religious and moral visions seem worlds apart. The debate proceeds both in public and in private conflicts of conscience. It often concentrates on understandings of family and sexuality, the place of religion in education, or the relation between Christian ethics and domestic and international policy. Occasionally it touches on broader questions of the church's role in public life.

In recent years, the debate has become increasingly heated and polemical, as is apparent to anyone who has followed the last two presidential campaigns or the recent national assemblies of prominent denominations. Sociologists point to genuine hostility between two main groups: one comprises fundamentalists, evangelicals, and religious conservatives; the other consists of religious liberals, progressives, and humanists. This in turn is closely related to talk of a "deep cultural divide" or "cultural cleavage," and to struggles to define both America and its soul.[1]

The contentious climate is not likely to dissipate very quickly. For one thing, fractiousness is by definition an element of "mainstream Protestant decline." The present pluralistic environment makes it nearly impossible to conjure up a united Protestant front at the religious and moral center of American society. As the nation has become more and more ethnically and religiously diverse, as Roman Catholicism in the Americas has emerged to champion elements of the historic liberal agenda, as conservative Protestantism has made an impressive "post-Scopes Trial" bid to become a culture-shaping force, and as growing numbers of Americans find spiritual meaning in experiences, explorations, and ideas apart from established institutional forms, the cultural mainline—the mainstream, or whatever one prefers to call it—simply has become too fragmented for that.[2] For better and worse, American Protestantism clearly is not united today, if indeed it ever was. Americans have begun to face the strong claims to attention of other traditions and perspectives, and American society finds itself without any obvious, common, or implicit religious/ideological backdrop.

My chief concern in this book is not what all of this may mean for the ethos of the American nation, the moral fabric of American society at large, or the quality of its public discourse—important questions being addressed today by everyone from Pat Robertson to William Greider, James Davison Hunter, Stephen Carter, and innumerable columnists and politicians. It is rather to provide a theological interpretation of the vital spirit and commitment of "reforming Protestantism," a particular strain of Christian piety that is not a product of current "culture wars" and that often seems lost in the scuffle.[3] In a sense, my purpose is to *reform* reforming Protestantism itself. I propose to provide a normative theological interpretation of its vital commitment, an interpretation that will identify and advance the distinctive form of faithfulness that ought to characterize the reforming movement in America today.

Reforming Piety

It is important to begin with first principles. Reforming Protestantism is theocentric. Its leading affirmation is that first and foremost, we belong to God. By this first principle, reforming piety means *metanoia:* not thinking first about ourselves and our isolated groups, but being caught up in the messianic event of Jesus Christ—the person-for-others who embodies a way in life oriented by radical devotion to God, the Word who discloses the faithful God-for-others. Reforming piety means that the earth is the Lord's and that we are not our own. It means that genuine faithfulness is a living-for-others, a life reordered and reformed by the messianic pattern of devotion to God and God's all-inclusive commonwealth.

Thus, from the very outset we see that the theocentric piety of reforming Protestantism affirms the transformative lordship of Jesus Christ, and I can think of no more appropriate understanding of that lordship than Allan Boesak's:

> Christ is the Lord of all life, even in those situations where his lordship is not readily recognized by wilful humans. . . . All of life is indivisible, just as God is indivisible, and in all of life—personal and public, politics and

economics, sports and art, science and liturgy—the Reformed Christian seeks the lordship of Christ.[4]

All of life is to be reordered and reformed. That is why reforming Protestantism always entails a Christian commitment *in* the world.

This basic insistence reflects a number of further convictions. Reforming piety affirms that we are created good, equipped for an abundant and good life together in God's encompassing reign, and fitted and sustained for conscious and responsible interrelations with God and others. Our chief end, we might say, is to enjoy communion with God in community with others. Caught in the grips of a warping tendency, we become narrowed, curved in upon ourselves, unresponsive, irresponsible, and isolated. Community with neighbor and communion with God are broken. Sin is a radical corruption of what we are equipped and sustained to be, a turning away from God and God's interdependent commonwealth, a dimunition and fragmentation of the abundant and good life that befits us. Where this goes unrecognized, then so do the corruptions and the persistently destructive tendencies of persons, communities, and institutions.

The good news of the gospel is that the faithful God refuses to abandon creatures to sinful corruption. In Jesus Christ, we are enabled to turn again toward God and the inclusive commonwealth of interdependent neighbors; we are restored to our chief end. In Jesus Christ, God's great faithfulness extends to sinners, to those who betray the fundamental vocation for which they are fitted and sustained. Thus, if sin means derangement, grace means rearrangement. If sin means inordinate constriction, grace means enlargement. If sin means the brokenness of human relationships to each other and to God, then grace means the transforming divine power and initiative that overcomes brokenness and that elicits a new responsiveness to God and neighbor. Grace means regeneration: the conversion, restoration, and rehabilitation of faithful participants in the divine commonwealth. Grace means the renewal of genuine communion. Where the possibility of grace goes unrecognized, so too does the promise of persons, communities, and institutions.

Within the frame of reforming Protestantism, then, all are subject to criticism even as all are affirmed. All are summoned to repentance and new life. Indeed, those who consciously acknowledge God's transformative way with the world in Jesus Christ are called to reform all persons, communities, and institutions by relating them both critically and constructively to God and to one another. They are called to denounce and restrain corruption, and to announce and pursue promising possibilities for genuine communion and renewal. They are called to participate faithfully in God's world. The spirit of reforming Protestantism, then, is a theocentric piety that issues in a commitment or bias toward faithful participation in God's encompassing reign or inclusive commonwealth.

A Rich and Varied Heritage

This reforming spirit has a rich American heritage of varied theological expressions and institutional embodiments. Indeed, different elements or dimensions of reforming piety have been drawn out and emphasized at different times and under different circumstances. For our purposes here, however, we should recognize that these changing emphases may be understood as varied accents or dialects of the same dynamic orientation and bias toward faithful participation.

PURITAN BEGINNINGS

Reforming Protestantism's American pilgrimage began when a wide spectrum of Puritans, holding to the theocentric belief that all of life should be reordered in relation to the reign of the sovereign God, emigrated to a "new world" where they might make explicit a new social order and form its predominant ethos. In response to challenges of common purpose, identity, and stable institutions, transplanted congregationalists, separatists, Anglicans, and Quakers devised holy commonwealths. During this initial period, then, the faithfully participatory spirit of reforming Protestantism came to mean contributing to the work of social construction.[5]

From the Bible colonies of New England to nonconformist Rhode Island to William Penn's "Holy Experiment" in Pennsylvania, this constructive work was guided by variations of a broad principle of Christian constitutionalism that furnished mutually accepted structures of responsibility and freedom under God. The first, and most famous, expression of Christian constitutionalism was the Mayflower Compact of 1620. By signing that document, the Pilgrims committed themselves to a common enterprise. They claimed that "in ye name of God" they had undertaken "a voyage to plant" a colony "for ye glorie of God, & advancement of ye Christian faith." They promised "solemnly & mutually in ye presence of God, & one another, [to] covenant and combine our selves together into a civill body politik for our better ordering & preservation, & furtherance of ye ends aforesaid." Furthermore they pledged "to enacte, constitute, & frame such just & equall lawes, ordinances, acts, constitutions, & offices, from time to time, as shall be thought most meete & convenient for ye generall good of ye Colonie, unto which we promise all due submission & obedience."[6]

Soon a basic and implicit assumption of this constitutional principle was significantly challenged and revised. Roger Williams, whose life was changed in unanticipated ways by his banishment from Massachusetts and consequent founding of Providence, claimed that it was "the express duty of the civil magistrate" to remove enforced "payments and tithes" to support ministers, as well as all religious oaths and ceremonies from courts of law. Moreover, he insisted that the magistrate should support "a free and absolute permission of the consciences of all men, in what is merely spiritual, not the very consciences of the Jews, nor the consciences of Turks or Papists, or pagans themselves excepted."[7] Representing Massachusetts' orthodoxy, John Winthrop and John Cotton argued that, since sinful human consciences are prone to error, the magistrate legitimately places limits on religious toleration. Williams countered that, as the magistrates themselves are therefore also likely to err, the only appropriate civil limits are those that prevent persons from unjustly injuring one another.[8] The question of freedom of religious expression also was raised by Anne Hutchison's claims to an immediate revelation of God's Spirit.[9]

Williams's revision proved to be a harbinger. Prompted by the experiences and convictions of congregationalists, separatists, Quakers, Baptists, and humanistic deists, by fears of established intolerance, and by the exigencies of living together in an ecclesiastically diverse society, reforming Protestants came to affirm the independence of the church from institutions of civil government. Baptists eventually were joined by Presbyterians, as well as by statesmen such as Thomas Jefferson and James Madison, in an ultimately successful fight against religious favoritism in Virginia. This had a direct bearing on the religion clauses of the First Amendment to the Constitution of the United States.[10]

No single ecclesiastical blueprint emerged from all of this, although the general result proved immensely important for the institutional pattern of reforming Protantism in the American context. Early American Protestants invented denominations: voluntary, relatively fluid religious associations centered on congregational tasks of preaching, teaching, and care (discipline). These distinctly American ecclesiastical institutions developed diverse internal structures and made important contributions to the broad separation of powers that became characteristic of the new republic. They envisioned themselves at the religious and moral center of the emerging society, even as they also implied and sustained an environment able to tolerate a significant measure of predominately Protestant theological diversity. They depended on voluntary patterns of participation and support and consequently proved remarkably sensitive to and engaged in the sociocultural contexts, values, and concerns of their lay constituents.

EVANGELICAL PROTESTANTISM

In a subsequent period, characterized by emancipated individuals, westward expansion, and relaxed social conventions, the reforming movement turned toward an invigorating apprehension of renovating grace in Christ. Evangelicals joined heirs of earlier Puritans and emphasized personal conversion toward God and neighbor. Thus figures such as Jonathan Edwards, John Wesley, George Whitefield, Lyman Beecher, and Charles Finney held a common assumption that fallen persons need to be reoriented and redirected toward the true good by the rule of Christ in human hearts and wills. The essence of Christ's reign was faith working by love, a dynamic that came to be expressed in varied ways by John Woolman's universal love to fellow creatures, Edwards's true virtue, Wesley's reverence for life, and Samuel Hopkins's principle of disinterested benevolence, as well as in ideas about holiness, Christian perfection, and "entire sanctification."

The evangelical period thus marked an important shift in predominant social vision. Through waves of revivals, evangelists aimed to win not only individuals but also the nation for Christ. The reforming spirit of faithful participation now came to mean manifesting the fruits of a new birth in qualities of character and in voluntary social involvements. The result they hoped would be "Christian America," a chosen and righteous nation, a beacon to the world.

Denominations now took on the form of missionary societies, producing a steady stream of preachers, church founders, and educators aimed at the formation of Christian character and conviction. This redirection of persons in Christ supported a new voluntarism that assumed a variety of institutional embodiments. Evangelical Protestants established worshiping congregations, as well as Sunday schools that soon became familiar features of American culture. They organized public or "common" schools and colleges, as well as voluntary societies concerned with everything from religious tracts regarding "salvation" and pamphlets against the use of alcohol and tobacco, to the character formation of youth, women's rights, prison reform, better hospitals, and peace.[11]

With the rise of abolitionism, the new nation experienced what Sidney E. Ahlstrom called "its first truly fundamental moral encounter," one that divided the country in civil war, as well as many of the Protestant churches.[12] The issue put the meaning of "Christian America" to a severe test of substance, and the results were decidedly troubling. At one level, the new voluntarism could be relatively impressive. Antislavery societies and sentiments had been present in the country since the 1770s, particularly among Quakers, and the American Anti-Slavery Society was organized at Philadelphia in 1831. Amid increasingly polarized attitudes and suppressed slave rebellions, prophetic and politically aware witnesses were put forth by Protestant leaders such as William Lloyd Garrison, Angelina and Sarah Grimke, and Theodore Dwight Weld.[13] Harriet Beecher Stowe, herself "an able lay theologian," wrote *Uncle Tom's Cabin,* a book of immense influence for the antislavery cause.[14] In general, however, the mainstream denominations, ever responsive to the opposing interests and sensitivities of their constituencies, found prophetic stands elusive, exceptions being the Congregationalists, Unitarians, and Universalists, whose constituencies were almost entirely northern. Southern church leaders, including one at my own seminary, offered impassioned defenses and apologies for slavery as an institution.[15]

Nonetheless, the abolitionist movement enlisted the energies of a number of feminists such as Elizabeth Cady Stanton, Susan B. Anthony, and Lucretia Mott, an experience of public leadership that focused their attention on human rights and institutions. In 1848, the Seneca Falls Declaration insisted on the equality of women and men in marriage, ministry, property, and more. Antionette Brown became the first fully ordained woman in a mainstream denomination (Congregational), in 1853. And in the sermon he preached on that occasion, the Rev. Luther Lee, a well-known Wesleyan Methodist, made the following claim. "I have now proved that there were a class of females in the Primitive Church called prophetesses, that is, there were female prophets, and these prophets were preachers or public teachers of religion."[16] Lucretia Mott, who was a minister in the Society of Friends, held that women in the church had been subordinated by priestcraft, while the Methodist advocate of temperance, Frances Willard, noted that Jesus' utterances and actions point in the direction of opening all positions in the church to women.[17]

By mid-century, the influx of immigrant labor also began to command attention in the industrial north, and because many of the immigrants were Roman Catholic, the meaning of the word "Christian" in "Christian America" again was tested with less than satisfactory results. Protestants argued over whether religious instruction in the public or "common" schools should accommodate Catholic interests, and few were sympathetic to Catholic schools. The Protestant League (later renamed the Christian Alliance), which included ministers such as Lyman Beecher, Joel Hawes, and Horace Bushnell among its prominent supporters, vacillated between plainly anti-Catholic aims and the hope that Protestants together with Catholic liberals would modify Roman authoritarianism. Many Protestant leaders, accustomed to making the case for religion in patriotic terms, believed that Catholicism imperiled America itself.[18]

THE PROGRESSIVE ERA

The rise of "new knowledge," especially in the forms of Darwinian biology, historical investigation, and emerging social sciences, combined with the advent of industrial America to constitute something of a watershed in the story of the reforming movement during the later nineteenth and early twentieth centuries. Ecclesiastical responses were varied and deeply divided. Essentially, however, the reforming spirit of faithful participation came to mean a progressive willingness to reformulate and revise inherited theologies and ethics in order to engage these new developments. Liberal scholars and theologians questioned such things as traditional ascriptions of biblical authorship, the historicity of Adam and Eve, and the appropriateness of classical doctrines, as they attempted to interpret texts, figures, communities, and dogmas in relation to historical settings and new scientific theories. Proponents of the social gospel movement drew on new interpretations of Jesus and the prophets, recent currents in sociology, economics, and political science.

Most Protestant progressives shared important elements of the evangelical vision of "Christian America," although they modified it by understanding society as a web of interdependent interests and relations, rather than a simple collection of individuals to be won for Christ. That perception of organic unity helped to energize criticisms of competitive individualism and laissez faire capitalism, as well as attempts to elicit commitment to new possibilities for reforming the social order. In its effort to address an age of industry characterized by massive suffering and an expanded matrix of economic relations, the social gospel made use of the evangelical themes of renovation, conversion, and benevolence, but combined these with ideas of social discipleship. The movement included interdenominational spokespersons such as Josiah Strong, reform-minded sociologists such as Albion Small, moderate theological ethicists such as Francis Greenwood Peabody, directors of urban settlement houses for immigrants and the poor such as Jane Addams, and radicals such as George D. Herron, who once expounded "The Political Economy of the Lord's Prayer."

Richard T. Ely, an economist with theological interests, developed an idea of "social solidarity" that he claimed had roots not only in contemporary social philosophy and sciences but also in biblical notions of the disobedience of all in Adam and the redemption of all in Christ. Walter Rauschenbusch, the movement's leading exponent, regarded God's kingdom as the divinely empowered, inherently social reality at the center of Jesus' teaching and mission. The kingdom, said Rauschenbusch, is a dynamic *telos* of mutual service and cooperation that opposes sin's "private kingdom of self-service." Upheld by the Spirit, the church is the kingdom's emissary, and it pursues a prophetic mission to the whole of society by encouraging human impulses toward greater solidarity through the formation of persons' characters, the exemplary organization of its internal affairs, the promotion of humane attitudes and customs, and support for useful public institutions and reforms. In short, the principle of the kingdom entailed "a thorough regeneration and reconstitution of social life."[19]

Many of these impulses gained important institutional footholds in seminaries and divinity schools before the United States entered World War I. They also led to the creation of *The Christian Century* (as a nondenominational liberal journal), the adoption of social creeds and offices of social service in a number of denominational bureaucracies, and the establishment of the ecumenical and reform-minded Federal Council of Churches. The cumulative influence was impressive.

> The social gospel tradition . . . [was] reflected in the training of ministers, the staffing of denominational agencies, and the operations of the Federal Council of Churches, whose presidents were all drawn from its ranks. Although the social gospel found its largest following among Congregational, Methodist, Disciples, and Presbyterian leaders, it made inroads in the Episcopal, Baptist, and Lutheran denominations as well.[20]

Nonetheless, liberal, socially active, and ecumenical progressives clearly did not represent American Protestantism as a whole. Indeed, partly in response to their advances, fundamentalism had emerged as early as the 1870s, and pamphlets called *The Fundamentals* began to appear in 1910. The Churches of Christ, emphasizing opposition to instrumental music and biblical inerrancy, broke with The Disciples of Christ in 1906. A series of secessions and expulsions from Methodist ranks contributed to the formation of The Church of the Nazarene, with its emphasis on holiness and an initial aversion to higher learning. Further Methodist divisions contributed to the first national meeting of Pentecostals, who emphasized the outpouring of the Spirit as a sign of Christ's imminent return, as well as a belief in scriptural infallibility.

These divisions proved lasting and serious. Even as the fundamentalist controversy reached the boiling point among Presbyterians and Northern Baptists during the 1920s, progressives entered into expanded ecumenical ventures aimed at recognizing and cooperating with Roman Catholics and Jews in American society.[21] In subsequent decades they continued to respond to the encounter with modernity, while fundamentalists "organized new denominations and Bible schools, and developed ministries aimed at individuals and groups hungering for traditional faith."[22]

PROTESTANT REALISM

The reforming movement entered its "post-liberal" phase during a period marked by severe economic depression, World War II, and the emergence of the United States to international prominence. As totalitarian
regimes swept into control of powerful European states, Protestant realists sought to disentangle Christian ethics from unholy alliances with the
social programs and interests of Western civilizations. Invigorated by a renewed appreciation for the meaningfulness of classical theological symbols
and ideas, theologians and ethicists such as Reinhold Niebuhr, John Ben-
nett, and H. Richard Niebuhr criticized the naive optimism of earlier liberals. Although no single formula captures their nuances and differences,
the reforming bias toward faithful participation began to be closely associated with a witness to the radical priority of God and sinfulness of human beings that relativized social interests and achievements and illumined
the precariousness and disorder of the human condition.[23]

While it led to the creation of important new journals, such as *Radical
Religion* (later renamed *Christianity and Society*) and *Christianity and Crisis,*
for the most part, the new realistic mood did not lead to the formation of
new institutions, but it exerted influence on institutions and ventures that
were already in place. It made its presence felt at progressive seminaries
and divinity schools, in the writing of denominational Sunday school cur-
ricula, and in ecumenical associations and conferences (most notably at
Oxford in 1937 and the First Assembly of the World Council of Churches
at Amsterdam in 1948). By the end of the war, realists had the attention
of powerful politicians and important national publications, and they
helped to generate popular support for a vigorous plan of European re-
covery.

Indeed, from the 1930s to the 1960s, liberals and realists continued to
play significant roles as American society became more self-consciously
secular and pluralist. However, they proved incapable of mobilizing anything approaching a united Protestant witness. The Federal Council
Committee on Goodwill cooperated with various Jewish organizations in
a study of Protestant textbook references to Jews in the early 1930s, and
in 1938–39, the Committee became the National Council of Jews and
Christians. Vigorous and sustained criticisms of modern views of human
nature and history launched in the 1930s came to powerful expression in
Reinhold Niebuhr's influential Gifford Lectures, published in 1941 as *The
Nature and Destiny of Man.*

In 1944, Benjamin Mays, the president of Morehouse College who
had attended the World Conference of the YMCA in India and the Oxford Conference on Church, Community, and State in 1937, was elected
vice president of the Federal Council of Churches. Mays also delivered an

important address on "The Church Amidst Racial Tension" at the Second Assembly of the World Council of Churches at Evanston, Illinois, in 1954. Partly through the ministrations of black leaders such as Mays, in 1946 the Federal Council denounced "the pattern of segregation in race relations as unnecessary and undesirable and a violation of the Gospel of love and human brotherhood."[24]

Developments such as these helped to put some elements of reforming Protestant leadership in a position to present to a wider public an understanding of human rights and social justice that transcended current laws and practices during the civil rights movement of the 1950s and early 1960s. Nonetheless, it is well to remember that Martin Luther King Jr.'s famous "Letter from Birmingham Jail" was addressed to white moderates and liberals who recoiled from his campaign of nonviolent confrontation and legal pressure. As the decades continued to unfold, reforming Protestants debated the Vietnam War and also supported less dogmatic approaches to the comparative study of religions. More recently, they have been concerned with world missions that relieve hunger and cooperate with indigenous churches, support for women's rights, views on sexuality, promoting economic fairness, protecting the environment, opposing oppression in the third world, fostering inter-religious dialogue, and the control of nuclear weapons.

Characteristic Faults and Strengths

"There is no innocent tradition," and it would be dishonest and destructive to romanticize the American heritage of reforming Protestantism and thus overlook its considerable and characteristic shortcomings.[25] Many of these may be regarded as variations on a basic fault that emerged early and often. Puritan jeremiads that referred to "an *uninhabited Wilderness, where* they had Cause to Fear the *Wild Beasts, and Wilder Men,*" were emblematic of a continued, often violent failure on the part of American Protestants to acknowledge the integrity of others who remain truly "other."[26] This persistent constriction contributed to the lethal combination of missions and wars resulting in disasterous consequences for North America's native inhabitants. It has had dire consequences also for African Americans subjected to centuries of slavery and injustice, and it has contributed to recurrent bouts of anti-Catholicism, anti-Semitism, and sexism.

If Puritan social covenants contributed to a lasting and vital civic ethos and set of institutions, then, as Williams and others soon discovered, they could also harbor an oppressive intolerance of diversity. To a degree, the voluntarist and individualist bent of nineteenth-century evangelicalism may be said to have mitigated the intolerance of earlier social covenants.

The abolitionist movement, as well as the emergence of other voluntary missionary and benevolent societies, certainly afforded women opportunities for leadership that helped generate controversy about women's proper participation in the church.[27] Nonetheless, as William Lee Miller notes, quite often the contribution of evangelical voluntarism to American civic culture

> has been not perspective, wisdom, depth of insight, but the rousing of the sentiments and energies for particular acts of charity, generosity, and social reform. The characteristic vices have been those of a vulnerably over-simple implicit social conception: a radical pietistic individualism of the change of heart, which knows too readily what is "moral" and expects too easily to persuade people to do it—and topples into cynicism when that does not happen.[28]

Behind and beneath this pattern lay the troubling tendency of those committed to the social ideal of "Christian America" to uphold disturbingly narrow visions and moralities. Thus Horace Bushnell, a creative representative of the reforming establishment, could understand the suffering of civil war with sensitivity and grace, and he also could note the increasingly inclusive progression from a "Puritan" to a "Protestant" and then a "Christian America." But he also mixed nativist and nationalist appeals on behalf of true religion with racist and anti-Catholic sentiments.[29] Again, though he believed that women should be educated, he also thought that home was their proper place, and in 1859 he published *Women's Suffrage: The Reform Against Nature,* arguing that women are not qualified to do men's work or to enter the world of politics.[30] Similar ambiguities beset Rauschenbusch's early calls to "Christianize" society, although in his mature work, he could praise Catholics committed to the cause of social reform, and his solidaristic conception of sin underscored the evils of bigotry.[31]

Consequently, if reforming Protestantism in America has proved remarkably flexible, it also has displayed troubling tendencies toward the accommodation of predominant ethnic, class, regional, and political interests.[32] Indeed, its denominational sensitivities to voluntary constituencies and patterns of support often have resulted in adulterations of the gospel with foreign loyalties, practices, and commitments. Faults such as these help explain why, in the midst of an often brutal age of industry, there was no lack of Protestant support for prerogatives of capital and wealth. As later realists often observed, even when they adopted progressive postures, many reforming Protestants attempted to alter entrenched economic and political powers with naive calls for changed individual attitudes and acts of benevolence. Nonetheless, more than a few realists themselves came to represent equally typical failures of denominational Protestantism by cultivating the company of leadership elites and sometimes becoming closely aligned with the established social agendas of power politics, democratic capitalism, and the "Cold War." It should not surprise us, then, that by the 1960s, some "were beginning to suspect that Protestant reform had won the right to speak in the councils of the mighty, only to discover that there was no longer much to say."[33]

In spite of all these faults, however, the reforming movement has not doubted that God sends both opportunities and challenges for faithful response in every time and circumstance. Its theocentric vision has appealed to diverse communities and sensibilities, so that, over time, reforming Protestants have been Puritans, Quakers, Baptists, Episcopalians, Congregationalists, Presbyterians, Methodists, Disciples, and more. It also has demonstrated a certain dynamism or capacity to learn from others and to respond to changing currents. Thus, Puritans did not start out as abolitionists or as "new school" proponents of evangelism and revival. Neither did theocratic New England encourage societies and associations aimed at the voluntary formation of public life. Progressive heirs of evangelical individualists learned to attend to systemic socio-economic interdependencies, and at least some were willing to cooperate with Catholics and Jews in addressing important issues. Realists struggled to estimate the demonic powers of fascism and the massive destruction of World War II in ways that often transcended mere nationalism as well as their own ethnic backgrounds.[34] More recently, many reforming Protestants have come to question persistent patterns of racial discrimination, the stockpiling of massively destructive weapons, and our lack of concern for the earth's ecology. They have also been responsive to wider social currents and pressures to invite the full participation of women in ministry and they have begun to recognize the pervasiveness of sexism.

Reforming Protestants, although with considerable conflict, have proved willing to nurture the distinctive confession that we belong to God, that sin's corrupting power is both radical and universal, and that the true meaning of the messianic event is transformative. In different ways under different circumstances, they have endeavored to relate persons, communities, and institutions both critically and constructively to God and to one another. They have tried to denounce and restrain corruption and to announce and pursue promising possibilities for renewal. At different times and with different emphases, they have nourished a distinctive bias toward faithful participation in the encompassing reign or commonwealth of God. They have attempted to uphold a distinctive quality of Christian commitment *in* the world.

Competing Alternatives

This reforming stance is at odds today with three movements that are receiving a good deal of press and attention: reductively therapeutic spiritualities, evangelical moralism, and radical Christian communitarianism.

REDUCTIVELY THERAPEUTIC SPIRITUALITIES

In the midst of changing lifestyles and a pervasive ethos of modern individualism, many people find that contemporary life lacks compelling meaning and purpose. Because of this, they come to envision the church and other religious associations as havens for pieties centered on wholeness and personal growth, understanding faithful participation as the attempt to maintain a healing presence that bolsters self-acceptance and self-esteem.

Howard J. Clinebell, Jr., commends this kind of a stance, as do some other advocates of the pastoral counseling movement. They interpret our situation as one in which impersonal organizations block personal growth and diminish self-esteem. Thus, Clinebell decries life on the "success treadmill" and the suppression of the "feeling side" of life (to the impoverishment of men's lives especially). He also criticizes the stereotypical assumptions about marriage and family that oppress many women, and he favors marriage agreements or contracts that emphasize "equal growth."[35] The church, he says, should be a community of nurture that heals our estrangement, an association where persons experience authentically loving, trustful, and dependable relationships. It should affirm doctrines that emphasize love, self-acceptance, and self-esteem; it should sponsor practices that maximize human potentialities.[36]

In a somewhat similar way, M. Scott Peck focuses on the importance of spiritual growth, something he relates to responsibility for solving life's problems and to loving and mutual relationships. He claims, for example, that marriage is a cooperative institution requiring mutual contributions and care, "but existing for the primary purpose of nurturing each of the participants for individual journeys toward his or her own individual peaks of spiritual growth." Indeed, "the ultimate goal of life remains the spiritual growth of the individual." He adds, "marriage and society exist for the basic purpose of nurturing such individual journeys," grace is a powerful force that "nurtures the spiritual growth of human beings," and "God's will is devoted to the growth of the individual human spirit."[37]

The vital concern evident in therapeutic spiritualities is for the quality and depth of personal life and relationships. Human spirits need healing in every age. And today there exists a genuine need to address the chronic stresses, strains, and brokenness that many experience in the midst of bureaucratized social systems and at the hands of personally destructive communities, practices, customs, and attitudes. The danger in this movement, however, is that it will reduce Christian piety to a source of self-worth with few doctrinal and moral standards, and that the church will be transmuted into what Clinebell himself recommends, "a smorgasbord of small groups, workshops, classes, and retreats designed to meet the needs for nurture and growth support of individuals and families."[38]

Therapeutic spiritualities play a critical role in traditionalist enclaves committed to inherited institutional forms, particularly in the areas of marriage and family. But too often they merely furnish emotional nurture and support to people whose everyday lives continue to be dominated by routinized roles and institutions. Moreover, to the extent that they interpret more public issues, they combine a piety centered on wholeness with relatively uncritical commitments to individual choice, fulfillment, and mobility—values supported by selected cosmopolitan features of contemporary culture.[39]

EVANGELICAL MORALISM

A diametrically opposed trend is that many Protestants, traumatized by cosmopolitan institutions and values as well as a pluralistic cacaphony of communities, commitments, and lifestyles, are being drawn toward a resurgent evangelical moralism. These people envision contemporary America as a culture beset by apostasy and instability, and they envision the church as that association called to restore spiritual righteousness to our society. Faithful participation becomes a moralistic campaign to reclaim and reconstruct "Christian America."

This is the stance advocated by Jerry Falwell, Pat Robertson, and other proponents of "the Christian right," who emphasize "biblical principles" that will shore up structures of moral accountability and thus continue America's favor in God's sight. They interpret the present situation as anti-Christian and chaotic, claiming that the religious and moral foundations of our society have been badly shaken. Robertson writes of a "war on the family," and he decries feminism's "unnatural" agenda. He claims that the ultimate spiritual guidance for the family comes from God through the husband and that when disagreement arises, the wife should submit to the husband's wisdom. Believing that the father is the God-ordained "spiritual leader," "decisionmaker," "servant," "provider," and "protector" of his wife and children, Falwell bemoans the instability of the family at a time when the roles of women and men are fluid. According to him, laissez faire capitalism and the work ethic are also mandated by Scripture and are inextricably connected with freedom and limited government. Falwell decries secular humanism, the new "religion of

America" that legitimates an egalitarian, all-sovereign state, and so supports burgeoning bureaucracy and welfarism. He warns of decline and judgment, and he calls Christians to mount a moral crusade to turn America around.[40]

Against the background of appeals to personal growth as a "master goal," we can recognize the legitimate concern represented by evangelical moralism.[41] Human beings need structure and direction in every age. And in a society of cosmopolitan individualists, it is easy to forget that our responsible participation whether in a family or in a nation, entails commitments to the well-being of communities and institutions that may require adjustments in what we want and desire. The dangers, however, are that Christian piety may be reduced to a moralistic legitimation of rigid and authoritarian social forms that are too easily identified with God's will, and that the church may become the spiritual guardian of a reactionary American way.

Evangelical moralism sometimes offers important criticisms of cosmopolitan commitments. But too often it merely "baptizes" certain features of a narrow American mythos. Social contexts are interpreted by combining a piety centered on "biblical principles" with uncritical commitments to a hierarchical family, laissez faire capitalism, and American super-patriotism—institutions and attitudes that allegedly support righteousness and gain support from selected conservative features of modern American culture.

RADICAL CHRISTIAN COMMUNITARIANISM

Some of those who are dissatisfied with the accommodationist tendencies of therapeutic and moralistic stances are trying to divest themselves of unholy alliances. Calling for a new rejection of fallen powers and institutions, they have come to envision the church as a community that confesses and embodies a different way. They emphasize how Christian communities sustain practices that form Christians as a distinct and faithful people.[42]

In the hands of Stanley Hauerwas, this is a vibrant alternative. With the passing of a society where many thought "American values" fit "into a loosely Christian framework," Hauerwas believes that "we have an opportunity to discover what has been and always is the case," namely, that the church is "a colony . . . a beachhead, an outpost, an island of one culture in the middle of another" that trains persons in an alien lifestyle and politics.[43] Liberal society, he says, encourages individuals to discharge roles that contribute to the well-being, unity, and survival of a "tolerant" civil community. It makes people into bland, light-minded, and pragmatic reflections of liberal civility who will support (or at least not challenge) patriotic nationalism. Liberal democracy produces people who value free-dom in the private sphere and who finally are willing to kill for the state. Thus, Hauerwas argues, the education of Christians requires the "telling of a counter-story" centered on Jesus Christ, a story that exposes the lib-eral fiction of national communities that transcend cultural differences. In Hauerwas's view, again, the liberal presumption that families are volun-tary communities of privileged emotional intensity existing only for themselves means they are vacated of educational, moral, and political functions in order to create an individualistic economic and political or-der. By contrast, Christian families should train children in a tradition, serve "the ends of the more determinative community called church," and so operate as checks on the state.[44]

The vital concern of radical communitarianism is to check the recur-rent tendency of denominational Christianity to align itself with prevail-ing economic, political, and cultural interests. At a time when many Christians are trying to retain cultural significance by means of therapeu-tic and moralistic stances, the prophetic dimensions of our communities are at risk. This is why Hauerwas's communitarianism needs to be directly engaged by those who intend to be theologically serious. From the van-tage point of reforming Protestantism, however, the danger in his posi-tion is that Christians will falter in their commitment to participate faith-fully in the world of commercial, civil, and other institutions. Thus Christian piety may be reduced to a church-based cultural criticism that neglects the task of making a fuller, more constructive, and even worldly response to the One who finally is the creative, providential, and re-demptive presence in every situation and environment.[45]

Strengths and Weaknesses

From the perspective of reforming piety and its distinctive spirit of faith-ful participation, then, each of these movements has strengths, but each also harbors a debilitating flaw. Therapeutic stances appropriately empha-size empowering nurture and care, but they confuse loyalty to God and God's commonwealth with a constricted commitment to personal growth. That is why proponents of therapeutic spiritualities have difficulty deal-ing with basic requisites for life together such as "the limits or boundaries of the acceptable and unacceptable" and "the language of obligation and moral concern." Evangelical moralists correctly emphasize institutional structures and moral standards, but they confuse loyalty to God and God's commonwealth with a constricted commitment to inherited institutions and attitudes. That is why they are so ready to set limits and boundaries that exclude diversity. In short, both link deficiently critical theologies with accommodations to already prominent, even though mirror opposite, cultural agendas. That is the reason they are so easily co-opted in current "culture wars" to define America.[46]

Radical communitarianism correctly criticizes these accommodationist tendencies and insists on the church's participation in movements against war, hunger, and other forms of inhumanity. It is unfortunate, however, that it confuses loyalty to God and participation in God's commonwealth with a constricted commitment to and participation in the church. It therefore fails to encourage and guide our participation in civic and economic institutions in order to fashion lasting, stable, relatively equitable, and prosperous societies that might effectively address the scourges of our time. To recall an old Calvinist idea: radical communitarianism is better at decrying institutions as sinful corruptions than at envisioning them as corrupted goods susceptible to reform. It misses the point that, by our participation in families as well as in economic and political institutions, we may be stewards of one another's personal, material, and civil goods in ways neither easily nor appropriately annexed by the community called church and its practices.

Equipping Faithful Participants

One important point, therefore, is that the deep differences between reforming Protestantism, therapeutic spirituality, evangelical moralism, and radical Christian communitarianism are profoundly and explicitly theological. Their diverse attitudes toward American culture stem in part from different understandings of the first principles of Christian believing. Those of us imbued with the spirit of reforming Protestantism, however, must do more than estimate the strengths and weaknesses of competing alternatives. We need to equip ourselves with reforming interpretations of the many communities, institutions, practices, and roles of contemporary life. And we need to show how these may be situated within the expansive frame of living-to-God and others within God's universal commonwealth.

We should interpret our churches, confessing that they often are corrupted by inordinately constricted devotions to self, ethnic community, nation, Christian community, or what have you that subvert the meaning of the messianic event and God's regenerating grace. As noted earlier, during the course of its American pilgrimage, denominational Protestantism often has been marked by a failure to acknowledge the integrity of others who remain truly "other," a persistent constriction that has had dire consequences for North America's native inhabitants and for African

Americans. This constriction has contributed to recurrent bouts of anti-Catholicism, anti-Semitism, and sexism. It too often has led to rigid polities and/or leadership networks that discourage the participation of women and others who do not mimic particular lifestyles. Moreover, it has tacitly, and sometimes openly, supported polemic rhetorics that beguile us into thinking that our enemies in times of war amount to morally depraved subhumans unworthy of our concern, for example, Krauts, Japs, Gooks. In short, denominational Protestantism too often has contributed to breaches of communion with God in community with neighbor by uncritically distinguishing and bolstering the worth of an "in-group" at the expense of an "out-group." For this and other reasons we should recognize that faithful participation requires the continual criticism of our churches and the pieties they engender.

At the same time, we should announce and pursue the dynamic promise of our churches as avenues by which we may come to acknowledge God's transformative way with the world in Jesus Christ, commit ourselves to a life-for-others, and nurture others in the wisdom of reforming piety. We ought to insist on the reforming theological integrity of our services of worship, our Christian education, our polities, and our missions. We should maintain that the church stands in a tensive, multivalent relationship with its surrounding environments. It does not merely embrace prevailing attitudes and practices in a fallen world, but neither does it reject God's good creation. It refuses to give up on what God refuses to give up on.

For this reason reforming churches will welcome responsible restructurings of institutional forms, restructurings that break down rigid hierarchies and support the emergence of more genuine communities and spiritualities. This is also why reforming churches are purposely mixed into the world, without becoming havens for growth groups, spiritual legitimators of the American way, or colonies of resident aliens. They are (1) with the world, confessing our common faults; (2) against the world, criticizing idols and corrupting constrictions; (3) attentive to the world when it exposes their own failures and corruptions; (4) for the world, pursuing a critically constructive and reforming mission to increase the love of God and neighbor, embody genuine communion, and so equip people to participate faithfully in God's commonwealth.

We should interpret the other contexts and institutions in which we participate as well. We should, for example, interpret our civil governments, confessing that they may succumb to inordinately partial interests, malignant ideologies, and nationalistic passions. No citizen should need to be reminded of the horrifying and oppressive practices or the escalating and immoral threats that nations and governments may support. Neither should we ignore the ethnically and religiously inspired violence that may follow on the dissolution of the state at the hands of inordinately narrow interests and groups. And we should not fail to acknowledge the ways in which centralized modern governments and their culture-standardizing agencies may erode the distinct identities and traditions of particular communities. Neither should we fail to observe the ways in which these same agencies may help to break down traditional barriers to the political and social enfranchisement of particular groups and minorities. Genuinely faithful participation requires that we critique these realities and sometimes oppose particular governments and policies.

Along with this, however, we should also announce and pursue the genuine promise of civil communities and governments as avenues by which we may participate faithfully in God's commonwealth. Pursuing that promise does not mean reducing politics to the goal of enhancing individual fulfillment or to an endorsement of "my country right or wrong." We must not confuse it with the creation of a civil community that reduces other communities, institutions, and traditions to common denominators that press few disturbing questions and concerns. Where we are fortunate enough to be citizens of a relatively just constitutional democracy that is significantly accountable and responsive to the will of the people, we may participate in a fabric of freedoms and responsibilities that provides a stable environment for families, businesses, schools, and other institutions at the same time that it allows for and respects conscientious dissent.[47] We should commit ourselves to furnishing basic levels of support and opportunity to all. We should protect, honor, and enhance the elective social "space" needed for voluntary associations of religious, political, social, and other kinds. We should uphold equitable courts of law. We should participate in representative institutions that help to restrain the inordinate interests of each by enfranchising all, and that train persons and groups in deliberative and mutual practices of decison-making. We should support international agreements, balances of power, and assemblies that help restrain the inordinate appetites and objectives of our own nation and of others, even as they encourage governments in practices of domestic responsibility and limited cooperation. As citizens, we may be stewards of one another's political well-being, enhancing genuine life together in ways that are not easily duplicated by other institutions.[48] That is why faithful participants in God's world affirm that our civil communities and institutions entail standards of equity, justice, and representation that illumine and restrain corruption even as they enhance political practices that may contribute to the well-being of a wider commonwealth.

Conclusion

We need to interpret these and other features of our common life if we are to meet with faithfulness both the everyday and exceptional challenges confronting us. The spirit of reforming Protestantism today does not mean choosing sides in current "culture wars" to define America. It does not mean rejecting the culture with a few exceptions, and it does not mean remaining silent in the midst of controversy. It means assuming a faithful and participatory stance that emerges from theocentric piety and is willing to contribute its critical and constructive voice in wider, pluralistic, and often contentious conversations. It means a vigorous, genuinely critical, and constructive Christian commitment in the world.[49]

When addressing the first world assembly of the World Council of Churches at Amsterdam in 1948, Reinhold Niebuhr insisted that "Christian life without a high sense of responsibility for the health of our communities, our nations, and our cultures degenerates into an intolerable other-worldliness."[50] Those of us imbued with the reforming spirit of faithful participation should agree. That is why, although reforming piety is not a product of current "culture wars," we should not shun contemporary conversations and debates about Christian faithfulness and American culture. Indeed, in the course of these conversations, and as loyal adherents to our distinctly reforming confession, we should support the principled well-being of persons, societies, and institutions. We should try to contribute to a revitalization of our culture's fragmentary ethos and often quite shallow public discourse. We probably shall also find ourselves opposed to many misguided and reductive attempts on the part of some Christians to do these things.

The essential point, however, is that we adopt this participatory stance and attempt these and other things because we know that neither our communities, our nations, nor our cultures lend final meaning to life. The essential point is that we first uphold theological principles.[51] First and foremost, we belong to God. Genuine faithfulness means reordering all life in devotion to God and God's commonwealth, a living-for-others that strives for true communion and refuses to give up on what God refuses to give up on. A community equipped with these convictions will be caught up in the transformative meaning of the messianic event of Jesus Christ and in the bias toward faithful participation. It will have theological reasons to care for the health of our communities, our nations, and our cultures. It will denounce corruptions and announce and pursue promises. It will make a vibrant reforming witness.

2
Reforming Protestantism: Identity and Relevance

T he spirit of reforming Protestantism is a theocentric piety that issues in a transformative bias toward faithful participation in God's all-inclusive commonwealth. At different times and under different circumstances, this orientation or bias has taken on different accents or dialects. For early Puritans, it meant contributing to the work of social construction; for evangelicals in eighteenth- and nineteenth-century America, manifesting the fruits of a new birth in voluntary associations; for progressives, transformative engagement in a new age of science and industry; and for realists, a sharp insistence on the precariousness and disorder of civilized achievements and the human condition. Today, in the midst of "culture wars" and competing alternatives, the spirit of reforming Protestantism means a faithful and participatory stance that is willing to contribute its critical and constructive voice in wider, pluralistic, and often contentious conversations.

The above statements provide a synopsis of my basic argument thus far. Any attempt at renewal and revitalization, however, brings us face to face with a vexing difficulty. In the midst of a contentious culture, the reforming movement currently suffers severe internal strains and conflicts. It often resembles a house divided, and divided houses are difficult to mobilize around shared visions and common causes.

A Polarized Ecclesiastical Ethos

Our basic internal division in many respects parallels a "deep cultural divide" in contemporary American society. The widespread polarization in

23

American life between conservatives, who are committed to traditional attitudes and institutions, and progressives, who want to revise these attitudes and institutions to address changing situations and realities, constitutes a major axis of cleavage in contemporary Protestantism.[1] Indeed, it is possible to arrange American denominations on a cultural morality scale ranging from the most conservative (Assemblies of God and Nazarenes), to the most liberal (Unitarians and Christian Scientists).[2]

Scales of this sort, however, need to be viewed with appropriate caution. Much depends on just how one interprets "cultural morality," and generalizations about the attitudes of entire denominations and families of churches inevitably obscure significant diversity within virtually every communion. Even so, what remains instructive for our purposes here is that the cultural divide between conservatives and progressives (liberals) poses special challenges to those religious communities caught in the middle, not falling to either end of the spectrum. It puts them, in effect, in an embattled position, plagued by internal divisions while trying to hold together divergent impulses that often emanate from disparate constituencies.

This is roughly the situation among reforming Protestants. Reforming conservatives tend to support traditional activities and programs aimed at the formation of distinct Christian identity, such as increased emphases on Bible study, denominational heritages, prayer, and evangelism. Reforming progressives tend to support ecumenical ventures as well as activities and programs aimed at developing dialogical engagements with cosmopolitan culture, such as studies of current politics and economic conditions, sexism, and racism. It is not surprising, then, to find significant tensions and mutual suspicions. Conservatives have misgivings about what they take to be the liberal and secular overtones of activities that interest progressives. Progressives are uncomfortable with what they believe to be the authoritarian and pietist overtones of activities that interest many conservatives.[3]

These divergent impulses, as well as the potential for conflicts between them, have been heightened by recent changes in a variety of institutions. Robert W. Lynn observes that, in an earlier era, "mainstream" churches relied on a circle of interlocking agencies and communities to educate their members. Many families engaged in regular Bible study and devotions. Public schools to a significant extent contributed to the formation of mainstream Protestant values, beliefs, practices, and attitudes. Congregations provided regular services of worship, as well as religious instruction for children. Church-related colleges and universities offered educational environments that further probed and reinforced mainstream heritages and beliefs in dialogue with the sciences and humanities, and they also furnished "traditioned" candidates for ministry. Seminaries and divinity schools offered advanced theological training for ministers and church professionals. Church-related journalism furnished an avenue whereby each of these points along the circle could remain in contact with one another, and it also offered regular discussions of current issues and events according to mainline Protestant perspectives.[4]

Today, all of these institutions have changed, and many have dropped out of the circle altogether. A variety of economic and cultural pressures have rendered the family a beleaguered community, particularly when it comes to passing on particular heritages and traditions. Attempting to serve plural constituencies, as well as the exigencies of a modern economy, the nation's public schools have adopted a nonreligious stance. Responding to the mobile and cosmopolitan objectives of their constituents, as well as to the cultural utility and prestige of autonomous, "nonsectarian" inquiries, many church-related colleges and universities no longer furnish distinctive religious environments. The consequent decline in theologically literate, reforming Protestant readership has contributed to a decline in significant reforming journalism, and where such journalism does survive, its basic audience has been reduced to religious professionals.

The "institutional ecology" of reforming Protestantism, therefore, has changed as basic communal contexts for theological discourse have been significantly narrowed and reduced. Reforming Protestants now look almost exclusively to congregations and seminaries to form traditional identities and to engage and interpret the wider culture. There also are clear indications that our expectations exceed the capabilities of these two institutions.

Our congregational leaders are caught in an ever-widening spiral of programs and responsibilities. They prepare sermons and lead services of worship. They socialize. They visit the sick and comfort the bereaved. They meet with committees and administer both programs and budgets. They help raise funds. They participate in extra-congregational judicatories, conferences, and assemblies. They staff retreats for youth, families, and officers. They teach confirmation classes, lead youth groups, and oversee Sunday schools. They scramble to find, and often also to train, qualified teachers for programs on everything from Abraham to aging, Pentecost to professions, worship to war, and evangelism to ecology.

Our seminaries are caught in a similar spiral. We ask them to foster scholarship, offer continuing education, facilitate satellite programs, and even provide lay education. We expect them to make their faculty available to congregations and to denominational studies and task forces. At the same time, and ordinarily within a three-year program, they are asked not only to train students in Bible, theology, church history, and practical tasks of ministry, but also to nurture them in the formation of their traditional identities, as well as in their abilities to interpret the contemporary world.

The consequence, then, is that conservative impulses for distinct identity formation and progressive impulses for relevant engagement are locked in competition for highly limited and strained resources. In the absence of church-related colleges and universities to strengthen students' acquaintance with their Christian heritages and traditions, the responsibilities of seminaries for traditional formation increase. Most seminary faculty members cannot assume that the majority of their students have strong backgrounds in biblical study, that they have taken a course in the Protestant Reformation, or that they have anything more than a passing acquaintance with Augustine, Wesley, and the meaning of the word "Puritan." Most ministers cannot assume that many of their adult members have backgrounds in these areas either. But there are further pressures. For example, one commentator laments a lack of attention to seminarians' personal relationships with God, and recommends that seminaries employ "trained spiritual formation teams" and offer courses "in the history, theory, and practice of spiritual direction."[5] Another notes that spirituality often "becomes something added to an already overloaded program," and he wonders "if there is a seminary that would have enough courage to abolish the field-work program."[6] Still others favor increased commitments to and course offerings in evangelism, youth ministry, church growth, and so on.

Similar pressures arise from progressive demands for relevant engagement. Here again, institutional erosion takes a toll because interpretative labors that once were undertaken, at least in part, by church-related colleges, universities, and journalists are also left to congregations and seminaries. Denominational bureaucracies attempt to contribute in this area with varied humanitarian relief efforts, reports on domestic and international social conditions, studies, and position papers. Their efforts, unfortunately, are hampered by declines in support and credibility, especially among more conservative churchgoers. Moreover, the usefulness of studies and position papers often depends on the availability of qualified interpreters and expanded programs that, in turn, place additional strains on congregations and ministers.

A growing literature also presses demands for relevant engagement in seminaries and divinity schools.[7] We read that "theological education must be intentional inquiry into the global situation," into threats of nuclear war, world hunger, exploitation, debtor nations, ecological crisis, sexism, racism, and population growth.[8] This too places burdens on limited resources such as international exchange programs and travel.[9] Indeed, some propose "the addition of new subjects to the curriculum," such as "economics, sociology, politics, and the study of non-Christian traditions," even though this will mean that "some of the present 'core' subjects (Bible, Systematics, History) will have to be taught at a simpler level."[10]

These, then, are some of the pressures and strains that result from a polarized ecclesiastical ethos and that have been intensified by the erosion or reduction of communal contexts for reforming education and theological discourse. Although some congregations and seminaries are sufficiently aligned with one or the other camp to escape significant tensions (a strategy, that is almost never available to denominational offices and bureaucracies), many find themselves caught in the middle, if not also in the crossfire. More than one president, administrator, or professor has found it necessary to assure both conservative and progressive constituencies that his or her school is responsive to their leading interests and concerns. Many ministers and Christian educators find the uneasy politics of dynamic educational programming and preaching both professionally and personally taxing. (One prudent rule of thumb is that congregational programs on oppressive conditions in the third world need to be balanced by others on more traditional topics. Another is that highly divisive issues such as abortion and homosexuality should be directly addressed, if at all, only by visiting speakers who are removed from the immediate politics of that particular congregation.) To summarize, the polarized ethos of reforming Protestantism today requires exceptional institutional balance, personal energy, and creativity if one is to avoid the dangers such as bland education and lukewarm leadership that typically accompany uninspired attempts to avoid controversy.

Broader Trends and Developments

The polarized ethos of reforming Protestantism parallels prominent lines of fissure in American society. We may also observe that divergent impulses have been intensified by competition for the scarce resources of congregations and seminaries. Moreover, our current tensions and divisions have important antecedents in earlier splits between theocratic Massachusetts and the advocates of religious freedom and toleration in Rhode Island, "Old School" representatives of scholastic Calvinism and "New School" proponents of experiential piety, as well as controversies between fundamentalists and modernists. Nonetheless, in order to understand why conservative/progressive fault lines have been activated with such force in our own time and place, we also need to look beyond our local American context and history to broader trends and developments. Only then will we be in a position to estimate their fuller meaning for reforming piety and its distinctive participatory spirit. Let us begin by thinking of our present situation in terms of *globalization,* or the emergence and recognition of a single circumstance of world interdependence, and *pluralization,* or the emergence and recognition of varied communities, identities, viewpoints, and values.

GLOBALIZATION

Globalization is connected with a variety of factors. For example, there is a growing international web of economic interdependency. This can be illustrated by the intricate relationships that now exist between financial markets in Tokyo, Hong Kong, London, Toronto, New York, Mexico City, and so on. Or think of the number of late-model automobiles that are imported, manufactured by companies in international partnership, and/or built with parts produced around the world. Markets and manufacturing have become truly global, as is evidenced by worldwide growth in international investments, imports and exports, and by the emergence of multinational corporations and corporate arrangements.[11]

Interconnected economic realities go hand in hand with a political environment that also exhibits an increasing tendency toward interdependence. At a fundamental level, it is apparent that political relationships and decisions made at almost any point around the globe can have far-reaching consequences. Power is significantly dispersed, as is evidenced by the fact that heretofore "regional" issues and conflicts often have worldwide significance. One reason for this is that economic interdependencies invest particular communities and locations with additional political significance—the prime, but by no means sole, example being the oil-producing lands of the Middle East. Another factor contributing to the dispersal of power is the advent and proliferation of technically sophisticated, highly destructive, and comparatively inexpensive conventional, chemical, and nuclear weapons. Then too, intricate systems of trade, travel, communication, and electronic information seem particularly susceptible to sporadic disruptions, e.g., terrorism. Under these circumstances, no spot or community on the planet can be disregarded without considerable risk. The fates of many are increasingly in the hands of many.

At the same time, we are more and more aware that the web of interdependency in which we live and move and deploy our powers is one that includes significant interactions with a delicate and shared natural environment. We live at a time when political, production, and development decisions have enormous impact on countless birds, fish, and plants; in which spray cans, automobiles, and factories appear to deplete the ozone layer; in which the practice of drinking from polystyrene cups apparently will ensure a nonbiodegradable store of waste for hundreds of years to come; and in which the disposal of toxic wastes threatens the long-term ecological integrity of an increasing number of sites. Prosperous societies have so threatened the welfare of their populations with landfills and air and water pollutants that barges loaded with tons of refuse languish at sea for months, trying to find someplace to unload their sickening cargo. A growing belt of space garbage already encircles the earth.

It is obviously impossible even to outline economic, political, and ecological dimensions of our global circumstance without paying special attention to the holistic implications of our immense and increasing technological capabilities. Mass media and travel have changed the "feel" of life on planet earth. The many faces of achievement, beauty, cruelty, tragedy, and starvation are routinely accessible and concrete. Contemporary medicine and biology alter the very boundaries and genetic constitutions of life. Perhaps the most forceful illustration of the global significance of our technological powers is the enormous destructive capability of modern nuclear arsenals. Our capacity to bring about the very long-term destruction of almost all known ecological balances and planetary life forms is genuinely unique, and it is one of the more ominous factors making for the crystallization of contemporary notions of human and global unity.[12]

Thus we live in the midst of a single interdependent social and natural ecology, and our awareness of that fact underscores a wide variety of promising and troubling realities and questions. For example, severe economic disparities among national societies are thrown into sharp relief, and one wonders whether prosperous nations get and remain that way only at the expense of poor nations. Again, how shall we understand the inevitable mixture of political, economic, and moral factors entailed by the practices of international cooperation, joint manufacturing, and investment among societies with diverse internal politico-social policies and situations such as the United States and China or Mexico? Additional matters of economic, political, and moral importance emerge with the availability of advanced technologies, as well as our awareness of significant interactions with the natural environment. How shall we distribute medical systems and technologies able to remove the specter of unnecessary suffering and untimely death from so many? How shall we understand complicated interrelationships between pollution, economic development, population, and consumption? Can we devise an effective and responsive world agriculture and food-distribution system that will take advantage of significant recent advances in technologies of production?

Note also that our present global circumstance puts a distinctive stamp on somewhat more traditional philosophical and existential questions. How, for example, shall we understand nature and nature's claims (both human and otherwise) in a world that daily grows more artificial and more dependent on humans? In the face of impressive and expanding life-extending technologies, how shall we understand life and death? How shall we understand the meaning of human life, agency, and responsibility now that we clearly have the ability to bring the histories of our own and other species to an end?[13]

Particularly in what Richard R. Niebuhr calls a "radial world," where a global nervous system transmits images and messages from people and places well beyond the bounds of any local horizon, the sheer magnitude and complexity of our present circumstance can easily become overwhelming and desensitizing.[14] Nevertheless, it simply will not do to complain that matters such as these are exotic and far removed from ordinary life. Those of us involved in science, education, technology, law, agriculture, management, labor, finance, medicine, government, and so on, operate daily in the midst of globally linked professions and institutions.[15] Indeed, the intricate and encompassing web of world interdependence infiltrates even the most personal choices and fabrics of our lives such as where we live, what we consume, how many children we have, the way we spend our leisure time, and decisions about medical treatments and interventions.

PLURALIZATION

Although we acknowledge the pull toward globalization, we also note that our present situation is further complicated by a related tendency toward pluralization. It is true, of course, that the world always was more diverse than many insulated and sometimes elitist communities were prepared to admit. Nevertheless, under the rubric of pluralization, I mean to do more than simply point to a diversity that was already there. The current general recognition of plurality closely connects with many of the factors already mentioned such as economic interdependencies and the dispersal of political power that have enabled diverse societies, subcultures, and groups to command significant attention. Contemporary individuals, businesses, governments, and churches are not paying attention to a larger number of distinctive communities and viewpoints just because they can; they are also responding to new distributions and configurations of opportunity, competition, and power. Consider, for example, our recently increased awareness of the different perspectives and loyalties among varied Arabian societies and groups, current American interest in Japanese corporate stuctures and styles of management, or our heightened sensitivity to the multinational and multiethnic characteristics of eastern Europe and what used to be the Soviet Union.

In addition, the recent dynamics of pluralization have been distinctively stamped by conditions associated with the continuing rise and exportation of functionally "rationalized" and differentiated Western institutions. Consider the economic sphere of cultural activity. In traditional societies, economic functions are "combined in a number of different ways with familial, political, religious, or military functions."[16] By contrast, economic functions in industrial and postindustrial societies are carried out by business organizations independent of household, church, army, and so on. Thus the modern corporation devotes itself to the production of wealth in the forms of profit and dividends. Its structures, practices, and ethos are ordered or "rationalized" in accordance with that objective and with the exigencies of different environments. As such, the corporation is set apart from family, church, army, university, symphony—institutions that are ordered toward other functions.

One important consequence is that employment and advancement in the modern corporation tend to become matters of qualification and performance more than familial status, military rank, or religious affiliation. The corporation often is able and willing to retain productive employees regardless of their "private" involvements and commitments; where it is unwilling, it is often subject to serious moral and political criticism. This, in turn, has tended to increase economic mobility and to undermine traditional social dams separating unequal levels and groups—important conditions providing trends toward the enfranchisement of those who were once excluded such as women and minorities, and thus also for the emergence into prominence of additional communities, viewpoints, and values.

The other side of the coin, however, is that the modern corporation demands that its employees discharge roles largely defined by the instrumental values and rationality of corporate life. For this reason, it tends to require substantial levels of education and training of its employees. It also tends to bracket-out from the sphere of one's economic activity certain beliefs, commitments, and values that once were the cornerstones of integral personal identity. Indeed, these more traditional, "ideal" assets often are relegated to a mainly private and therapeutic significance. The modern corporation is willing to employ qualified Muslims, Catholics, Jews, Protestants, Mormons, Buddhists, and agnostics because it does not expect privatized religious affiliations and beliefs to challenge the corporation's understanding and expectations of an employee's job-related activities and responsibilities.

Recognizing the other cultural spheres and institutions in which people participate, an individual's role as corporate employee will be one of many that she or he undertakes, each with its own specific pattern or texture such as family member, student, churchgoer, citizen, or soldier. As the number of relatively distinct roles increases, it can become more and more difficult to retain a sense of wholeness, coherence, or integrity; personal identity may therefore become highly problematic.[17] The ensuing search for identity and commitment sometimes takes the form of quite individualistic and eclectic attempts at finding oneself.[18] It may also lead to the resurgence of more traditional bases for identity such as local community affiliations or ethnic and religious heritages that either were displaced or continue to survive at the margins of a differentiated and cosmopolitan society.[19] Consequently, even within modern societies where Western institutions are highly developed, personal identities, values, and viewpoints can be widely varied.[20]

Under these conditions, then, the modern state supports the development of effective mass media, near universal literacy, and an all-embracing and standardizing educational system—all of which are necessary for the occupational skills and social mobility essential to modern economic growth.[21] The state, in effect, becomes a sponsor and protector of a relatively common or cosmopolitan culture that furnishes people of diverse personal backgrounds and local involvements with a shared idiom, set of customs, and ideals. Like fast-food chains and the interstate highway system, the overarching culture cuts across regional and subcultural differences, functioning as a common denominator of public life in areas of employment, education, politics, entertainment, and more. This is yet another point at which secularism becomes an important force in relation to more local and traditional structures of personal identity.[22]

At the same time, participation in the interdependent world system of nations encourages the development of a strong, relatively centralized state that is able to express national societal interests in relation to other such interests, and is also able to articulate a national identity in relation to the global circumstance that will elicit the loyalty of its citizens. The nation needs to represent some cause or reality that its locally, and perhaps also ethnically and religiously, diverse citizens find distinctive and worthwhile such as democratic liberty or social equity. For this reason, and also because the secular state has taken on various existential and moral matters concerning social welfare and human well-being, (for example, education, the regulation of agriculture, big business, employment practices, medical and social insurance) the quasi-religious and ideological symbolisms and commitments of modern civil life become especially significant.[23]

Here again there are two sides of the coin, both of considerable consequence for the pluralization of societies, viewpoints, and values. On the one hand, the standardizing cosmopolitan culture and quasi-religious assets or ideologies of the secular state often have the effect of breaking down oppressive hegemonies supported by traditional and archaic social patterns, loyalties, and identities. In this sense, it allows individuals a significant degree of mobility and freedom from more traditional ties. On the other hand, the virtual monopoly of high culture, coupled with a successful development of ideological assets, means that other, more traditional sources of identity will be relegated to a mainly local or therapeutic status.

This last point means that under certain circumstances and in various ways the modern state, its attendant ideologies, and the cosmopolitan culture of differentiated and "rationalized" institutions and roles with which that state so often is associated, tend to supplant people's basic religious loyalties. Certainly, this public sociocultural context or system maintains values, practices, and assumptions that are able to orient and order much of life quite apart from the sense that there is a God. Thus, as Charles Taylor notes, "even in societies where a majority of people profess some belief in God or in a divine principle, no one sees it as *obvious* that there is a God."[24]

These, then, are some of the factors creating significant difficulties in relationships between religious associations and modern, state supported, cosmopolitan cultures and ideologies. In some instances, religious communities are rendered confused and tentative about the significance of believing in God. In others, religious believing, language, and practice are forced almost entirely into a privatized and individual sphere. In still others, fundamental tensions provoke virulent, antisecular reactions such as in theocratic Iran.

To summarize, pluralization not only points to increasingly intricate relationships of interdependence that require us to attend to many different historical communities, cultures, viewpoints, and values; it also indicates that they are differently structured and arranged within different sorts of societies, groups, and individuals. There are traditional societies in which modern secular institutions have not emerged and in which traditional religion, ethnicity, and territoriality furnish primary bases for solidarity. There are societies in which secular cultures and civil ideologies conflict in varying degrees with other, often local, ethnic, and religious orientations and loyalties. There are societies in which public life is more or less successfully oriented by cosmopolitan cultures and civil ideologies and in which other, more traditional assets have been relegated to essentially private individual significance; societies in which traditional religious loyalties have retaken the centralized state and its considerable culture-standardizing agencies; societies in which one or more of these different patterns are mixed or combined; and so on. Likewise, there are personal identities and perspectives centered on familial, tribal, and local

affiliations; identities rendered deeply problematic by a plurality of differentiated roles; identities and outlooks more or less successfully integrated
by a common cosmopolitan culture and civil ideology. There are dualis-
tic identities in which secular public roles are largely separate from varied,
often highly individualistic, therapeutic sources of private identity; persons whose lives reflect deep conflict among a variety of ideological resources; and so on.

A basic point, then, is that differently structured cultures and personal
identities make for a dizzying plurality of perspectives on human life, society, and the world. More colloquially put, in the United States we do
not find ourselves simply responding to generic Americans, but to Americans whose outlooks are variously influenced by Protestant, Catholic,
Jewish, Muslim, Buddhist, and secular commitments; Americans whose
public lives are ordered by instrumental cosmopolitan values but whose
private lives are structured by largely therapeutic religious affiliations;
Americans who join religious or cosmopolitan loyalties with strongly nationalistic ideologies; Americans whose personal identities and orientations continue to be shaped by predominantly local community-based
networks of interaction and affiliation, and so on. On the international
scene, we do not respond to generic Arabian states, but to Arabian societies in which secular economic and political institutions have emerged
and have been distributed to varying degrees and in which national cultures and ideologies are variously developed and related to differently understood local and Muslim loyalties and beliefs.

A Dual Challenge

With this in mind, we are now in a position to consider the following
question. What is the basic challenge that those of us imbued with the
spirit of reforming Protestantism confront in a pluralistic America where
countless global interrelations converge, and where modern Western institutions are highly developed? A short answer is that we confront the
task of participating faithfully in an environment characterized by intricate interdependencies and plural communities. As a consequence, we
face an intense dual challenge. We are challenged to maintain the integrity
of our own distinctive confession, orientation, and identity. But we are
equally challenged to interpret meaningfully and engage the many interdependencies, cosmopolitan institutions, and plural perspectives that characterize our present world.

We are challenged to maintain the integrity of our confession. At an
immediate and practical level, we have relatively little choice about this
matter. Americans today typically live and move amid a dizzying plural-

ity of perspectives on human life, society, and the world within the context of a relatively common, standardizing, and mobile cosmopolitan culture. In our daily lives, in our discussions and debates, we find ourselves interacting with persons and communities whose outlooks are variously influenced by diverse affiliations, experiences, and ethnic backgrounds, as well as by different religious and philosophical commitments. We also find ourselves participating in cosmopolitan institutions, roles, and practices that are able to orient and order much of life quite apart from any explicit religious sensibility. Regular contact and communication with different groups, their varied languages, vocabularies, outlooks, and practices can challenge and erode the distinctive orientation and identity of any particular person or community. So can regular participation in institutions, roles, and practices that tend to relegate more particular ethnic, local, and religious traditions to a largely private and elective sphere. Our identities often are rendered precarious by constant pressures toward compromise and eclecticism. This is the buzzing confusion, or to mix metaphors, the fertile soil from which conservative demands for distinct and traditional identity emerge with heightened intensity.

Reforming Protestants have good reasons to take these demands very seriously. The confession that we belong to God, that sin's corrupting power is both radical and universal, that the true meaning of the messianic event is transformative, and that genuine faithfulness is a living-for-others within God's commonwealth is a historic treasure borne by a particular community and tradition as subject to corrosive forces as any other. We shall not be faithful participants if we neglect it, and, in America today, we cannot plausibly expect people to know what this confession means or to be formed in its fabric of convictions simply by virtue of their participation in the plurality and popular culture of American society. Indeed, we can reasonably expect that the integrity of any particular tradition will be challenged. This presents our own community and tradition, as well as many others, with a host of practical pressures and problems. Yet for this very reason we find ourselves in a particularly good position to recognize the ineluctable particularity of reforming piety, and to explore what it means to be a distinctly reforming Christian community in the world. In this basic sense the conservatives are right; we ought to be especially concerned to engage in strategic practices aimed at the intentional formation in persons of a distinctly reforming piety and confession.

However, we are challenged also to engage and interpret the many interdependencies, cosmopolitan institutions, and plural perspectives that characterize our present world. This too is an immediate and practical demand about which we have little choice. Americans today typically live and move in the midst of globally linked economic and political realities, vulnerable natural ecologies, and interdependent and powerful technologies. Under these conditions, our traditional, inherited, and more locally bounded horizons, attitudes, and institutions regularly are subject to reevaluation and revision. We confront new possibilities and limits that insinuate themselves into even our personal choices. We confront troubling moral questions about severe economic disparities, international compromise and cooperation, new medical technologies, the distribution of food, and more. Almost no American physician, autoworker, stockbroker, farmer, student, soldier, executive, pilot, truckdriver, or office worker is entirely unaware of these things. Virtually any community enmeshed in the current American environment, especially one whose constituents tend to be educated and mobile participants in cosmopolitan institutions, will be pressured to take these things into account. This is the increasingly intricate, encompassing, and influential web from which progressive demands for relevant interpretation and engagement emerge with heightened intensity.

Reforming Protestants have important reasons to take these demands very seriously. After all, it is part of the distinct confession whose integrity we uphold to criticize inordinately narrow and constricted orientations and visions. Again, reforming piety itself affirms that genuine faithfulness is a living-for-others within God's all-inclusive commonwealth. We shall not be faithful participants if we do not pay attention to the meaning of these convictions in our own place and time. Moreover, in America today, we cannot plausibly expect persons to be unaware that they are linked with others, and others who do not share their own particular viewpoints and values by intricate and influential interrelationships of interdependence. Neither can we plausibly expect persons not to take up some stance in response to this compelling circumstance. This, again, presents many communities and traditions with a host of pressures and problems. Yet because of this we find ourselves in a particularly good position to appreciate the enlarging tendency of the new responsiveness in Christ enabled by God's regenerating grace. In this basic sense, the progressives are right; we ought to be especially concerned to interpret theologically and engage faithfully the intricate and expansive interdependencies that characterize our contemporary world.

This is why we are caught in the middle. Reforming Protestants have good reasons—theological reasons—to endorse the basic substance of both conservative and progressive impulses. One might even say that this double endorsement amounts to a point of contact between reforming piety and the contentious spirits of the age. Nevertheless, as soon as we say this, we must also turn around and say something apparently opposite. *Double endorsement implies double criticism.*

Within the frame of reforming piety, the progressive impulse is correct to maintain that faithful participation, a living-for-others within God's all-inclusive commonwealth, requires us to interpret and engage the threatening and promising realities of our global and cosmopolitan circumstance. Left to its own devices, however, this impulse underestimates the identity-diffusing and corrosive dimensions of our pluralistic situation, as well as the ability of cosmopolitan societies to deaden the sense that there is a God in relation to whom we should order our many activities and involvements. The conservative impulse recognizes these challenges and appropriately calls for renewed commitment to the strategic formation of Christians in a historically distinctive community and its particular piety or wisdom. Left to its own devices, however, this impulse often fails to recognize that the integrity of reforming piety requires us to engage our contemporary world in a manner that may call into question and even lead us to revise inherited attitudes and institutions.

Within the frame of reforming piety, then, conservative and progressive impulses ought not to be ultimately opposed. Fundamentally, they are different, mutually dependent aspects of the same thing. The progressive impulse to relevant engagement cannot survive apart from the conservative impulse to maintain a distinctly reforming confession that leads believers to envision the world as God's commonwealth. The conservative impulse to guard the integrity of a distinctly reforming confession cannot come to completion without leading to the progressive impulse to relevantly engage the world as God's commonwealth.[25]

This is why reforming theology ought to include both a confessional/dogmatic dimension and a dialogical theology of culture. It should explicate, promote, deepen, and extend a historically particular and faithfully participatory spirit. The need for theological work of this sort is not merely academic. Indeed, the currently contentious and polarizing politics of reforming Protestantism in both congregations and seminaries indicate we shall not be able to carry forward the reforming spirit of faithful participation in our own time and place without it.

Two Possible Futures

There have been more than a few places and times in which the reforming project of participating faithfully in God's all-inclusive commonwealth has been especially difficult, and in which different possible futures have hung in the balance. Moreover, there are good reasons to think that American society today is such a place and time.

One possible future is that current polarization between conservatives and progressives will become even more acute until the reforming stream separates into two channels of relatively discrete, more homogeneous associations and institutions. Theology matters. While a single issue or concern such as feminism or homosexuality may be the occasion for splits within particular denominations, the basic bifurcation of the reforming stream actually would be the result of radically different styles of theological discourse and reflection that have been nourished by disagreements over many issues and concerns. Conservatives, freed from the countervailing pull of progressives, might then adopt more defensive and provincial stances that accommodate selected traditional features of American culture and criticize cosmopolitan trends. Freed from the countervailing pull of conservatives, progressives might spawn extensive reformulations of belief and practice that accommodate cosmopolitan dimensions of the culture and criticize conservative trends. The result would be two diametrically opposed culture Protestantisms, an even more thorough division of American Protestantism into opposing camps, and a debilitating dissolution of the distinctive spirit of reforming Protestantism.

Under these conditions, the position advocated by Stanley Hauerwas and others likely would be more attractive to those who become sufficiently dissatisfied with the accommodationist tendencies of progressive humanism and of conservative moral crusades. Indeed, a radically communitarian "rejection of the culture with a few exceptions" would expose the implicit and unacknowledged hypocrisies of culture Protestantisms on both sides by pointing to the virtually complete co-optation of conservatives and progressives by the ideological interests of different segments of American culture. It would also confirm a prophetic remnant in a highly distinct, counter-identity.

Nonetheless, Hauerwas's option would not lead toward a revitalization or renewal of the faithfully participatory spirit of reforming Protestantism. That spirit's confessional and dialogical dimensions paradoxically might be forced to migrate beyond the bounds of American Protestantism altogether. Perhaps they would find fertile ground among American Catholics whose traditional commitments remain stronger than those of many Protestant progressives but who, nonetheless, seem more willing to dialogically interpret and engage our contemporary situation than are many Protestant conservatives.

A different future might emerge from a timely renewal of reforming piety that holds together our sometimes disparate and conflicting impulses in a manner that advances the spirit of faithful participation. I believe that theologically this would require the kind of confessionally dogmatic and dialogical stance mentioned earlier. It would therefore also require the frank acknowledgment that the current polarization between conservatives and progressives represents a culturally accommodating and theologically bankrupt denial of both the integrity and the dynamism of reforming piety. It would require conservatives to recognize the need for renewed attention to and dialogical engagement in the encompassing web of interdependencies, plural communities, and cosmopolitan institutions that characterize our present world. It would require progressives to recognize the need for renewed attention to the traditional formation in persons of reforming piety and believing.[26]

This second future also would entail the kind of vigorous, sustained, and creative attention to the institutional ecology of reforming Protestantism that has been characteristic of some of the movement's most dynamic periods. It would demand a commitment to building up communal contexts and structures no less impressive than earlier Puritan commitments to constitutional construction, evangelical commitments to voluntary associations, and progressive commitments to ecumenical ventures and assemblies. This commitment would have to be made initially in congregations, seminaries, and denominational bureaucracies by energetic laypeople, church professionals, and educators. But it is vitally important to recognize that the already strained resources of these institutions, at least as they are presently constituted, plainly are insufficient. To meet the dual demand for confessional integrity and relevant engagement will require not only the prudent stewardship and renewal of theological discourse in our congregations and seminaries, but also the renewal, revision, and creation of additional institutions and communal contexts.

Expanded educational programs cooperatively supported and staffed by consortia of congregations and local judicatories, lay academies, theological institutes or "think tanks," church-related schools, college student associations, and church-related journals—these are some of the institutions that might be tried in different places according to perceived needs and available resources. The characteristic marks of these ventures should parallel the confessionally dogmatic and dialogical dimensions of reforming theology. That is, our renewed and expanded communal contexts should institutionally embody the commitment to forming persons who are able to live out of the tradition of reforming Protestantism in our contemporary world. They should furnish opportunities for training and discussion aimed at helping people recover that tradition and its distinct confession. They should furnish opportunities for genuine debate and dialogue about contemporary social contexts and public issues. They should attempt to provide ethical and theological training to those who combine valuable experiences in politics, business, helping professions, and so forth, with reforming piety and commitment. They should devise programs that expose seminarians, pastors, and church leaders to the wisdom and expertise of public leaders, as well as to persons with experience in the careful analysis of the interdependencies, cosmopolitan contexts, and plural communities that characterize our present environment.[27]

It may be that this second future is nothing more than a pious pipe dream, and that reforming Protestants in America today had better busy themselves trying to identify their disparate niches in variations of future number one. Certainly, profound tensions and conflicts remain, and there can be no guarantee that we shall succeed in revitalizing the reforming spirit of faithful participation and its distinct quality of Christian commitment in the world. Nonetheless, I remain convinced that this is the direction that both *can* and *should be* tried in faithful response to the challenges of confessional integrity and relevant engagement that have been visited upon us in our place and time. In the following chapters we will explore a theological stance that lends support to the attempt.

3
A Theology for Reforming Protestantism

My understanding of our current circumstance basically comes to this: The distinctive spirit of reforming Protestantism, a transformative orientation or bias toward faithful participation in God's commonwealth, is at odds with therapeutic, moralistic, and communitarian movements that threaten to undermine its basic commitment in the world. Moreover, in the midst of a contentious American culture, conservative demands for distinct identity and progressive demands for relevant engagement threaten to fragment the confessional and dialogical impulses that are integral for reforming commitment. These developments raise a host of important questions regarding the present condition and future prospects of reforming Protestantism in America, but the basic challenge is *theological*.

My purpose in this chapter, then, is to outline a preliminary interpretation of reforming theology as a mode of reflection. I shall contend that Christian theology in the reforming stream is no neutral enterprise but a disciplined reflection in the service of the distinctive orientation of reforming piety. It is a confessional and dialogical effort to explicate, promote, deepen, and extend the dynamic spirit of faithful participation.

A Theocentric Piety

Note, once again, that the particular strain of Christian piety supported by reforming Protestantism is decidedly theocentric. Its leading affirmation is that, first and foremost, we belong to God. This is why reforming piety strives for *metanoia:* not in the first place thinking about ourselves and our

41

isolated groups, but being caught up into the messianic event of Jesus Christ—the person-for-others whose way in life is oriented by devotion to God, the Word who discloses the faithful God-for-others.[1] Reforming piety encourages a new quality of responsiveness to God-in-Christ, a communion with God in community with others. It endorses genuine faithfulness as a living-for-others, a life reordered and reformed by devotion to God and the well-being of God's inclusive commonwealth.

Jesus Christ points to God, our Father in heaven whose name is to be hallowed, who feeds birds and clothes lilies, who creates all things and also faithfully sustains them, and whose historic reign culminates in the coming kingdom (Matt. 6:9–13, 25–33; Mark 1:15). God alone is God, and we should have no others. Clearly, there are many other things of importance: personal growth, the civil society and nation, and the church. But personal growth is not the source and center of meaning and value. The nation is not God and neither is the church. As H. Richard Niebuhr insisted, God is the One beyond the many on whom the many depend. The true value and importance of the many other things that occupy our energies and attentions can be properly understood only in relation to God.[2]

Sin may be understood as our failure to recognize this with all of our hearts, minds, and wills. As sinners, we substitute something other than the faithful God for the source and center of meaning and value. We fail to uphold the First Commandment. We have gods other than God, with the result that our lives are oriented by constricted devotions to lesser realities such as self, nation, or church. In this way, we turn our backs on the project of being faithful persons-for-others, and become persons who are only for *some* others. Communion with God is broken, as is community with those who do not share our partial relations to ourselves and to our isolated groups.

God alone is God, and we should have no others. Equipped with this conviction, we will not capitulate to the idolatrous devotions, constricted visions, and fragmented patterns of responsibility that besiege the world and all of us in it. Even as we become inextricably enmeshed with misdirected desires, willfully limited attentions, and fractured promises, we will not fail to subject ourselves and all others to genuine criticism. Even as we participate in the partial commitments, self-invested interpretations, and skewed responses of persons, societies, nations, and churches, we will not fail to look for the judgments of God. We will not fail *critically* to relate to God and God's purposes all persons, communities, and institutions. God alone is God, and we should have no others. Measured by this plumb line, we ourselves, all of the peoples, nations, and churches will be subject to criticism, and all will be called to repentance.

A constructive corollary is that God always stands in relation to all, therefore, all things belong to God. In Dietrich Bonhoeffer's phrase, God is the integrity of reality; "when I encounter the world it is always already sustained, accepted and reconciled in the reality of God."[3] Thus, if nothing other than God is God, and if everything other than God is caught in the grips of broken communion and community, then nothing other than God is without God either. The God whom we come to know in Israel and preeminently in Jesus Christ, the person-for-others, is the God-for-others who refuses to abandon any thing. This God of everlasting covenant has been faithful, is faithful, and will be faithful. All things stand in relation to God and to one another in God's all-inclusive commonwealth because God always and already stands in relation to all things. All things in nature and in history are caught up in the intricate and encompassing web of divine power, presence, and grace. This is what renders the many things other than God a *uni*verse, and in this basic sense, nothing is godless, nothing profane.[4]

This also is why sin's universal and radical corruption is never the only or the last word. Jesus Christ is good news for sinners. The great faithfulness of God-in-Christ, God's refusal to abandon any thing, extends even to sinners, to those who betray the fundamental vocation for which they are fitted and sustained. If sin means brokenness, then God's great faithfulness means grace, the transforming divine initiative that overcomes brokenness and elicits a new responsiveness to God and neighbor. Grace means that within the intricate and encompassing web of divine faithfulness and presence we encounter promising possibilities for renewal. Grace also means the restoration of inordinately partial and constricted persons, communities, and institutions as faithful participants in communion and community within God's expansive commonwealth.

Equipped with this conviction, even in our criticisms of self, others, societies, nations, and churches, we will recognize, respect, and love them all as companions in God's good world. We will not fail to pursue promising possibilities for true communion in community. Precisely in the midst of criticisms and calls for repentance, we will not fail to relate *constructively* to God and to one another, rich and poor, weak and powerful, righteous and unrighteous, suburb and city, family and profession, corporation and government, church and world. Understood in the light of God's steadfast faithfulness, we ourselves, all of the peoples, institutions, plants, animals, and stars are caught up in an encompassing web of grace. All are affirmed; all are summoned to hope.

Reforming piety is theocentric because it affirms that, first and foremost, we belong to God, that God alone is God, and that God always already stands in relation to all. It is Christ-formed and even Christocentric in the sense that each of these affirmations in its fullness is both provoked by and made in Jesus Christ. Thus equipped with these convictions, persons endeavor to relate *critically* to God all persons, communities, and things, and they endeavor to relate *constructively* to God all persons, communities, and things. They try to relate all things *appropriately* to God and to one another. They are faithful participants in God's great commonwealth who are both critical and generous. They try to embody communion with God in community with others. They witness to God's no and to God's yes. They point to sin and to grace, to the cross and to glory, to judgment and to mercy. They call for the dynamic ordering and reordering of all of life in faithfulness to the One on whom we depend, to whom we belong, and from whom nothing can separate us.[5]

Living to God and Faithful Reflection

This particular strain of Christian piety accords with a certain understanding of Christian theology. If reforming piety is a life reordered in faithfulness to God, then in William Ames's Puritan phrase, reforming "theology is the doctrine or teaching of living to God."[6] Reforming piety is a kind of living that is caught up in the epic of God's dealings with Israel and in the messianic event of Jesus Christ and that is mediated to persons in Christian community. It is a socially shaped and interactive orientation pregnant with implications for understanding God, the world, and ourselves that issues in a particular practice. Christian theology in the reforming stream is a faithful reflection: the reflective effort of believers and their communities to explicate, promote, deepen, and extend this particular theocentric strain of Christian piety. Reforming theology thus is reflection in the service of a theocentric and reforming piety.

Reforming piety more specifically may be understood as a particular qualification of heart, mind, and will. Affectively, it is centered on a Christ-formed devotion to God and to the community of all things in relation to God. Imaginatively, it entails a Christ-inspired vision of God as the One beyond the many who always stands in relation to all, of the world as divine commonwealth, and of ourselves as participants in that commonwealth. Practically, it issues in an active, Christ-directed disposition of benevolent regard for God's all-inclusive commonwealth, or in a pattern of universal responsibility.

In this manner, Christian theology in the reforming stream is no neutral intellectual enterprise but a passionate reflection in the service of faithful participation, or the particular orientation of reforming piety. Reforming theologians reflect on an affectively charged, imaginatively visionary, and actively disposing orientation that has emerged as believers and their communities have wrestled with the classic resources of scripture and tradition in their continuing efforts to specify and to form the texture of faithful living to God within the divine commonwealth. This faithful orientation is decisively shaped and determined by Jesus Christ, the Word of God, the person-for-others and pioneer of true faithfulness; and it is preserved and communicated in and through the many practices and resources of reforming Christian communities.

It follows that as a biased and faithful reflection in the service of reforming piety, reforming theology is confessional, theocentric, critical, and constructive. It is *confessional* because it self-consciously depends on a historically particular, messianic, and socially mediated formation of affect, imagination, and responsibility in Christian community. It is *theocentric* because it serves a stance in living that is centered on a dominant devotion to God. It is *critical* because a basic corollary of this theocentric stance is that God alone is God and we should have no others. And it is *constructive* because of the corollary that God always stands in relation to all, and that, therefore, nothing is godless or profane.

Interactive Orientations and Reflections

Christian piety, whether of the reforming variety or any other, is not the only historically particular and socially formed interactive orientation that animates persons, and so Christian theology, whether of the reforming variety or any other, is hardly the only form of biased or committed practical reflection. Indeed, the world of dynamic human interrelations and interactions is also a world of faithful orientations and reflections sustained by various communities and institutions. So reforming piety and theology are not distinctive because they are matters of faithful orientation and reflection borne in community, but because they comprise one specific interactive orientation and faithful reflection among the many others that vie for human hearts, minds, and wills.

Consider the pragmatic assertion that persons are engaged in responsive interactions with their social and natural environments. These interactions are almost endlessly varied, and often they are characterized by accident, confusion, and deception. Even so, they are not entirely haphazard. Our responsive interactions display patterns that express our life-orientations or stances. They express our deep-seated devotions, visions, and dispositions. We might say that the morphologies of our lives express particular configurations of affect, imagination, and responsibility. This is why arguments and debates about matters of practical importance are deeper than mere reasoning or logic. It is also why we do not really understand people, their inactivities and patient endurances, their acts of creativity and sacrifice, unless we grasp the passion that tempers their hearts, the vision that enlightens their minds, and the disposition that directs their actions.

It is not difficult to understand why this should be so. For one thing, the social and natural environments with which we interact present us with many possible objects of devotion, and often we want, need, and are devoted to many different persons and things. Consequently, if we are to lead lives that are not constantly at cross-purposes, we must prioritize, order, and balance our many affections. In this sense, to be oriented rather than haphazard, to have some particular energy and way of negotiating life, is to be gripped by some orienting passion(s) or devotion(s).

Our social and natural environments, however, also confront us with so many possible and different objects of attention that we clearly cannot attend to all of them at once. If we are to lead lives informed by any coherent view of our circumstances at all, we need to attend selectively to limited samples and configurations. In this sense, to be oriented rather than haphazard, to engage our environments with some pattern and coherence, means to have an imaginative vision that orders our attentiveness to the many realities, persons, events, and interactions that surround us.

In much the same manner, we also find ourselves enmeshed in many interdependent relations of trust and responsibility. Not all of these depend equally on our immediate participation, and we clearly cannot be engaged in all of them at once. So if we are to lead lives that are practically responsible, we need to weigh, prioritize, and order our many responsibilities. In this regard, to be oriented rather than haphazard, to negotiate life with some direction, is also to be disposed in some more or less definite manner toward the many interrelations in which we participate.

It is critically important to understand that we do not construct our interactive orientations in isolation. Our personal orientations, our interactive skeins of affect, imagination, and disposition are socially located and socially formed. They are shaped and sustained in particular communities that introduce us to objects of devotion, visions of our environments, and patterns of responsibility. A community cherishes its particular heritage. It appropriates and interprets a cause or object of devotion, a vision of the encompassing world, and a pattern of responsibility that its heritage embodies and conveys.

This is why a community's vitality depends on the continuing viability of its traditions. If persons do not appropriate a community's heritage and extend its devotion, vision, and responsive disposition to engage, illumine, and order the challenges and realities of their present experiences, then the community and its distinctive orientation is threatened with extinction. When a community's tradition ceases to be reappropriated and extended, the characteristic orientation or stance of that community dies. What ceases is the dynamic of interpretation and appropriation, the vital willingness of persons to engage in the sustaining practices that allow them to be formed by the heritage in question and to embody its devotion, vision, and responsive disposition. A living tradition, then, enters into the constitution of meaningful personal life because by persistent practices of appropriation and interpretation, it continues to furnish an orientation that orders the continuing experiences of a society of people.

The interactive orientations of those who participate faithfully in a nation, for example, are shaped in converse with patriotic companions and interpretations of the nation's cause or object of devotion. Patriots are devoted to the nation, rejoicing over its existence, thankful for what it gives them, reverent of its integrity, and loyal to its cause. They are attentive to the nation, envisioning its citizens, institutions, ideas, cultural assets, and geographical areas as both historic and present elements of the beloved community in which they participate. They are responsive to the nation, understanding themselves to be bound to it and to their companions by special bonds of commitment and interdependence. They even are disposed to endure trials and risk actions that preserve and promote the nation's well-being.

Those individuals, institutions, communities, and realities that are not internally related to the national community and its cause are "foreign" because they stand in tangential relationships to civic devotion, vision, and responsibility. The affective commitments of patriots to these "others" therefore tend to be more diffuse and largely subordinated to their nationalistic devotion. Except as they are believed to impinge on the well-being of the nation and its cause, these outsiders occupy more or less displaced locations in patriots' fields of attention.

Moreover, it is always possible for one or another outsider to be elevated to the status of a quintessential evil that threatens a kind of demonical attack on both soul and substance. Such transmutations of others into monsters may bolster the solidarity and identity of an in-group, and they are often the staple of wartime propaganda. Some groups in contemporary America apparently envision gay people in this way. The problem here is not a simple failure to attend to the other, but a kind of inauthentic, wrong, and demonizing attention. Such demonizing attention, however, ordinarily seizes on a lack of any genuine interaction with and attention to the other that might call it into question. Indeed, we might say that the lack of genuine interaction and attention creates the social-psychological "space" for an almost entirely fabricated imaginative construction that functions to justify problematic actions, controls, and coercive demands. "We have to do this or you must do that in order to combat this invidious evil."[7]

Even apart from dire external threats (whether real or imagined), patriots endeavoring to live to the nation typically confront a number of significant difficulties that may precipitate faithful reflections. Conflicting judgments about particular courses of action may reveal that different groups within the patriotic community hold divergent interpretations of the nation and its cause. Or because patriots ordinarily are also members of other communities—families, ethnic groups, regional communities, religious associations, and so on—they may experience some difficulty in relating these other communities and causes to their nationalist affection, vision, and disposition.

The following excerpt from an article in *The Washington Post* regarding debates within the U.S. State Department concerning policy toward Iraq points to different judgments about particular courses of action that imply divergent interpretations of a nation and its cause.

> . . . three top State Department officials . . . prepared a confidential memorandum for Secretary of State George P. Schultz arguing against congressional efforts to impose tough economic sanctions against Iraq following that government's use of poison gas against hundreds of Kurdish citizens.
>
> "Iraq could [react by suspending] . . . repayment of the $1.5 billion of principal" on outstanding U.S. agricultural commodity credit, wrote . . . [the] senior officials. "The result would be the unraveling of the U.S.-Iraq economic relationship" to the benefit of European competitors.
>
> This position was unsuccessfully opposed at the time by the State Department's Bureau of Human Rights and Humanitarian Affairs, which published grim, unvarying accounts throughout the 1980s recounting the Iraqi government's systematic torture and killings of those it disliked, as individuals or as members of ethnic and religious groups.[8]

The understanding behind the alleged memorandum virtually identified the cause of the American nation with national commercial and political interests. Within the vision or field of attention supported by this understanding of patriotic devotion, the fate of the Kurds occupied a highly tenuous and peripheral place that was overshadowed by risks concerning commodity credit and potential European competition. By contrast, the actions of the Bureau of Human Rights and Humanitarian Affairs implied another interpretation, one that linked the cause of the United States with a concern for human rights that might not entirely coincide with the nation's more immediate commercial and political advantage. Within the field of attention supported by this understanding of nationalist loyalty, then, the plight of the Kurds might exert a more profound influence on American policy.

The difference between the authors of the memorandum and the Bureau points to differences in political philosophy or ideology. These, in turn, can only be addressed by intentional reflections about the piety or interactive orientation of the American national community.

As noted earlier, entirely consistent nationalists are rather rare. Among patriots, as among other groups, families, ethnic ties, regional affiliations, religious associations, and more also vie for some measure of heartfelt devotion, imaginative attention, and disposing intention. These other communities and their causes need to be ordered somehow in relation to the practical frame of living to the nation and its cause. And the more usual development is that they do not fit with complete harmony within the nationalist frame. Diverse centers of devotion, imagination, and disposition, therefore, tend to complicate life even for ardent patriots. These complications may also precipitate serious conflicts.

This is yet another reason why persons often are led to engage in intentional reflections about the spirit, character, and ethos of the national community. These reflections may be pursued by the emperor's court, offices within a national bureaucracy, political parties, poets, academics, journalists, or what have you. Their basic purpose is to explicate, promote, deepen, and extend the particular orientation entailed by a specific national devotion. They are not detached or neutral intellectual enterprises, but practical political philosophies, ideologies, and even civil theologies in the service of a nation's particular bias.

Consider the following paragraph from a recent essay by Robert Hughes, titled "The Fraying of America."

> America is a construction of mind, not of race or inherited class or ancestral territory. It is a creed born of immigration, of the jostling of scores of tribes that become American to the extent which they can negotiate accommodations with one another. These negotiations succeed unevenly and often fail: you need only to glance at the history of racial relations to know that. The melting pot never melted. But American mutuality lives in recognition of difference. The fact remains that America is a collective act of imagination whose making never ends, and once that sense of collectivity and mutual respect is broken, the possibilities of American–ness begin to unravel.[9]

Hughes's remarks amount to intentional reflections in the service of the civic piety and orientation of the United States of America. He alludes to a heritage: the formation of the nation around an idea, cause, or "construction of mind," rather than a simple extension of (initially European) ethnic, class, or territorial loyalties. Indeed, the American nation is a "creed," a cause that results from "immigration" and the "jostling" of diverse "tribes" or ethnic communities that become faithfully "American" to the extent that they find their places in a responsive pattern or polity of mutual respect and recognition of differences. To a significant extent and degree, this continuing and "collective act of imagination" does battle with other loyalties and causes that lie just below the surface of American life, as is indicated by "the history of racial relations." We might say that the American "sense of collectivity" promises to accommodate plural subcommunities with their specific loyalties, visions, and responsive dispositions, so long as these plural subcommunities and tribes accommodate themselves to an overarching cause or devotion called "American mutuality." When this does not happen, "the possibilities of American-ness" or for an inclusive national orientation and identity "begin to unravel."

My fundamental point here is that distinct interactive orientations are promoted by many different communities, institutions, and associations. In each of these social groups, persons share a particular heritage. They are bound to companions by shared devotions, imaginative visions, and patterns of responsibility. Thus disagreements may emerge that betray different understandings of the community's basic orientation. Moreover, since persons ordinarily belong to more than one community, they often experience some difficulty relating their different centers of devotion, attention, and responsibility. Consequently, in each of these communities, conflicts and difficulties may precipitate intentional and faithful reflections. So the world of dynamic human interrelations and interactions is also a world of faithful orientations and reflections sustained by various communities and institutions.

Revision, Assimilation, Disintegration, and Conversion

A critical question arises at this juncture. Are we simply fated to uphold our socially formed interactive stances come what may? There are reasons to think so. After all, we always find ourselves with specific orientations formed by our participation in particular communities and informed by their affectively charged and disposing interpretative visions or frameworks for interpretation. Thus, we are never entirely open or neutral agents and observers, but instead are predisposed to attend to and interact with persons, situations, and realities in certain ways. Furthermore, genuine faithfulness, whether to God, nation, family, or what have you, often demands that we hold fast to our devotions, imaginative visions, and disposing patterns of responsibility even in the face of pressing, occasionally attractive alternatives.

Nonetheless, as we continue to interact with changing circumstances and realities, our particular practical wisdoms—our socially formed orientations, biases, or stances—sometimes are subject to challenge. This is so because, as noted, persons and communities engaged in the push and shove of nature and history continue to reason and reflect in the service of their interactive orientations. They consider and reconsider their heritages and traditions. They ponder their chief causes and purposes in relation to other objects of concern. They interpret the significance and importance of changing situations, events, and realities. They estimate the shifting and interdependent lines of responsibility in which they participate.

In the midst of these continuing reasonings and reflections, challenges may arise in connection with our own preferred interactive orientation or in conjunction with persons and communities who represent other, equally particular interactive orientations. In either case, challenges emerge when, for one reason or another and to some significant extent and degree, we recognize that our patterns of responsibility, imaginative visions, or dominant devotions are called into question. Challenges begin with a felt dissonance or perception of dissonance.

Some challenges precipitate revisions in our patterns of responsibility and imaginative visions that enable us skillfully to assimilate changing circumstances, realities, and ideas in ways that largely preserve and extend our devotions and the particular interactive orientations they nourish.[10] So, for example, accustomed patterns of responsibility and received interpretative visions may be called into question when they fail to encourage us to uphold certain relationships of interdependence and trust, and when they fail to direct our attention toward certain pressing realities. To return to "American-ness" as a "construction of mind," this is one way to describe what happened to at least some Americans as a consequence of the civil rights movement. Received and established patterns of interaction and responsibility, as well as received and established visions of the American political community, were altered and revised in ways that were understood to be consistent with the preservation and extension of devotion to the United States and the cherished cause of democratic equality or even mutuality expressed in its heritage and political tradition.

Revisionary assimilations such as these can be highly significant, and it would also be a mistake to underestimate their complexity. They often are responsive not only to changed conditions but also to ideas, visions, and confrontational and symbolic actions offered by particular communities such as black Americans. It may be better to say that contributions such as these often are among the circumstances that we strive to take into account. Then too, revisionary assimilations often are achieved only at the cost of significant conflict and suffering, since they involve adjustments in persons' cherished causes, familiar visions, and customary patterns of responsibility. They also often require adjustments in the ways communities understand their classical heritages, as is apparent to many Americans today when they ponder the meaning of the sentence, "All *men* are created equal."

Regardless, revisionary assimilation does not entail the decisive dissolution of a particular orientation, its radical displacement, or its replacement by another. These more radical possibilities amount to exchanging one object of devotion for another, one imaginative vision for another, and one pattern of responsibility for another. They involve more than revisionary assimilation and the extension of a particular orientation, and they are therefore better understood under the rubrics of disintegration and conversion.

Like a revisionary assimilation, a disintegration or conversion may begin with challenges that call into question some aspect of a particular pattern of responsibility or imaginative vision. True disintegrations, however, do not stop there, since they entail challenges that, for one reason or another, are not assimilated within the frame of our dominant devotion. Moreover, to the extent that a given disintegration leads to conversion, that it leads not only to relinquishing a dominant devotion, but also to adopting another, it takes place in conjunction with affections, images, and patterns contributed by some other, equally particular interactive orientation.

Consider again the situation of a committed nationalist. Her interactive orientation has been shaped by participation with companions in a particular national community that offers certain interpretations of its heritage and its cause. She therefore is predisposed to envision and interact with persons, communities, and circumstances in ways consistent with her patriotism. Nonetheless, she may encounter anomalous and troubling circumstances and realities.

Suppose, then, that she finds her particular pattern of responsibility called into question by some train of broken trusts, occasions of malice, injustice, and oppression. Perhaps her initial discomfort will emerge during visits to communities ravished by violence and war that ordinarily lie at the periphery of her patriotic vision. Perhaps she feels accosted by the consequences of things done or left undone by her national community and compatriots. Perhaps on her return to her own community she engages patriotic companions in conversations about these conditions. To her dismay, she finds her companions largely unresponsive. They seem unable to conceive of any change in their patriotic vision and tradition that might take into account her experiences and yet accord with their devotion to the nation and its cause.

At this point, our protagonist has reached an impasse. If she is unable to disregard or repress the force of her recent experiences, she may find herself edging toward a crisis, not only of responsibility and vision but also of patriotic faith and devotion. If that crisis persists and her sorrow and concern intensifies with respect to circumstances and trusts that her compatriots apparently deem insignificant, then her nationalist orientation may begin to disintegrate and unravel.

This is only a crisis, or an instance of emerging disintegration. For a conversion we need to introduce contributions from some other orienting framework. Let us say, then, that our protagonist comes into contact with a relief agency and organization that is actively engaged in trying to address the very conditions that have elicited her concern and precipitated her crisis. She encounters persons whose responsible actions uphold the trusts with which she recently has become concerned. In conversation, she finds that their pattern of responsibility or practical disposition points toward an imaginative vision appreciably different from the one to which she is accustomed. She hears them speak of "universal human rights" that reach across national borders even when the recognition of such rights does not entirely accord with the interests of particular nation-states. Perhaps in and through her interactions and discussions with these people she surmises that their particular interpretative vision of the circumstances calling for action is centered on a devotion to the human species.

She still is not necessarily converted, although she has within her field of attention all of the elements needed for conversion. She is troubled by what she regards as the bad consequences and inadequacies of the nationalist orientation into which she was socialized, and she has interacted with persons who represent another orienting devotion, vision, and disposition that seems better able to take into account much that has been troubling her. If she then "converts" to this alternative orientation, she will become a humanist of sorts rather than an entirely committed nationalist. In order to nourish, sustain, and extend her newfound practical wisdom, she probably will need to seek the company and community of others who share a similar orientation.

All of this may mean that this woman now turns her back almost completely on her previous center of devotion, vision, and disposition. It may mean that she comes to regard her nation and her previous devotion to it as entirely incompatible with her humanism, and therefore false and pernicious. On the other hand, it may not mean exactly that. It may mean that she now endeavors to "situate" her patriotic devotion, vision, and responsibilities within the wider context of her newfound humanism. For example, she might come to regard her nation's cause as a particular formation and expression of the more fundamental cause of "universal human rights." (This might be relatively close to the understanding of the cause of the American nation that apparently helped motivate some persons in the State Department's Bureau of Human Rights and Humanitarian Affairs to publish accounts of Iraqi government atrocities during the 1980s.) She may even come to interpret her nation's heritage and classical documents this way. In that case, her nationalist center of devotion will not, in her judgment, have been relinquished or destroyed, although it will have been significantly reconfigured. This, in turn, will enable her to criticize more narrow nationalist orientations, even though she does not now regard all nationalism as utterly evil.

Similar things may happen to communities. A society's particular and unifying orientation may be challenged by diverse commitments, visions, and patterns of responsibility that come to expression in the midst of bitter internal conflicts. It may be challenged by suspicions that it is being used to further the isolated interests of power-seeking persons and groups, by the emergence of a compelling critique of its heritage and mythologies, or by encounters with more powerful and persuasive communities and their orientations. Circumstances such as these constitute crises of social faith.

Under these circumstances, the troubling consequences and implications of holding to a particular and established orientation may prove too severe for at least some critical mass of a community's participants. Difficulties such as these have recently emerged for many whites in South Africa, whose civic pieties, legal, political, and commercial patterns of responsibility were decisively shaped by a national heritage and constitutional government self-consciously devoted to an exclusive racial cause that deliberately disenfranchised a vast black majority. Difficulties such as these have emerged also for many of those who supported the Nazi cause of Aryan nationalism and then experienced the decisive military defeat of their nation, as well as international disclosure of the holocaust of the Jews. In any event, disintegration sets in when a community's particular orientation fails the test of revisionary assimilation. Conversion becomes possible, both for individuals and communities, when that test is failed in the presence of other equally historically and socially particular orientations.

Thus continuing reasoning and reflection in the service of our interactive orientations and biases sometimes lead to challenges, revisionary assimilations, crises, disintegrations, and conversions. This is why, although our interactive stances remain historically and socially conditioned, we are not simply fated to uphold our socially formed and interactive stances

come what may. This is also why we can justify standing fast in a particular orientation, revising it, or abandoning it in favor of another. Our justifications will be passionate and deeper than mere reasoning or logic.
They will combine appeals to the affectively charged and practically disposing interpretative vision that we presently affirm with accounts of how
it adequately addresses certain significant situations and realities. These
justifications may also include polemics or criticisms of alternative orienting frameworks of which we are aware and that we believe do not address
these situations and realities with the same integrity, helpfulness, or effectiveness.

To put these same points another way, our faithful orientations and reflections are historically particular and socially located, but they are not
simply and utterly incommensurable. They need not remain esoteric and
obscure to those who do not share our specific pattern of devotion, vision, and responsibility. They need not imply a vicious relativism. They
may be rendered intelligibly, in ways that enable us to enter into conversations with people who represent other, equally historically and socially
particular interactive stances.

Reforming Piety

My general suggestion, then, is that we regard the interactive orientations
of personal agents as historically particular and socially formed wisdoms or
practical ways of negotiating life that may be rendered intelligibly in conversations with others. These wisdoms entail devotion to some object or
objects, some vision of our environments in relation to our object(s) of
devotion, and some corresponding active disposition or pattern of responsibility. My further suggestion is that Christian piety in the reforming stream may be regarded as one, historically particular, socially mediated, and practical wisdom among others.

Like other interactive orientations and practical wisdoms, reforming
Christian piety entails a specific formation or qualification of personal affect and imagination that issues in a particular pattern of responsibility. It
comes to us by participation in a particular community of devotion, imaginative interpretation, and practice that is sustained by a particular heritage
and tradition. It has proved capable of accommodating revisionary assimilations. It is capable of entering into ecumenical conversations and debates. There also have been instances in which, for some persons and
communities, reforming piety has been subject to disintegration and displaced by conversion. What makes reforming piety distinctive is that it
entails devotion to a specific object, a particular imaginative construal of
ourselves and our environments in relation to that object, and a specific

corresponding disposition or active tendency. These are mediated to people in the church and sustained by a continuing appropriation and interpretation of its scriptures and traditions.

A normative description of this particular orientation thus can only be given in conjunction with reflections on the church's scriptures and traditions. We might note that in the library of literatures known as the Hebrew scriptures a particular skein of devotion, vision, and responsibility comes to expression. There emerges a radical faith in the God who brought Israel out of bondage in Egypt, who creates the world and all that is in it, and who governs the histories of nations and empires. Particularly in the prophetic literature, this theocentric devotion comes into conflict with devotions to things other than and less than God, such as the Ba'alim, the monarchy, and the class interests of the comfortable. Yet devotion to God remains the primary affective vector that is both vindicated and recommended by the literatures we have received. Here, we find the affirmation that God alone is God, and we should have no others.

Similarly, the Hebrew scriptures both express and provoke a vision of all creation—both nature and history—as the reign or dominion of the one God. "The earth is the LORD's and all that is in it, the world, and those who live in it" (Ps. 24:1). Indeed, the Lord "looks down from heaven on humankind" (Ps. 14:2, 53:2). Kings are not saved by their great armies; neither are warriors delivered by their strength (see Prov. 21:31). The Lord rules in glory and in might. Here all human relations, whether among persons or among communities and institutions, are envisioned and depicted as covenantal relations of promise making and promise keeping in the presence of the one faithful God. A particular pattern of responsibility emerges in which persons and communities are responsible and answerable to one another at the same time that they also are answerable and responsible to the One who stands in relation to all.[11]

It is within the indispensable context of Jewish monotheism that the theocentric orientation or wisdom of Christian piety comes to decisive articulation in Jesus Christ, the person-for-others, the Word who discloses the only faithful God. Thus, Jonathan Edwards wrote of "the Christian spirit" in Jesus' teaching, example, and last sufferings, claiming that this spirit is based in "the love that Christ has to the Father."[12] H. Richard Niebuhr insisted that the virtues of Jesus Christ—love, hope, faith, obedience, and humility—can only be understood in terms of his radical devotion to God.[13] It is in this sense, for Niebuhr, that Jesus Christ incarnates radical faith in God.[14] Somewhat similarly, James M. Gustafson says that Jesus incarnates theocentric piety.[15]

We might say that Jesus Christ is devoted to God and God's purposes, even unto death on a cross. By his radical devotion to God, he testifies that God alone is God, that we are not our own, that all things belong to God, and that we too should subordinate all other devotions and concerns to God and God's purposes. This is one way to interpret Mark 8:34b–36 and its parallels. At stake here—in denying oneself, in taking up one's cross, in following Jesus, and in losing one's life in order to find it—is an abiding and orienting dominant devotion. If one gains one's life-orienta-tion, interactive movement, and identity from devotion to a cause, then the figure of Jesus in the Gospels constantly poses the prime practical ques-tion of life, because his own orientation so transparently depends on his radical devotion to God. And it is precisely this life-orientation and iden-tity for others, this decisively new creation, new person, or new human-ity that is vindicated by resurrection.

It is crucially important to understand that this dominant passion does not reduce to mere emotion. Like other devotions, it works to set us go-ing, to direct and sustain our behavior.[16] It orients us; it connects us with the world around us by engendering both interpretations of and interac-tive responses to objects, situations, and contexts. To put this another way, passionate devotion to God has imaginative and active dimensions; it en-tails a particular faithful vision and a specific faithful disposition.

For Edwards, the imaginative dimension entailed by devotion to God is a sense for the beauty and excellence of divine things. Christian believ-ing, Edwards thought, involves a vision of all things "in connexion with the whole" that has its subsistence in God. So Edwards could write that "the child of God is graciously affected, because he sees and understands something more of divine things than he did before. . . . "[17] The eigh-teenth-century Quaker and abolitionist, John Woolman, in his eloquent "A Plea for the Poor," wrote of being enlarged and so regarding all oth-ers as "our fellow creatures" under God.[18] In a similar way, H. Richard Niebuhr maintained that radical faith in God involves a reinterpretation of our "total context" or "environment," a reading of "that community of which the universal God is the head" and of the ultimate history within which we live and move.[19] Again, Richard R. Niebuhr links believing and enlargement, or what he calls the experience "of being on the way to membership in an ultimate society."[20]

We might say that Christian piety in the reforming stream involves a particular imaginative discernment. To be more specific, it discerns the God in whom we live and move and have our being to be the One who stands in relation to all, directing creatures toward their appropriate rela-tions to God and to one another. In light of this discernment, reforming Christians imaginatively interpret a world created, sustained, and re-deemed by the one God, a universe of integrity and purpose, a world as divine commonwealth on the way toward its consummation. They discern what Gordon D. Kaufman calls "the interdependence and self-giving which underlies and makes possible all creativity and life."[21] They glimpse what Martin Luther King Jr. called "the beloved community," an "inescapable network of mutuality" and interrelatedness, "a single garment of destiny."[22] This is the capacious eye, the imaginative vision of our surrounding environment entailed by Christian believing.

The active correlate of these devotional and imaginative dimensions of reforming piety is a disposition to live in accord with God's own cause or purposes. This is the heartfelt and passionate obedience that reverses sinful constriction. Edwards called it "benevolence to being in general," while Woolman wrote of "a universal regard to our fellow creatures." The nineteenth-century revivalist and abolitionist, Charles Finney, spoke of a turning toward "God and the interests of his kingdom," a formulation not unlike ones later employed by Walter Rauschenbusch as he advocated the social gospel. H. Richard Niebuhr referred to a pattern of universal responsibility.[23]

Consequently, Christian piety in the reforming stream may be understood as an orientation in life characterized by devotion to God and God's purposes; an imaginative vision of the world in which we live and move as God's reign, commonwealth, or city; and an active tendency or disposition of universal regard, benevolence, or responsibility to all things in relation to God. This is what I mean by the reforming orientation of faithful participation: an orientation that emerges in Israel and is decisively embodied, displayed, and provoked by the messianic event. Jesus Christ, the Son with whom the Father is well-pleased, the person-for-others, embodies an orientation in life centered on devotion to God and love of the community of all things in their appropriate relations to God and to one another. Precisely in the event of this embodiment vindicated by resurrection, he decisively discloses the faithful God-for-others who refuses to abandon the community of creatures. In a world gripped by sin, fragmentation, and conflict, Jesus Christ teaches, embodies, and empowers *metanoia;* God's continuing revolution in human minds and hearts that supports a distinctive stance of faithful participation in God's universal commonwealth.

As a reforming Christian, then, my interactive orientation is decisively shaped in Christian community by means of practices that continue to appropriate and consider the scriptural accounts of Israel and Jesus Christ with the aid of the church's extracanonical tradition. I am devoted to God-in-Christ, rejoicing over God's existence, thankful for God's faithfulness, reverent of God's integrity, and loyal to God's cause, or to the commonwealth of all things under God. I endeavor to be attentive to this universal community and to the persons, things, structures, and relationships that are past, present, and potential participants in the beloved community in which I participate. I try to be responsive to this universal society, understanding myself to be bound to it and to my companions by bonds of affection and interdependence. And I am disposed to endure trials and risk actions that promise to enact, preserve, and contribute to the well-being of the universal community.

Within this particular frame of reference, then, there is no person, place, power, or reality that is not, in some potentially relevant sense, internally related to my community and its cause. For this reason, I realize that all of my partial and selective commitments, fields of attention, and patterns of responsibility stand in need of continual correction toward the expansive compass of the universal commonwealth. I recognize that the many other foci of my devoted affection, imaginative attention, and active disposition—my family, my nation, my race, and so on—need to be situated and reordered within the expansive frame of living-to-God within the universal commonwealth. This is one reason reforming churches often encourage and support reflections on the character and ethos of the divine commonwealth or in the service of reforming piety. These are not neutral intellectual enterprises, but reforming theologies that attempt to explicate, promote, deepen, and extend the particular wisdom, orientation, or bias of faithful participation.

Indeed, it is this particular, theocentric, and practical orientation or bias of faithful participation that ought to be preserved, exercised, communicated, and promoted by the practices and patterns of interaction in the reforming churches. It is this particular and practical wisdom that ought to be borne by the reception and interpretation of scripture and tradition in these communities. It ought to be exercised, communicated, and internalized in services of worship and in sermons, in song and in prayer, in classes and in fellowship, in care and in counsel, in meditation and in mission. And it is explicated, promoted, deepened, and extended by reforming Christian theology, or by the primary reflective enterprise that ought always to accompany and be supported by reforming churches, communities, and institutions.

Reforming Theology

Reforming theology is roughly analogous to the faithful reflections supported by other communities. Like them, it is not a neutral or detached intellectual enterprise. Its fundamental aim is to explicate, promote, deepen, and extend a particular interactive orientation or bias in living. What makes reforming theology distinctive is its reflection in the service of the theocentric bias of reforming Christian piety. Christian theology in the reforming stream aims to explicate, promote, deepen, and extend an interactive orientation characterized by radical devotion to God-in-Christ, a vision of all things in their appropriate interrelations with God and one another, and a disposing pattern of universal responsibility. It is reflection in the service of the spirit of faithful participation.

Reforming theology, in pursuit of this aim, examines the practices of reforming churches. It examines their preaching, worship, teaching, care, administration, fellowship, and witness. It examines their continuing appropriation and interpretation of the scriptures and of their extrabiblical traditions. It examines their continuing interpretation or construal of the encompassing world as the divine commonwealth within which we live and move and respond to God and to others. And the normative criterion in all of this is Jesus Christ, the person-for-others who decisively discloses the reality of human living-to-God, the Word of God who decisively discloses the reality of the faithful One beyond the many who always stands in relation to all.

As such, Christian theology in the reforming stream has significant cognitive dimensions. One of these is exegetical. With the aid of the church's tradition, reforming theology requires continuous and disciplined reflections on the scriptures. These indispensable reflections move toward normative specifications of living-to-God, of faithful participation, or of theocentric devotion, vision, and responsibility. They include the claim that this particular interactive orientation accords with the biblical witness, as a witness to God's transformative way with the world in Israel and in Jesus Christ.

Nonetheless, and here we come across a matter often obscured by the modern differentiation of theological subdisciplines (for example, biblical studies, church history, systematics, and practical theology) as well as by the "scientific" study of religions; our exegetical reflections are not ends in themselves. These reflections are theologically significant to the extent that they contribute to the fundamental aim of reforming Christian theology. They are theologically valuable to the extent that they help point persons and communities toward the living and only Lord, to whom the scriptures themselves point.

Thus we arrive at the constructive dimension of Christian theology. Reforming piety purports to orient persons and communities toward the many objects, situations, and realities with which they interact in a manner that is faithfully responsive to the God disclosed in the scriptures, the One who always stands in relation to all. It claims to shape individuals and communities into faithful participants in God's world—a constructive claim that does not reduce to a matter of exegesis or biblical interpretation alone. Or expressed another way, the socially formed and practical wisdom of reforming piety entails a distinctive vision of God and world. Therefore, in its constructive dimension, and as a biased reflection in the service of reforming Christian piety, reforming Christian theology offers an interpretation of the world, or of all things in their appropriate inter-relations with God and with one another.

Gustafson gives an account of this constructive dimension when he says that the world may be construed in many ways and that theology is a way of construing the world. Revising a sentence of the contemporary philo-sophical theologian, Julian N. Hartt, he writes of "an intention to relate all things in a manner appropriate to their *relations* to God." Theology, says Gustafson, is primarily "an activity of practical reason" that has cog-nitive and intellectual elements because it tries "to make sense out of a very broad range of human experiences, to find some meaning in them and for them that enables persons to live and act in coherent ways" in the presence of God.[24]

In a similar manner, Hartt maintains that Christian theology may be understood as "a conceptualization of the Christian outlook." This con-ceptualization can and ought to be tested in relation to other conceptual schemes and interpretations. Nonetheless, we need to remember that "the case the authentic believer is committed to making assumes the form of a personal justification or verification of a truth claim." This "is not so much a matter of being proved right in holding to certain beliefs as it is of be-ing warranted in holding to a course of life."[25] Holding to a Christian course of life involves an interpretation of the setting for human life.

We might say that Christian piety in the reforming stream is a histor-ically particular and practical wisdom that includes a distinctive vision of the many contexts, relationships, loyalties, loves, sufferings, and involve-ments of life in relation to God-in-Christ. Christian theology, as reflec-tion in the service of this piety, tries to interpret a broad range of experi-ences so as to enable persons and communities to live to God. It is an intellectual enterprise that aids believers in holding to a particular course of life, and in doing so, it constructs an interpretation or construal of the world that can and ought to be compared with other interpretations and construals.

The distinctive orientation or piety of the reforming movement, then, is tied to an apprehension of the living Lord whose commonwealth or do-minion includes all things in nature and in history, past, present, and fu-ture. Given this conception of God in relation to humanity and the world, theological reflections in the service of reforming piety cannot eliminate from consideration things other than the historical Christian tradition and scriptures. To inquire about God from the perspective of the historic vi-sion supported by reforming Christian piety is always also to inquire about other things with which we interact and the varied ways in which they may be understood. It is in this sense that reforming piety mandates continuing intellectual engagement with the world. What is presently known about anything in nature, history, and society is potentially relevant for understanding God and God's purposes, as well as the orientation in human life that is faithfully responsive to the living Lord.

This would not be so if Christian piety in the reforming stream took a limited reality as its cherished object of devotion—if, for example, it was a matter of devotion to the clan, the nation, the church, or even to the human race. Then the field of mundane interrelations that would need to be faithfully ordered and envisioned in relation to the cherished object of devotion would be less than universal. One or another aspect or interrelation within nature and history might then be left out of account because it would not count in relation to the cherished object. Yet the object in relation to which the reforming movement affirms that we live and move and have our being is no limited reality but is the One who bears all things in a single commonwealth.

First and foremost, we belong to God. God alone is God, and God always stands in relation to all. For reforming Christian believers, this means that no corner of nature or history is of no account as we try to relate all things in a manner appropriate to their belonging to God. Indeed, in the service of theocentric piety, reforming Christian theology is inherently dialogical. It is an intellectual venture, *habitus,* or sapiential reflection especially disposed to engage the many challenges that sometimes precipitate revisionary assimilations.

For example, to be open exegetically to considering and reconsidering diverse interpretations of the scriptures is part of attempting to live-to-God, the One to whom the scriptures point. It is a way of checking to find out whether our customary interpretations of scripture have been skewed or compromised by an object of concern, imaginative vision, and pattern of responsibility that banishes some significant aspect of the biblical witness from our field of attention. With respect to the constructive dimension of reforming Christian theology, to be open to attending to realities, situations, and interrelations that may appear anomalous and troubling is part of what it means to relate all things both critically and positively to God. This is a way of estimating whether, as a consequence of some constricted concern, we have failed to attend to one or another significant aspect of our responsive interactions within the divine commonwealth.

Engaging diverse interpretations or construals offered by other communities is also part of what it means to interpret all things in their appropriate interrelations with God and one another. These other interpretations or construals may bring to our attention matters of importance that we have neglected, and the diverse communities and disparate visions with which we interact are themselves among the things to be interpreted in relation to God. As an inherently dialogical reflection, then, reforming Christian theology tries to correct the reforming community's own historic lapses of attention and so enhance its participation in the all-inclusive commonwealth of things in relation to God.

At the same time, however, it is important to remember that these admittedly wide-ranging reflections are never without their specific focus and direction. This is so because reforming theology, even in its dialogues, remains confessional and dogmatic. It denies that devotions to lesser realities—gods other than God, such as family, nation, or even humanity—are appropriate organizing centers for life. It subjects reforming piety or believing to criticism in light of radical devotion to God-in-Christ, the One beyond the many who always stands in relation to all. It criticizes all conceptual schemes and visions that, in virtue of devotion to some finite reality, arbitrarily select for exclusive attention some communities, situations, and realities that appear to have no greater claim to centrality than do others. It is especially on the lookout for ways in which such partial visions and devotions may skew the theological reflections and practical orientations of those who participate in reforming Christian communities. And, in all of this, it is guided by the dogmatic confession that Jesus is the Christ, the person-for-others who decisively discloses the reality of human living to God, the Word of God who decisively discloses the reality of the faithful One beyond the many who always stands in relation to all, the God to whom, first and foremost, we belong, and the One from whom nothing can separate us.

First and foremost, we belong to God. God alone is God, and God always stands in relation to all. A reforming movement equipped with these convictions will support a distinct quality of Christian commitment in today's world. It will not split apart over disparate conservative demands for distinct identity and progressive demands for relevant engagement. Instead, it will recognize that its distinctly reforming Christian identity and its relevant and dialogical engagements are integral and complementary aspects of reforming piety. It will therefore renew its commitment to the continued explication, promotion, deepening, and extension of the theocentric wisdom of reforming Christian piety in human hearts, minds, and wills. It will do so in worship and in witness; in fellowship and in care; in meditation and in mission; in families, committees, offices, judicatories, and retreats; and in new institutionalizations aimed at the cultivation of its distinctly reforming spirit. It will engage in *dogmatic* reflections, knowing that these must finally lead to genuine dialogue and engagement with the circumambient world. It will engage in *dialogical* reflections, knowing that these finally are motivated and nourished by the dogmatic confession that Jesus is the Christ, the person-for-others who decisively discloses the reality of human living-to-God, the Word who decisively discloses the faithful and only God who always stands in relation to all. In dogma and in dialogue, criticism and construction, it will renew the meaning of an old affirmation. *Ecclesia reformata, semper reformanda.*

4

Responsible Realism and Creative Responsibility

C hristian piety in the reforming stream is a historically particular wisdom that orients individuals in Christ toward God and all things in their appropriate interrelations. This is the basic sense that it finds in life. Thus, the conviction of divine sovereignty, or that, first and foremost, we belong to God, is the central element of this wisdom. God alone is God, and we should have no others. Therefore, all of the constricted devotions, visions, and patterns of responsibility that are centered on things other than God are subject to prophetic criticism. God always stands in relation to all. Therefore, nothing is godless, nothing profane; all things are caught up in the intricate and encompassing web of divine power, presence, and grace.

Equipped with these convictions, those who would respond to God find themselves called to relate all things both critically and constructively to God and God's purposes. They are called to participate faithfully in the full field of natural and cultural interrelations. Within the frame of reforming piety, then, the divine power and presence meets us at every turn, and we are called to be faithfully responsive to God in all of our activities and involvements. Reforming piety elicits a pattern of responsibility as broad as the divine governance. It supports an orientation, stance, framework, or bias that lends life meaning and coherence.

Particularly in our current circumstance, however, there is considerably more that needs to be said. A large part of the reforming movement's present difficulty stems from our inability to *deliver* theocentric sensibilities into all of life in the midst of our pluralistic and interdependent setting.

Indeed, many of us are drawn to therapeutic, moralistic, and communitarian movements that salvage only a portion of reforming piety by narrowly joining a felt sense of God and God's purposes with one or another partial dimension of life. One consequence is that we have difficulty believing that God meets us at every turn, partly because we have forgotten how to live faithfully to God in all our activities and involvements. We have difficulty showing both ourselves and others precisely how our Christian commitment makes a difference.

This chapter helps connect a distinctively reforming and theocentric piety with all of life by exploring a tensive polarity near the heart of reforming piety that further specifies the stance of faithful participation. Properly understood, the dynamic of sin and grace points to the persistent corruption of human life, as well as to a transformation that bestows "newness of life" (Rom. 6:4). It recognizes a disruption of the fundamental community between God and world that ultimately is overcome in redemption, a history of fragmentation and conflict transfigured by regenerative possibility. In short, the dynamic of sin and grace combines attitudes of pessimism and optimism in such a way as to lend to the stance of faithful participation the twin qualities of responsible realism and creative responsibility.

The result, I believe, is a practical stance that makes a difference in every aspect of life, whether personal or institutional, ecclesiastical or cultural. Unlike the stances supported by therapeutic spiritualities, it does not accept personal growth as a master goal, because it recognizes that faithful participation in communities and institutions often requires significant adjustments in what persons want and desire. Moreover, faithful participation specified as responsible realism and creative responsibility also differs from the practical stances supported by moralistic and radically communitarian pieties. Unlike the former, it sharply criticizes easy and immediate identifications of God's purposes with authoritarian and nationalistic attitudes and structures. Unlike the latter, it criticizes ecclesiocentric loyalties, and it affirms that corrupted institutions may be turned toward equitable and good purposes.

Sin as Multifaceted Corruption

John Calvin correctly insisted that "sin is not our nature but its derangement."[1] The reforming Christian conviction of sin presupposes that humans are created good and are intended to occupy a distinctive and creative place in the dynamic whole of God's good world. As befits their significant, even wondrous, powers and capacities, humans are intended for conscious, intentional, and creative interrelations with God and with others. They are created for abundant and good life.

We might say that the human fault is a corruption of what we are equipped to be, a turning away from God and others, a diminution of the abundant and good life that befits us. Humans are equipped to be faithful and creative participants; we are fitted for covenantal relationships of attentiveness, fidelity, and responsibility with God and with others. We are fitted for true communion with God in community with others. Sin means that, although we are fitted and sustained for this distinctive vocation, we are chronically confused, misoriented, and misdirected in the ways we live and move and deploy our powers. We are in the grips of a corrupting tendency, an impeding influence that keeps us from living the truly abundant and good life. Sin means the way toward *death,* or the diminution of *life* in its fullness.

There are additional terms, metaphors, and concepts that may help us explore the meaning of sin. Paul Tillich wrote of sin as "man's estrangement from God, from men, from himself."[2] We might call it the estrangement of persons from God, from others, and so also from their own best and true life or possibility. Gustavo Gutiérrez writes of "the fundamental alienation, the root of a situation of injustice and exploitation" that has both personal and collective dimensions. Sin, for Gutiérrez, may be understood as a basic "breach of friendship with God and others."[3] We might say that this breach of friendship is itself a turning away from that abundant and good life for which we are fitted and sustained. It is the fundamental alienation from true communion with God in community with others. Leonardo Boff writes in a similar way of "disgrace" as a "closing in upon oneself" that constantly threatens a drive toward openness and communion inherent in grace.[4]

Mary Potter Engel notes that we probably should resist any overly sharp reduction of our understanding of sin to a single term. The variety of destructiveness in human relationships, as well as in human relations with nonhuman life-forms and realities, is truly protean. We need to keep before us "the many ways we go astray as we travel together the path toward greater, deeper, and more just relatedness," particularly if we are to find and create "a variety of ways to combat these destructive powers" and also "point toward the multifarious ways God graces the world."[5]

Sin's corruption is multifaceted. James M. Gustafson notes that the longer theological tradition has identified at least four interrelated facets of the human fault.[6] Two of these are direct corruptions of affect or devotion. Thus, *idolatry* refers to a corruption of confidence and loyalty. It is a matter of placing our confidence and loyalty in inappropriate objects, or of misplaced degrees of confidence in and loyalty to otherwise proper objects such as race or nation. *Concupiscence* points to a corruption of love and desire. Wrongly ordered loves and desires orient persons toward inappropriate ends or toward the right ends wrongly, such as health, wealth, and power. In matters of the heart, then, we often devote ourselves to the wrong things, or to the right things with either excess or defect.

Two further facets of sin, although they are not directly matters of corrupted devotion, have their roots in skewed affectivities. *Corrupt rationality* refers to "the wrong depiction and interpretation of the particular 'world' that attracts our attention and that evokes our activity." Wrong confidences, loyalties, and loves skew our rational interests so that our interpretations of contexts and circumstances in which we participate often are slanted and incomplete. Finally, *disobedience* indicates a related corruption of our moral interests. Skewed devotions and depictions encourage us both to transgress and participate deficiently in personal and social relationships of obligation and responsibility.

Gustafson also points out how these varied facets of sin may be joined together by means of the Augustinian and Edwardsian metaphor of *contraction*. The deep root of the human fault is a contraction of the human spirit. As sinners, we shrink from the devotion to God that can enlarge us toward a genuine comprehension of and participation in the community of all things in their mutual interdependence and common dependence on God. Our souls become narrowed as we turn from God toward ourselves and toward our isolated or partial communities. Consequently, *idolatry* may be understood as a contraction of human trust and loyalty, and *concupiscence* as a contraction of human loves and desires. *Corrupt rationality* may be understood as a constriction of human vision, and *disobedience* as a contraction of our moral interests and responsibility.

Radical, Universal, and Original

Sin's corruption is not only multifaceted, it is also radical, universal, and original. From the perspective of reforming Christian wisdom, sin infects all our capacities, as well as every aspect of human society, so that the entire human project is unavoidably skewed. Although aspects of the traditional doctrine of sin frequently are misunderstood, and although some of the specific theories associated with it have proved untenable, these basic affirmations continue to furnish a helpful and illuminating commentary on the human condition.

Sin is radical. It is a matter of actions and inactions, of things done and left undone, and yet, fundamentally, it is more than a matter of discrete, external deeds. As Jonathan Edwards noted, sin is an active and persistent tendency, a disposing alignment of our powers, or an orienting impulsion.[7] Sin has to do not only with the surfaces of life but also with its depth and personal center. Sin is not just a matter of the hands, the feet, and the mouth; it is more than a matter of words and deeds. It is a matter of mind and heart and will, so that no aspect of human nature is exempted from sin's effects.

It, therefore, is not the case, as rationalists occasionally imply, that only the emotions and passions are disordered and that our reasoning capacity can be trusted to hold them in check and bring them to appropriate order. Neither is it the case, as emotivists sometimes claim, that only our reasoning is distorted, and that our deepest affections or our hearts remain a reliable guide. As Augustine insisted contra Pelagius, our capacity for choice is perversely misdirected because the right will or well-directed love has been transmuted into the wrong will or ill-directed love. Peel away our actions and our habits, and you will find not a neutral capacity for good or evil, but a corrupted elective capacity enslaved to wrongly biased affections.

A relatively common misunderstanding of reforming Christian wisdom exists that says the radicality of sin refers to the utter destruction of human capabilities and powers, and that, therefore, we are unable to accomplish anything of value. To the contrary, traditional orthodoxy insisted that, even after the fall, humans retain significant intellectual, moral, and technical abilities. Thus, both Calvin and Edwards, boosters of the notion of total depravity though they were, recognized in persons the continuation of impressive abilities in the arts and sciences, as well as certain basic social affectivities and a rudimentary sense of justice or fairness. These persistent abilities were understood as evidences of God's preserving care that remain essential for the levels of personal, social, and moral flourishing that humans generally are able to attain.

The rather more subtle meaning of sin's radicality is considerably more disturbing than mistaken notions of the utter destruction of human capabilities might indicate. Humans wield very significant abilities and powers, so that evidences of creativity, achievement, and even heartfelt sensitivity abound. For example, many parents love and care for their children; many citizens contribute to relatively just and flourishing societies; many business people and workers have labored to fashion a productive, worldwide system of economic interdependence. Scientists have harnessed the atom; physicians have begun to unlock the secrets of genetics. Yet even our best achievements, both as individuals and as communities, are corrupted by sin's constriction. Even caring parents sometimes neglect and inappropriately manipulate their children, and then again, there are many parents who participate deficiently in or even flagrantly violate important familial obligations. Even a relatively just and flourishing society will tend to regard other societies almost exclusively through the spectacles of its own partial interests, and many societies are neither relatively just nor prosperous. Our global economy is littered with notorious imbalances, injustices, and ecological disasters. The deep ambiguity of human scientific and technical achievements is one of the more profound lessons of modern history.

Consequently, it is apparent that the goods that individuals and communities endeavor to secure and protect, even at best, remain partial, and that, more often than not, our partial goods conflict with the partial goods pursued and protected by others. This is part of the meaning of finitude. The radicality of sin indicates that, even in the midst of our impressive achievements and accomplishments, we rarely are at our best. Indeed, at our worst, our impressive powers and abilities can be turned toward terrible injustice and terrifying evil as we struggle to protect and enhance our partial goods in the face of significant competition and conflict. The radicality of sin points to a world of human accomplishment and achievement that is also a world of destructive fragmentation, conflict, and evil.

Understood in this way, sin's radical corruption is also universal; there is no person or aspect of human society that is exempted from sin's effects. It is not the case, therefore, as social reformers occasionally imply, that a particular leader, community, movement, or institution is free from constricted rationality, devotion, and responsibility. There is no sin-free society; our lives as individuals and in families, in voluntary associations and in nations, all are infected by sin's corrupting tendency. Indeed, as Augustine pointed out, the universality of sin puts the lie to a pious refusal to admit that the church too, like other institutions and groups, is subject to sin's effects. The universality of sin means that we confront corrupting tendencies in every aspect of every human society and group. It is a confession of universal corruption that cannot and ought not be reduced to an ideology of Christian superiority.

Here, again, the historic wisdom of Christian believing has sometimes been subject to significant misconception. Sin's universality does not mean that every social and institutional arrangement is ineluctably futile, and that therefore all social and institutional arrangements are equally inappropriate. It means instead that attempts to combat the protean and destructive powers of sin are basic to every genuine form of faithfulness. Although no society is sin-free, some structures are better able than others to restrain corruption and to encourage more genuine participation. So, for example, as reforming Protestants have learned, particularly in the course of the American experiment, the universality of sin makes it appropriate to adopt certain social principles and strategies.

In light of our tendency both to neglect and transgress relations of mutual trust and accountability, it seems appropriate, in family and in church, as well as in economic and political communities, to adopt the *constitutional principle* whereby there are institutionalized clear and binding statements of commonly accepted and mutual responsibilities. The *principle of participation and the dispersal of power* assumes that perennial human tendencies toward self-aggrandizement and injustice are enhanced by concentrations of power in the hands of a few, and that representative structures check and balance the exercise of power by enfranchising the participation of all interested parties. Finally, the *principle of plurality* disallows monolithic and authoritarian hierarchies. It requires that basic institutions and associations remain relatively independent of one another, and it thus encourages their mutual restraint and participation.

There may be other ways of limiting corruption and enfranchising more genuine participation. My point here is simply that the affirmation of sin's universality underscores the ambiguities present in every human society, even as it rejects all counsels of quietism and despair. No society is sin-free. None avoids sin's constriction and its pernicious consequences. Therefore, none can be affirmed as good without qualification, and none should be exempted from criticism. Nevertheless, the affirmation of sin's universality encourages us to adopt realistic and responsible social strategies that take into account sin's pervasive contraction of the human spirit, as well as admittedly limited, but real, possibilities for fairness and justice.

When we combine the affirmations that sin is radical and universal, we arrive at the further point that, in some sense, sin is original. For traditional orthodoxy, the doctrine of original sin was connected to implausible theories about the historical Adam and Eve, an initial act of disobedience, and the manner of sin's transmission from generation to generation. It is not my intention either to imply or affirm those things here. Instead, like many modern theologians, I take the story of the first human pair, as well as the meaning of the traditional doctrine, mythically and symbolically. The symbolic and mythic meaning of original sin is that the corruption of our selves and our societies is both unavoidable and inevitable.[8]

To put this same point another way, sin has a basis in the finite condition of human persons and groups. Both as individuals and communities, the social and natural worlds in which we live and move confront us with multitudes of realities, events, and interrelations. As finite minds, we are unable to attend to everything at once, and so if we are to make sense at all out of our environments, we need to attend selectively to limited samples and configurations. In this instance, the unavoidability of sin means that, in the midst of our involvements with the encompassing world, we not only select, but our selections are persistently controlled by inordi-

nately partial interests and purposes. Our interpretations and depictions of
circumstances and contexts calling for action, therefore, chronically leave
out of account interrelations, situations, and consequences that are important to others. We fail to envision our interactions within the context
of an encompassing web of interrelations under God. Original sin means
the inevitable constriction and confusion of our practical reasoning.

Again, both as individuals and as communities, we want, need, and are
devoted to many different objects, causes, and ends. If we are to lead coherent lives at all, we must, therefore, prioritize, organize, and balance our
many confidences, loyalties, and desires. In this case, the unavoidability of
corruption means that, in the midst of negotiating the many challenges,
threats, and promises of the surrounding world, we chronically prioritize,
organize, and balance our trusts, commitments, desires, and loves in inappropriate ways that diminish, skew, and debilitate the good and abundant life. We invest our trust or confidence as well as our loyalty in the
wrong things and in the right things wrongly. We want and pursue the
wrong ends and we want and pursue the right ends wrongly. We too often find that the causes in which we trust are unable to lend life meaning.
We too often are mired in defensive patterns of participation as we attempt to protect our insecure confidences.

To recall Augustine's famous phrase, we become curved in on ourselves and our communities. We are disposed toward interacting with
other persons, communities, things, and conditions in ways that are centered on our own isolated wants, needs, and interests. We tend to find
pleasing those things that are favorable to ourselves and our communities,
even at the expense of others. Too often, we remain unmoved by those
actions, occurrences, and situations that are favorable for others. We are
disloyal to the all-encompassing community of God and neighbor. Original sin means the inevitable constriction and misorientation of our hearts.

Finally, in the midst of our many interactions and involvements, we
confront a plurality of interdependent relations of responsibility and trust.
Not all of these depend equally on our direct participation, and we clearly
cannot be actively engaged in all of them at once. It therefore is basic to
human participation to rank and to weight varied responsibilities. Here,
the unavoidabiity of sin means that, being curved in on our private and
communal interests and being inordinately partial in our depictions of our
contexts, we not only rank and weight our responsibilities, but the moral
interests in terms of which we rank and weight them are persistently
skewed. We chronically participate deficiently in, and even transgress, important relationships of accountability and trust. We too often lack both
the commitment and the attention required by our many interactions and
involvements with others. We too often are untrustworthy, deceptive,

and unjust. We fail to be fully responsive to the inclusive community of God and neighbor. In this sense, original sin means the inevitable constriction and misdirection of human responsibility.

In sum, the basic meaning of original sin is that, to some extent and degree, this story of multifaceted corruption is the story of "everyperson" and of every human community.[9] Despite our significant abilities, we inevitably fail to envision the wider community of things in its mutual interdependence and common dependence on God. We unavoidably are devoted to the wrong things or else to the right things wrongly. We inevitably transgress and fail to participate faithfully in the relationships of interdependence and trust in which we stand. We chronically betray the good and abundant life for which we are fitted. We diminish *life* in its fullness, and we travel along the way toward *death*. For these reasons, any responsibly realistic stance, ethic, or strategy, whether for individuals or groups, needs to take into account our persistent tendencies toward corruption.

Grace as Multifaceted Renewal

As a word of grace, the gospel is good news, because grace means that sin's corruption is neither the only nor the last word. If sin means derangement, then grace means rearrangement. Reinhold Niebuhr's mythical approach again makes a good guide. "The idea of grace can be stated adequately only in mythical terms," and in the mythos of Jesus, redemption means that we are "in the embrace of divine love" in spite of our sin.[10] We might say that if sin means an impelling tendency toward corruption, then grace means the emergence of a new tendency. If sin means a world of fragmentation and conflict, then grace means the realignment of our partial cities and partial goods within God's all-inclusive city. Grace means regeneration, the re-turning of persons and communities toward abundant life, toward true communion with God in community with others, or toward God and all things in their appropriate interrelations. Grace means the divine presence, power, and reality "that breaks down all the narrow barriers which we use to describe realities, dimensions, and worlds. Grace establishes one single world where opposites meet: God and humans, Creator and creatures."[11] Grace means transformative renewal, a conversion, restoration, and rehabilitation of persons and communities to their appropriate vocations as faithful participants.

Like sin's corruption, this transformative renewal is multifaceted. Indeed, a detailed account of multifaceted transformation begins with the observation that idolatry and concupiscence are related aspects of corrupted affectivity. Thus, when considered in light of our basic human capacities, the four facets of sin indicate three fundamental dimensions of sinful corruption. Sin, or the human fault, refers to a *contraction of mind* or constricted imagination and vision, a *contraction of heart* or constricted devotion, and a *contraction of will* or constricted responsibility. Regenerating grace precipitates a renewal of mind and heart that elicits a changed practice and responsibility. Grace means the emergence of a new cast of mind, a new temper of heart, and a new configuration of responsibility.

As an illumination and enlightenment of our minds, grace is a convictional knowledge that awakens a new vision of the encompassing world. Regenerating grace includes a discernment of the faithfulness and dependability of the power who bears all things and in whom we live and move and have our being. It therefore entails the recognition of a new imaginative totality. The cognitive inspiration of transforming grace is that all persons and things live by grace, and that the world itself is God's commonwealth of grace.

Edwards means something like this when he writes of a new sense whereby persons apprehend the excellency of God as well as of "the universal system of existence."[12] Spiritual understanding discerns "the glory of all God's works," and so "when the true beauty and amiableness in divine things is discovered to the soul, it opens as it were a new world to its view."[13] The world becomes a doxology of divine presence, power, and goodness. Nature and history become the sacrament of God's wisdom, purity, and love.[14] Again, in the words of H. Richard Niebuhr, through grace we discern "that [universal] community of which the universal God is the head."[15] We are given eyes to see the true excellency, beauty, and interrelatedness of God's world. As Richard R. Niebuhr puts it, "our vision becomes single or capacious and generous."[16] No longer thwarted by the blinding curvature of misplaced confidences, disordered loves, and inordinate self-concern, our eyes become "generous" so that the world that attracts our attention and action is expanded to include the entire system of things under God.

Through generous eyes it becomes apparent that there are many events and realities that call our restricted attentions up short and that suggest possibilities for truer vision. These include the costs to ourselves and to others of gross inattention. Thus, for example, whole towns, cities, and societies suffer the consequences of inordinate inattention to interdependent relationships with natural ecologies. Children, the weak, the dependent, and the "invisible" poor often suffer the consequences of others' neglect. Experiences of overlooking and of being overlooked may raise passionate and troubling questions that prompt reconsiderations of the contexts within which we live and move.

Again, possibilities for a more genuine and broader attentiveness also may be suggested by reliably attentive persons and institutions that refuse to let us drop out of their fields of vision and concern. Perhaps one has encountered a teacher who consistently strives to keep in view the needs, feelings, experiences, and interests of her students. Perhaps one has experienced a corporation that strives to attend not only to interests of its shareholders but also to those of its employees, as well as of various other publics affected by its operations. Perhaps a neglected and "forgotten" people will cherish memories of those occasions on which their plight was remembered. As occasions of regenerating grace, events and realities such as these comprise emergent possibilities for extending constricted visions beyond their pernicious and parochial scopes. They are indicators that God refuses to give up on corrupted persons and communities.

For reforming Christians, these emergent possibilities, these reconsiderations of context and circumstance always are accompanied by Israel and by Jesus Christ. With respect to the reformation of our visions, the Hebrew scriptures become a great gift to the imagination in poetry, story, and song. They portray God as the mighty creator and governor of the world and all that is in it; the saving power and liberator who hears the cries of an oppressed people and delivers them into a land of promise; the covenant partner who requires justice and mercy for the weak, the poor, the stranger, and the outcast; the Lord of history who attends to the destinies of all peoples.

Jesus Christ also becomes an imaginative gift, a prophet from Nazareth whose teaching recapitulates the truth about God's dynamic way with the world, the crucified and risen one who promises that God is faithful and that the fundamental aim of the faithful God is new life and true life.[17] In word and in deed, Christ teaches that the world is a realm of grace in which God both brings into existence and sustains every creature; a realm where birds are fed and lilies clothed, although neither birds nor lilies labor. So in Christ, God's world is a commonwealth of grace rather than merit, in which rain falls on the fields of the just and the unjust, and in which gifts and burdens are distributed without regard to our accomplishments. In Christ, we come to envision ourselves within a dynamic order of gratuity in which we and all that we have are dependent on God. This is one reason why the gospel is good news for sinners, the downtrodden, the weak, the poor, the sick, and the outcast. One's relation to the God of Jesus Christ is not contingent on social position, physical health, merits, or faults. Instead, the God whose world is a commonwealth of grace stands in relation to all creatures without prejudice.

Likewise, Jesus Christ teaches the truth about history as God's government. He proclaims the kingdom whose time is coming and now is. He brings the message of the *telos* of God's reign, a radically transforming and inclusive community in which relations among creatures are appropriately ordered by their relations to God and to one another. He brings the message that God is for the kingdom of God. That message is one of judgment, because the coming kingdom contrasts with our present disorder and because it exacts a tragic price for our confused visions, misoriented hearts, and misdirected acts, namely, the suffering of the innocent for the sins of the guilty. At the same time, however, it is also a message of promise, because the coming kingdom holds out the prospect of true *life,* of a changed world in which love of God and neighbor motivates and orders visions, dispositions, and actions that truly attend to the good of others.

Therefore, in Jesus Christ, the great occasion of grace, people recover their sight. Eyes are opened to a new world and a new history in which appropriately responsive human existence is situated within a universally gratuitous commonwealth whose *telos* is the kingdom. Wherever one turns, the divine power and presence is there rendering all things a single whole or interrelated universe. Indeed, the discernments that God always already stands in relation to all and that the world is God's realm of grace underscore the interdependence of the community of creatures in their common dependence on God, even as the message of the kingdom underscores its common destiny. In this sense, Christian believing means a recognition of the solidarity and mutual destiny of creatures in their common dependence on God. It means a cast of mind that enlarges our visions beyond their partial and parochial scopes. It means a vision that elicits confidence, gratitude, generosity, and hope.

Beneath and behind this new cast of mind, grace is also, and perhaps fundamentally, a new temper of heart, a passionate dying and rising, a repentance and conversion by which persons are turned from their obstinacy and enabled to put on a new inclination. Regenerating grace means the emergence of a new dominant devotion; the elicitation in persons of a new bias toward God and God's kingdom, or toward all things in their appropriate interrelations to God and to one another. Grace means the rebalancing of our attitudes, dispositions, and intentions. Indeed, since "the failure of vision, of recognizing life, is rooted in a failure of love," the correction of our hearts is the indispensable accompaniment of corrected vision.[18]

In Edwardsian terms, the new spiritual understanding is accompanied by a new and holy disposition that consists in a love of God and of the excellency of divine things, and this new disposition displaces self-love as the wellspring for action. Just as spiritual understanding forms a foundation for new exercises of understanding and imagination, the new and holy disposition precipitates new exercises of inclination or will. Horace Bushnell has something like this in mind when he speaks of human spirit being "impregnated with a new power of life." Persons in Christ, says Bushnell, are brought to a new reigning love so that "life proceeds from a new center."[19] No longer curved in and living to ourselves and our partial communities, we are centered in God and living to God and neighbor. Our governing purpose is changed; the old character is put to death, and a new character comes to life.

Within the frame of reforming Christian wisdom, it becomes apparent that God's world of grace is filled with ways in which our wrong confidences and disordered desires may be called into question. Inordinate love of wealth and career often bring with them a train of bad consequences, if not for ourselves, then at least for others. Popular literature as well as the histories of nations and empires are filled with illustrations of the costly consequences of inordinate desires for fame and for power. No twentieth-century reader should need to be reminded of the horrors associated with inordinate devotion to nation or to race.

Correspondingly, more genuine patterns of love and loyalty are suggested by persons and groups that order their ends and their causes in ways that point toward more varied and inclusive societies of service. Perhaps one knows a parent who, at the cost of qualifying or even denying significant professional goals and satisfactions, remains faithful to his or her family. Perhaps one reads of an organization that, at significant cost to its members, pursues a course of nonviolent resistance and confrontation in order to advance the participation of an oppressed people and to witness to the possibility of a more blessed and just political community. As occasions of grace, these and other events and realities, constitute emergent possibilities for a redemptive bending of human hearts beyond the pernicious arcs of their persistent constrictions. They are evidences of God's faithfulness.

For reforming Christians, these emergent possibilities, the lesser failures and catastrophic holocausts of disordered loves and confidences, as well as the heartening examples and witnesses of truer devotions always are accompanied by Israel and by Jesus Christ. Now the Hebrew scriptures become the story of a longsuffering God, who time and time again recalls a recalcitrant people from disordered loves and misplaced confidences, a history of judgment and mercy in which prophets meet with confrontation and rejection in the service of repentant renewal. Now Jesus Christ, the great occasion of grace, becomes the one who recapitulates the way of repentance and sacrifice that comes to expression in Israel's journey. He becomes the high priest and perfect sacrifice; the suffering servant whose cruciform service turns sinners toward the God who always already stands in relation to all. Jesus Christ becomes the power of *life,* the power of God to change hearts, and so to engender love of God and neighbor.

The New Testament writers clearly understood that this is not the power of nations and empires or of princes and kings, but a power made perfect in weakness. In Jesus Christ, the power of God is perfected in a tragic suffering that punctuates the consequences of our constricted devotions. The crucifixion becomes the great occasion of innocent suffering unto death that hangs over the many occasions of innocent suffering that continue to be the results of sin in our history. This is the great parable or analogy, the discerning lens through which Christians look at the world, and when they look through that lens, they discern the many other calvaries, both great and small, that clutter the horizons of our world. Then they see the innocent still suffering for the sins of the guilty—for our sins—on many an obscure hill. Jesus Christ becomes the dangerous memory and occasion that subverts our inordinate loves and confidences because he punctuates and underscores and will not let us turn our gaze from the sight of their tragic consequences.

At the same time, Jesus Christ also becomes the inspiring memory and occasion who elicits and sustains renewed devotion to God and God's kingdom. Defeated in his own life, his very defeat proves that the power of goodness is not defeated. Jesus Christ becomes the moving demonstration that, in God's world of grace, there is redemptive power beyond tragedy in suffering service to the kingdom. Precisely because the crucifixion bears the power of repentance and remorse, the great occasion of suffering service unto death for God's great cause is not hopeless.[20] The historic efficacy of this passionate passage inspires us to hope in Christ that further witnesses may also be accompanied in some measure by transformative power and possibilities for renewal.

For reforming Christians, then, grace includes a passionate dying and rising with Christ in the conviction that God is faithful, a repentant displacement of our inordinate loves and confidences, and the emergence of a new dominant devotion. To all but the hardest of hearts, Jesus Christ is the power who is able to work a change of heart, the power to turn people from the constricted ways of inordinately partial devotions toward the inclusive way of enlarged devotion to God and God's universal commonwealth or kingdom. Grace means the bending of the affective cores of our persons, and in that heartfelt conversion, there is hope.

Finally, as a new cast of mind and temper of heart, grace precipitates a renewed practice, a new manner of dwelling and participating in the world. Martin Luther never tired of saying that justification is by grace through faith, and that faith is active in love; Calvin insisted that "our regeneration by faith" issues in an amendment of life; Edwards maintained that grace means true virtue, a habitual agreement with and consent to the excellency and amiableness of the interrelations that characterize God's world. The recognition that all life is interrelated under God situates our interrelations and interactions in a new context, even as the conversion of our loves and loyalties lends us a new attitude or disposition. Grace means the reconfiguration of human responsibility.

Reforming piety comes to recognize that, within God's world of grace, there are many ways in which deceptive and deficient patterns of interaction may be called into question and redirected. Lies, broken promises and confidences, experiences of malice, injustice, and oppression often are unforgettably disturbing. Redemptive reconfigurations of the texture of human responsibility and the scope of true participation may, therefore, be prompted by our experiences of transgression and betrayal when others fail to uphold our trust and when we fail to uphold theirs. Correspondingly, the many examples of promises, trusts, and obligations splendidly kept are important pointers to another way. Perhaps we become acquainted with the routinely moving fidelity of a husband who cares for his wife through years of trying illness. Or perhaps we have knowledge of a community that houses and hides hunted strangers in the midst of Nazi terror, and at significant risk to itself.[21] As occasions of grace, these realities and events comprise emergent possibilities for creative reconfigurings of human responsibility.

For the reforming Christian community, these emergent possibilities always are accompanied by the stories of Israel and of Jesus Christ. Now the Hebrew scriptures become the great epic of a God and a people bound together by covenantal bonds of fidelity. Now the law and its statutes become signposts along a way that people may walk and live (Deut. 4:1–2; 5:31–33). Now Jesus Christ, the great occasion of grace, becomes the pathfinder who recapitulates and extends a way in life that accords with the texture and tendency of God's universal commonwealth.

Jesus Christ becomes the pioneer whom we may follow and so become disciples of God's way with the world. He marks off a path in life that is oriented by trust in and loyalty to God and the great cause of God's kingdom. He embodies *life* directed by love of God and neighbor, a direction in life that comes to expression in dispositions and in attitudes such as patience and humility; in purposes and in patterns of action such as healing the sick, associating with the poor, the weak, and the dependent. The kingdom's pioneer remains faithful to God and to others. He accompanies victims of malice, prejudice, injustice, and oppression, even as he becomes the decisive historical and liturgical victim himself, the seal of a new covenant of faithful service and obedience.

When we follow in this way, the many interdependencies in which we live and move become lines of service to God and to others. The texture of our obedience becomes covenantal, so that, in any particular relationship we stand in relation to others in the context of the divine ordering. Now we comprehend, as Richard R. Niebuhr points out, that in all of our relations and interrelations with others, "God-Ruling" is also present.[22] This is why Calvin could insist that, in our relations with others, what ultimately is at issue is not simply what others may appear to deserve in a frame of reference exhausted by our partial personal and communal interests. What also is at issue is the service of God in and through the particular interrelation at hand.

> Now if [the neighbor] has not only deserved no good at your hand, but has also provoked you by unjust acts and curses, not even this is just reason why you should cease to embrace him in love and to perform the duties of love on his behalf. You will say, "He has deserved something far different from me." Yet what has the Lord deserved?[23]

Thus, in the midst of our relations of mutual trust and responsibility with others, we respond not only to them, but also to the Other who faithfully stands in relation to all. This is the graceful reconfiguration of responsibility, and in it there is the patience, courage, and creativity needed to walk in a way of promise and to pursue possibilities for new and abundant life.

Radical, Universal, and Inevitable

Within the frame of reforming Christian wisdom, grace indicates multifaceted and emergent possibilities for renewal throughout the ceaseless flux of all that we envision, cherish, and do. By grace, human minds may be illumined so that we begin to envision ourselves and our communities within a single, universal commonwealth of interdependence under God. By grace, human hearts may be turned so that we begin to be oriented by devotion to God and to all things in their appropriate interrelations. By grace, human responsibility may be reconfigured so that we begin to participate faithfully along covenantal lines of service and obedience. In sum, grace is radical, and the radicality of grace matches the radicality of sin's corruption. It is therefore not the case that only the mind, or only the heart, or only the will is subject to the renewing influences of grace. Regenerating grace is a matter of mind, but not only of mind; a matter of heart, but not only of heart. It is a matter of both mind and heart that issues in an amendment of life and action. There is no aspect or capacity of the human spirit that lies beyond the possibility of regenerative enlargement.

For the reforming Christian community, the many occasions of transformative possibility are accompanied by the great occasion of Israel and of Jesus Christ. The idea of grace comes to expression in this *logos* and this *mythos,* this special occasion that points to a truth in every occasion. Indeed, by the grace of this great occasion and through the faithful wisdom that it engenders, the entire world becomes God's commonwealth of grace whose transforming *telos* is the kingdom, a universe of transformative interactions and occasions calling persons and communities to newness of life. In this sense, grace is not only radical, it is also universal, and the universality of grace matches the universality of sin's corruption. In other words, the lordship of Jesus Christ—the graceful reign of God's faithfulness, wisdom, power, and purpose—extends to all of life and creation. No area or dimension of life—politics, commerce, education, sexuality, and so on—is apart from or beyond this lordship and the reach of its regenerative possibility. It is a primary feature of the depth and the mythical profundity of Christian faith to claim that the promise of regenerating grace is coextensive with sin's corruption.

Finally, if grace is radical and universal, it follows that it is also inevitable and unavoidable. This means that, to some extent and degree, the story of multifaceted and emergent possibility is the story of "everyperson" and of every community. Despite our constricted visions, hearts, and actions, grace abounds, and the inevitability and unavoidability of grace abounding matches the inevitability and unavoidability of sin. This, finally, is the reason why, within the frame of reforming piety, genuine responsibility is realistic, but not only realistic. Genuine responsibility also is creative, venturing to risk and even to sacrifice in order to bear witness to the kingdom of universal community and to emergent possibilities for new life.

Responsible Realism and Creative Responsibility

With this last statement, we have come full circle. Sin corrupts but grace renews. If no basic dimension of human spirit, no person, community, or institution is exempt from sin's unavoidable constriction, it is also true that no dimension of life and no corner of creation lies beyond the reach and the hope of graceful transformation. Boff says that concrete persons and communities are "simultaneously graced and dis-graced," or as we might say, they are both corrupted and renewed. If our world is one of fragmentation and conflict, it is also God's commonwealth of grace. The holding of these truths together in tension is fundamental for a reforming

Christian commitment in the world. And, holding these truths together in tension, we are now ready to further specify and define the practical stance of faithful participation.

The conviction of sin, or of a multifaceted, radical, universal, and inevitable human fault, means that the entire human project is persistently skewed. It means that persons, societies, and cultures are enmeshed in self-destructive constriction; that even "the saints are always sinners"; that all persons, communities, and institutions, including Christians and their churches, are plagued by the turn toward ourselves and our isolated interests. All fall short of the kingdom and its glory. "There is no one who does good," no, not one (Ps. 14:3). In short, the conviction of sin points to a world of fragmentation and conflict. It therefore elicits a pessimistic attitude, or a sense for the moral limitations of both individuals and groups, that lends to our faithful participation the quality of responsible realism.

The fundamental intention, aim, or objective of the responsible realist is to restrain evil, or to keep things from getting worse. From this vantage point, basic institutions and relationships become strategies for minimizing harm and disorder. Thus anticipated loss of credibility restrains persons from lying. The basic obligations and responsibilities of marriage and family set limits that may also illumine acts of betrayal. A system of civil laws becomes a set of limitations or restraints backed by penalties and punishments. Business contracts specify mutual obligations that, if violated, become causes for legal actions and settlements. The practice of war is intended to protect the innocent and to contain aggression. Environmental irresponsibility is restrained by our experiences of the costs to ourselves and our communities of ecological disaster. Responsible realism, then, is an effort to limit and avoid harm in ways that are informed by rudimentary senses for justice, fairness, and accountability.

A basic strategy in this effort is to balance powers. This strategy builds on the recognition that pernicious consequences of corrupted rationality, disordered devotion, and misdirected responsibility are intensified where the powers of persons and groups remain unchecked. As the world is one of conflict among competing parties and their partial goods and interests, balances of power help to set contexts of mutual restraint within which egregious harm is more likely to be inhibited, and approximations to fairness and justice are more likely to be achieved. So, anticipated losses of credibility and respect are more likely to deter dishonesty and infidelity where persons stand in acknowledged relationships of mutual interdependence with others. A court of law may be looked upon as an institution that tries to put contending parties on roughly equal footing. Labor unions may be understood as associations that balance the powers of management and capital. Representative and democratic assemblies become efforts to limit, restrict, and balance the powers of any particular individual or group by enfranchising all individuals and groups in the dynamics of decision making. In relations among nations, attempts to formulate and maintain mutual checks and restraints are hampered by the general lack of relatively impartial, representative, and effective international courts and assemblies, and responsible realism tends to become the less stable and more risky business of balancing powers by means of inherently partial and fluid alliances, treaties, and agreements.

Even in the midst of attempts to restrain evil, however, the conviction that persons and communities are in the grips of sin, or that sin's constriction remains an impelling tendency in all individuals and groups, requires the responsible realist to recognize that all the efforts and strategies of restraint cannot guarantee either that harm will be avoided or that fairness will prevail. The mutual balances and restraints are all provisional, continually subject to subversion and defeat. For this reason, the responsible realist learns to share the fears of the fearful and to weep with those who are weeping. He or she recognizes that the intentions behind even the most carefully structured representative assembly can be subverted by greed and by the undue influences of concentrated wealth. The realist knows that corrupt rationality clouds the visions and judgments of even the most attentive spouses, parents, and children. The responsible realist is not surprised that racism and sexism may exclude entire communities and groups from meaningful economic and political enfranchisement, or that beyond the reach of relatively just laws, corrupted devotions may continue to foster climates of exclusion, constriction, and hate. Neither is he or she surprised to learn that international balances and agreements can be wrecked by the shifting winds of economic, political, and military strength; or that even while such agreements remain in force their deterrent value is often rendered precarious because they motivate societies to extend the scope of national interests and to stockpile implements of mass destruction.

As a result, the conviction of sin not only motivates the responsible realist to restrain evil, it also supports an attitude of sorrowful vigilance and criticism. The conviction of sin accuses, and its accusation points to the perils and shortcomings in all strategies of balance and restraint. The conviction of sin accuses, and so the responsible realist has reason to resist temptations to conservative complacency that often accompany less thoroughgoing pessimisms. In the midst of the struggle against evil, the responsible realist glimpses the suffering of the innocent for the sins of the guilty, the horrifying holocaust that relativizes and finally destroys every claim to righteousness.

At just this accusatory and critical point, a point at which the pessimistic temper of responsible realism threatens to resolve itself into meaninglessness and despair, the practical wisdom of reforming piety turns to promises of grace and newness of life. It recalls Calvary and the cruciform suffering of the innocent one for the sins of the guilty, a suffering that, beyond tragedy, proves to be the power of God for repentance and conversion. In this recollection of resurrection there is reason to hope that, beyond all of the failed efforts and strategies of restraint, the terrible consequences of constricted visions, devotions, and patterns of action may yet become transformative occasions of grace.

Such hopeful sorrow turns again because, as we have seen, the conviction of grace points to multifaceted, radical, universal, and inevitable possibilities for renewal. It insists that persons, societies, and cultures enmeshed in self-destructive constriction, or the turn toward themselves and their isolated interests, may yet be turned again. It means that the world is finally an interdependent and transformative commonwealth of grace whose *telos* is the kingdom. The conviction of grace, therefore, elicits an optimistic attitude or sense for the moral possibilities of both individuals and groups, and so it lends to our faithful participation the quality of creative responsibility.

The fundamental intention, aim, or objective of creative responsibility is to pursue good. From this vantage point, basic institutions and relationships become strategies for motivating and guiding persons and groups in paths of more genuine attentiveness, fidelity, and service. Now it becomes apparent that the mutual interdependencies of friendship and community not only restrain lies and betrayals, but also train persons in virtues of honesty and fidelity. Marriage and family become schools of piety and virtue whose intimate relations train persons in sensibilities appropriate to genuine participation in wider social systems and communities. A system of civil laws becomes a set of practices or guides that encourages the formation of virtue. Business partnerships and contracts encourage enlarged appreciation and responsibility for the mutual interdependencies that characterize our economic activities and involvements. Environmentally sound practices, such as recycling usable wastes, encourage persons to attend to the well-being of natural ecologies. Thus, creative responsibility is an effort to do good or to make things better informed by a devotion to and appreciation for the common welfare and mutual interdependence of persons and communities.

A basic strategy in this effort is to associate or relate individuals as participants within interdependent communities, and communities as participants within wider communities and interdependent structures. This strategy builds on the recognition that possibilities for generosity (attentive practical reasoning, enlarged devotion, and covenantal responsibility) are enhanced where persons and groups acknowledge and participate in wider structures of mutual interdependence. Because the world is a commonwealth of interdependent creatures in common dependence on God, because the *telos* of God's world is the radically transformative and inclusive community, acknowledged relationships and communities of interdependence enhance possibilities for true virtue, for *life,* or for appropriately faithful participation in God's world.

The interdependent bonds of friendship, for example, enhance possibilities for the attentiveness of persons to one another's needs and interests. Participation in families often tempers ideals of individual self-fulfillment with devotion to the well-being of an intimate community. Negotiated settlements and structures of corporate organization and accountability associate capital, management, and labor as mutual participants in common economic enterprises. Participation in representative assemblies can train persons and groups in deliberative and mutual practices that pursue the well-being of a wider society. Participation in international agreements, associations, and assemblies encourages national governments to engage in cooperative relationships, practices, and policies aimed at the welfare of a community of nations.

Even in the midst of pursuing good, however, the conviction that grace abounds, or that the world is a commonwealth of grace whose *telos* is the kingdom, encourages creative responsibility to recognize continual prospects for improvement. For this reason, the Christian optimist learns to share the visions of the visionary as well as the hopes of revolutionaries. He or she recognizes (1) that persons devoted only to the well-being of their families often fail to take the well-being of others into account; (2) that cooperative agreements between capital and labor often advance the welfare of only a part of society; (3) that the legislative compromises of representative assemblies may overlook the welfare of noncitizens; and (4) that frameworks for international cooperation often favor the interests of limited communities of nations at the expense of others.

Thus, the conviction of grace not only motivates the Christian optimist to pursue good, it also nourishes an attitude of continuing and hopeful criticism. The conviction of grace brings hope, and its eschatological hope points to further possibilities for good beyond every reformation and every improvement. The conviction of grace brings hope, and so the Christian optimist has reason to resist temptations to complacency that often accompany less thoroughgoing optimisms. In the midst of the struggle for good within and among our partial cities, creative responsibility harbors a hope that strains toward God's all-inclusive city and therefore relativizes every claim to righteousness and success.

At just this hopeful and visionary point, where the optimistic temper of creative responsibility threatens to embrace utopian illusion, the practical wisdom of Christian believing turns again to the conviction of sin. It recognizes that persons and groups are constricted even in their virtues, and that therefore all the efforts to pursue good and to bring about the beloved community cannot guarantee that true virtue and cooperation will prevail. It recognizes that every witness to the cause of God's all-inclusive and universal city is provisional and subject to subversion, if not at the hands of powers that be, then at the hands of new possibilities for constriction. It therefore recognizes that every revolutionary witness to true good must reckon with the possibility of destruction and defeat. And so, in the depths of passionate sorrow, the practical wisdom of reforming piety turns again to the cruciform pattern of defeat in the service of God's great cause.

Here, indeed, is a gift to devoted imagination and to imaginative devotion, a defeated service that beyond destruction proves to be the transformative power of God, a moving occasion whose victory lies in the inspiration of further witnesses both great and small. In this recollection, there is reason to hope that any and all of the defeated efforts and vanquished witnesses may yet become transformative occasions of grace.

Last Things

All of which brings us to last questions. If all the efforts to restrain evil and pursue good are provisional, dogged by contingency, and subject to failure, why should they finally be meaningful and worthwhile? How and why do they witness to something more than one's own stubborn, and perhaps also heroic, determination?

Reforming piety furnishes a host of answers, many of which cluster around the appropriate gratitude of persons at being created, upheld, and regenerated by the great, good, and faithful God. If the story of "everyperson" and of every community is to some extent and degree one of graceful, multifaceted, and emergent possibility, then we have much for which to be thankful. In laboring to restrain evil and pursue good, we witness to the divine faithfulness that meets us at every turn; to relinquish the effort would be the height of ingratitude. As the Heidelberg Catechism puts it, we are redeemed and renewed "so that with our whole life we may show ourselves grateful to God for his goodness and that he may be glorified through us."[24]

However, the last answer of reforming Christian piety—one anticipated in the affirmation of the continued power even of cruciform defeats—ventures a step further. God, the divine power decisively disclosed in the histories of Israel and of Jesus Christ, is sovereign. For reforming piety, then, the arc of the universe is God's arc, and although we cannot always make out its curvature, this arc bends toward God's universal commonwealth, kingdom, or city. And so, neither without nor apart from cruciform passions, reforming piety supports a chastened, truly "cosmic optimism."[25] Even in the face of suffering, death, and destruction, faithful participation gains nourishment, courage, and strength from the conviction that the power of goodness is greater than the powers of evil.

This ultimately triumphal affirmation is as ancient as the Christian community itself.

> For I am convinced that neither death, nor life, nor angels, nor rulers, nor things present, nor things to come, nor powers, nor height, nor depth, nor anything else in all creation, will be able to separate us from the love of God in Christ Jesus our Lord (Rom. 8:38–39).

Or as Edwards puts it, redemption is God's greatest work, and the basis for redemption is "the constancy and perpetuity of God's mercy and faithfulness." That, for Edwards, was what it meant to say that "God is the Alpha and Omega, the beginning and the end of all things."[26]

Reforming piety vindicates optimism with realism because its vision is antidualistic. Within the frame of this vision, the powers of evil, whether angelic or mundane, are neither ontologically nor metaphysically fundamental. They are secondary, parasitic derangements of a good creation that is originated, sustained, and redeemed by the power of the great and good God. As at the outset of this chapter, Calvin remains a reliable guide, this time as he echoes Augustine's reply to the Manichean objection that it is wrong to ascribe to the good God the creation of anything evil.

> This does not in the slightest degree harm the orthodox faith, which does not admit that any evil nature exists in the whole universe. For the depravity and malice both of man and the devil, or the sins that arise therefrom, do not spring from nature, but rather from the corruption of nature.[27]

This ultimately optimistic affirmation has never been an easy one to make. In a world of fragmentation and conflict, not only we ourselves, but also the dynamic movement of grace toward blessed community are assailed and deflected on all sides. Frederick Denison Maurice described his own wager on the creative source by which all things are, the one God who is the power and principle of grace and redemption, in the following remarkable passage.

I am obliged to believe in an abyss of love which is deeper than the abyss
of death: I dare not lose faith in that love. I sink into death, eternal death,
if I do. I must feel that this love is compassing the universe. More about it
I cannot know. But God knows. I leave myself and all to Him.[28]

Somewhat similarly, H. Richard Niebuhr was concerned throughout
his career with the relations of power and goodness in the principle of
being.

The great anxiety of life, the great distrust, appears in the doubt that the
Power whence all things come, the Power which has thrown the self and
its companions into existence, is not good. The question is always before
us, Is Power good? Is it good to and for what it has brought into being? Is
it good with the goodness of integrity? Is it good as adorable and delight-
ful? . . . But our second great problem is whether goodness is powerful,
whether it is not forever defeated in actual existence by loveless, thoughtless power. The resurrection of Jesus Christ from the dead, the establishment of Jesus Christ in power, is at one and the same time the demonstration of the power of goodness and the goodness of power.[29]

Elsewhere Niebuhr wrote of "a strange thing [that] has happened in our
history," a "movement beyond resignation to reconciliation" that is "in-
augurated by Jesus Christ." Within the context of this strange movement,

. . . salvation now appears to us as deliverance from that deep distrust of
the One in all the many that causes us to interpret everything that happens
to us as issuing from animosity or as happening in the realm of destruction.
Redemption appears as the liberty to interpret in trust all that happens as
contained within an intention and a total activity that includes death
within the domain of life, that destroys only to re-establish and renew.[30]

This is the resurrection we can experience, the victory of radical faith
in God over the lesser confidences and loyalties that require us defensively
and despairingly to guard ourselves, our communities, and our world from
an ultimately loveless, thoughtless reality. This is a liberating and a saving
faith, one that lends life meaning even in cruciform passions. God is faithful, and the purpose of the faithful God is new and renewed being. Exis-
tentially, this affirmation entails a vivifying assurance and self-understanding. It expresses confidence in and loyalty to the one in whom we live
and move and have our being. It represents a courage to be, to participate
faithfully in God's great commonwealth of being, despite the anxiety,
doubt, and meaninglessness that so often beset us.

At earlier times, this is what reforming Protestants understood to be the trust and devoted assurance that almighty God is "a faithful Father."[31] This faithful parent and creative source, this power of redemption and abyss of love, whose arc compasses the universe is the one by whose grace, in the words of Martin Luther King Jr., "we are caught in an inescapable network of mutuality, tied in a single garment of destiny."[32] This great and good God, God-in-Christ and Christ-in-God, is the one in whose power is the grace to restore broken community. That is why King could write that "there is something in this universe which justifies William Cullen Bryant in saying, 'Truth crushed to earth will rise again.' So, in Montgomery, Alabama, we can walk and never get weary."[33]

It probably cannot be emphasized enough that this affirmation is a testament of hope that no faithful participant makes lightly, a statement of faith made in continuous risk and beset by passionate doubt on every side. In a world torn by the fragmenting and conflictual results of sin's constriction, reforming piety ultimately means to elicit the deepest possible conversion. It invites a nondefensive confidence that God is both good and great, that the Power who bears all things is good, and that the goodness that refuses to abandon a corrupted world is powerful. It requires that we sacrifice our defensive, self-centered visions and devotions.

Contemporary readers have good reasons to be mindful of just how strange a conviction and conversion this really is. They may note the grossly destructive, oppressive, and murderous patterns that have characterized far too much of the world during the twentieth century. They may note that in our nuclear age we have learned (and cannot unlearn) the terrible and threatening lesson of our capacities to bring about the long-term annihilation of our own species, as well as many other species. They may note further, as Gordon D. Kaufman so powerfully has, that our abilities to bring the human project to an end constitute "a momentous *change* in the human religious situation."[34] I do not disagree.

Nuclear holocaust (or perhaps some other, equally artificial hell of our own making) is not the end as our ancient tradition envisioned it. It has a vastness and finality about it that are truly unique in the annals of human history. It is not an end to be hoped for but a disaster for the human species and many other creatures, a chilling setback for the dynamic movement of grace that all informed and responsible peoples should labor strenuously to avoid. It therefore mounts a most serious challenge to even the chastened and realistic "cosmic optimism" of traditional Christian believing.

Nevertheless, not even nuclear inferno followed by nuclear winter is *the end* of those vaster realities—world, universe, and God—in which we have been blessed enough to live and move and have our being. Neither is it the annihilation of all possibilities for grace and for the city of creatures under God. God is good and God is great. The power of goodness is greater than the powers of evil. That affirmation does not gainsay the very real, terrible, and destructive consequences of sin, fragmentation, and conflict. As we now know, neither does it carry with it a guarantee that humans will not destroy themselves and much else besides. It is simply and devotedly a confession of divine sovereignty, a confession that God is God, that God will be God and so be faithful, with us or without us. That, finally, is enough to secure the passionate conviction that when we act responsibly to restrain evil and creatively to pursue good, we participate faithfully, we render genuine and hopeful witness in accord with the arc of God's world.

Conclusion: Related and Interdependent Qualities

To summarize, sin and grace, responsible realism and creative responsibility, go together. Apart from the pessimistic temper of responsible realism, faithful participants are prone to forget that persons and communities are constricted even in their virtues, and that, therefore, practical efforts to pursue good in communities of interdependence rely on mutual checks, balances, and restraints. Apart from the optimistic temper of creative responsibility, faithful participants are prone to forget that persons and communities may be enlarged even in their vices, and that practical attempts to restrain evil by means of mutual checks and balances may therefore also present possibilities for virtuous enlargement, cooperation, and community. Faithful participation without responsible realism tends toward an idealistic romanticism that fails to recognize that possibilities for renewal very often come only at the cost of cruciform defeats and failed witnesses. Faithful participation without creative responsibility tends toward a debilitating despair that fails to recognize cruciform possibilities for renewal beyond the sufferings, tragedies, and defeats.

Within the wisdom of reforming piety, within a frame of passionate sorrow bounded by cosmic optimism, responsible realism and creative responsibility go together as related and interdependent qualities of faithful participation in God's world. They are integral dimensions of a practical orientation in all of life centered on the affirmation that first and foremost, we belong to God. They are dynamic aspects of a historically particular stance that tries to reorder all of life, or to relate all things both critically and constructively to God and God's purposes. They are basic characteristics of an uncompromising faithfulness that actively engages and respects a fragmented and promising world of plural and interdependent communities and institutions.

Responsible realism and creative responsibility go together as integral dimensions of a distinctly reforming Christian commitment in the world that delivers us from utopian fanaticisms as well as from dull and disingenuous acquiescence to the way things are. This commitment will not support uncritical and therapeutic affirmations of personal growth as the master goal. It will not issue in uncritical and moralistic endorsements of inherited hierarchies and patriotisms. It will not reduce to the insistence that faithful Christians be formed by their participation in the practices of the community called church rather than by their participation in other communities, institutions, and practices. Responsible realism and creative responsibility go together. There is no better time for reforming Protestants to remind themselves of this than when their theocentric and participatory spirit has been rendered insecure and called into question by narrower, less dynamic pieties and commitments.

5

The Church In, With, Against, and For the World

T his chapter will explore the relationship between church and world
in light of the theocentric stance, orientation, or bias of reforming
piety. The focal point intentionally is not the church in isolation because,
in a reforming perspective, the church bears the Christ-formed spirit of
faithful participation in God's all-inclusive commonwealth. The church,
therefore, is an association of those who recognize that we never respond
faithfully to God without also participating faithfully in the world as God's
commonwealth, and that we never participate faithfully in the world
without also responding faithfully to God.[1]

Thus, like "sin and grace," "church and world" indicates a tensive dynamic near the heart of reforming Christian piety. This particular dynamic
concerns a multivalent relationship between the association of those who
explicitly acknowledge God's transformative way with the world in Jesus
Christ, and those persons, communities, and institutions that do not. It
names the association whose purpose it is to increase love of God and
neighbor and it asks about the relationship between this association and
the world. It points to the society of those who recognize that we are
equipped for true communion with God in community with others, that
we are corrupted by sinful constriction, and that by God's faithfulness and
grace we are afforded promising possibilities for renewal; it points to persons, communities, and institutions that do not recognize these things; and
it poses the question of the relationship between them.

A Preliminary Definition

Consider the following definition: The church is the association of those who acknowledge God's transformative way with the world in Jesus Christ, and whose purpose it is to increase love of God and neighbor.

"The church is the association . . ." It is not a solitary seer, a lone believer, or a mere collection of individuals. It is a society, since to be caught up in the messianic event of Jesus Christ, the person-for-others, entails an impulse to communion with God in community with others. Theologically understood, the society called church, its social nature, is not accidental but an essential expression of the community-forming power of God. Although we chronically are confused, misoriented, and misdirected in the ways that we live and move and deploy our powers, "the divine initiative elicits a new responsiveness that overcomes the brokenness of human relations to each other and to the divine."[2] The gathering or assembling of the association called church is an embodiment and a sign of the transformative grace and promise of God overcoming isolation.

This is what a number of commentators have in mind when they note that the early church was a new sort of community. Membership, participation, and leadership were not limited by one's social class, rank, wealth, nationality, or sex. In Christ, to paraphrase Paul, there is neither Jew nor Greek, slave nor free, male nor female (Gal. 3:28). Indeed, within its own ranks, the church gave new status to slaves and to women. It also organized charity for strangers, the aged, the sick, and the poor.[3]

We could say that a basic dimension of the society called church is signaled by the word *koinonia*. The church is a new fellowship in new responsiveness, a personal and hospitable community of sisters and brothers in Christ. It is an association with a common ethos or spirit, a fellowship in faith, a community of common devotion, vision, and disposition "where two or three are gathered" in Christ's name (Matt. 18:20). The church is a communion in which, as John Calvin put it, "the heart and soul of the multitudes of believers are one," and by participation in which we are kept "in the society of God."[4] Or again, as John Wesley wrote in commentary on both the Apostle Paul and the Nineteenth Article of the Church of England, it is a congregation of faithful persons who walk in a manner worthy of their calling and who bear one another in love.[5] The church is a coming together of individuals in a company of mutual interaction and cooperation that crosses boundaries and overcomes division in a new togetherness. It is a community of those who share a common outlook and orientation, a corporate life of mutual caring, communication, and service.

But that is not all. If the church is *koinonia*, it is also *ekklesia*, the assembly of God-in-Christ that generates regular organization and leadership as it discharges its mission. The church is a personal community, but it is also an institution that orders personal life and interpersonal relations. The church is an institution that expresses, shapes, and guides the spirit of community in Christ by means of practices, rites, and roles. It is a body with many members who perform different functions. It is a polity, a governance of structures, offices, and processes of decision making. The church is more than intimate personal fellowship. It is also "the household of God," a building or structure joined together as a holy temple. The church is tradition, regular services of worship, organized instruction, care, and mission. It is congregations, constitutions, committees, councils, budgets, and bureaucracies.[6]

The association called church thus is both *koinonia* and *ekklesia,* both community and institution, and we ignore either dimension at our peril. Consequently, it is possible to focus on ecumenical structures, bureaucracies, and offices to the neglect of the common spiritual and moral life that crosses boundaries and seeks to come to expression in these institutions. It is possible to emphasize membership in the church as participation in institutional forms and activities to the neglect of passionate personal engagement in common devotion and mutual communion. On the other hand, the opposite error is also possible. Spiritual and personal community can be emphasized to the neglect of polity and leadership. A vague, inchoate, and easily manipulated common life may be exalted to the neglect of institutional forms. Indeed, when institutional structures are neglected, personal communities chronically fall victim to the influences of factions, alien loyalties, and warped personalities.[7]

The structures and practices of the church as institution can preserve, strengthen, and shape the church as personal community, but they can also corrupt it. They can express, define, and direct the common spirit of Christian community, but they can also deaden it. Conversely, the church as personal community can enliven as well as corrupt the structures and practices of the church as institution. Particularly where the community's spirit is skewed by partial loyalties to clan, race, gender, and nation, it can twist the meaning and forms of Christian institutions. The church is an association where community and institution belong together.

We are now in a position to go a step further. "The church is the association of those who acknowledge . . ." The association called church confesses and recognizes something prior and more fundamental than itself. It is not, in the first place, an association of free or random creativity, but one that depends on a reality logically and historically prior to itself, from which it is gathered and takes shape, and without which it would lose both its form and substance. The church is the association that acknowledges this prior reality in that its passionate devotion is elicited by it, its imaginative vision is provoked by it, and its active disposition is shaped by it. The church is the association whose common spirit—the spirit of faithful participation in God's commonwealth that comes to expression in personal community and in institutional forms—is given by this prior reality. The church acknowledges this prior reality, it appropriates it and applies it, and so it becomes the Christian church, the community and institution, the association or society of those who are being caught up in the messianic event.

It follows from this that the association called church, the character of its community and the form of its institutional structures, radically depends on the prior reality that it acknowledges, confesses, recognizes, appropriates, and applies. So it is critically important to say that "the church is the association of those who acknowledge God's transformative way with the world in Jesus Christ . . ."

The church confesses "God's way," the way that creates, sustains, judges, and redeems creatures equipped for an abundant and good life together in communion with God and community with one another. It recognizes the great faithfulness of the God-for-others who refuses to abandon any thing, even those who betray their chief end or the fundamental vocation for which they are fitted and sustained. It appropriates God's way, the way of grace that crosses boundaries, journeys into the far country, and traverses the frontier in order to go over to the betrayer, to rehabilitate the betrayer, and to reestablish the possibility of abundant and good life.[8] It acknowledges the foolishness of God that is greater than human wisdom, the righteousness of God that goes beyond human reckonings of justice and fairness. It acknowledges that the gospel of Jesus Christ is a gospel of reconciliation that is good news for sinners.

This way, God's way in Jesus Christ, is transformative because it turns the tables on sin's constriction. In Jesus Christ, sinners who are curved in upon themselves and their isolated groups, whose human spirits are thus constricted and diminished so that they do not participate faithfully in God's commonwealth, confront true faithfulness. In Jesus Christ, they confront the person-for-others as well as the God-for-others. They confront an enlarging living-for-others in the midst of fragmentation and conflict, a passionate faithfulness that exposes and challenges constriction and corruption. And so, in the event of this confrontation, they are criticized and accused.

Nonetheless, and here we come across the gracious community-forming power and initiative of God, in Jesus Christ sinners are not rejected but accepted. They are accepted and drawn into participatory communion as the others for whom the faithful messiah lives and dies, the betrayers to whom God remains faithful. They are reconciled, and in the event of their reconciliation, they are called to turn toward capacious possibilities for enlargement and renewal. They are summoned to repentance and to new life, to reorder and reform their lives in response to God and God's inclusive commonwealth, a commonwealth that includes even sinners.

In Jesus Christ, God's transformative way with the world, sinners recover true sight. They glimpse God's world as a universally gratuitous commonwealth of interdependence in common dependence on God. In Jesus Christ, sinners recover true hearts. The affective cores of their persons are turned toward an enlarged devotion to God and God's commonwealth. In Jesus Christ, sinners recover true responsibility. They are initiated into a renewed practice, a manner of dwelling in the world as God's inclusive commonwealth. In Jesus Christ, the person-for-others, the Word who discloses the faithful God-for-others, sinners are provoked, invited, and encouraged to take up a faithful living-for-others. They are caught up in a messianic event whose transformative bias toward enlarged vision, devotion, and responsibility moves them toward faithful participation in a world of fragmentation and conflict that is nonetheless God's commonwealth of grace. When the church acknowledges God's way, it confesses, recognizes, and appropriates this transformative initiative.

The church acknowledges this way, God's transformative way in Jesus Christ, with . . . the world! As both *koinonia* and *ekklesia,* the community and the institution of those who are being caught up, called forth, and assembled by God's transformative initiative, the church is turned, biased, and oriented toward the all-inclusive reality of God's commonwealth, toward a reality greater than itself that reaches beyond itself. It is the reality of God's all-inclusive commonwealth that finally truly defines both the world and the church.[9]

The church recognizes the radicality and universality of sin's corruption. It knows that no human capacity, no person, movement, or institution (including itself) is sin-free. At the same time, it also recognizes the radicality and universality of redeeming grace. It knows that no human capacity, no person, community, or institution lies beyond the reach of regenerative possibility or beyond hope for renewal. It therefore harbors a profound and sorrowful pessimism bounded by a genuinely cosmic optimism.

Precisely because it acknowledges God's transformative way in Jesus Christ the church is the association of those who refuse to set limits where God refuses to set limits. It is the society that acknowledges and comes to recognize that the object of the faithful God-for-others cannot be only some others in isolation, but instead is and must be all others in their

appropriate interrelations with God and with one another. The church is
the subject that explicitly recognizes God's all-inclusive kingdom or commonwealth. It acknowledges that God creates the world, sustains the
world, judges the world, and redeems the world. It is the community and
institution that understands that it cannot either say or think "God" without also saying and thinking "world." It acknowledges that "the earth is
the LORD's and all that is in it, the world, and those who live in it" (Ps.
24:1). It comes to recognize the expansive meaning and significance of
John 3:16, "For God so loved the world . . ."

Indeed, just because it acknowledges and recognizes and appropriates
and applies these things, just because it is provoked, invited, and encouraged in Christ to take up a faithful living-for-others, the church endeavors to be responsible to all the others that participate and have their places
in the world as God's inclusive commonwealth. The church pays attention to the world, loves the world, and is responsible to the world. It in-
teracts with the world and it interprets the world. It endures the world
and it celebrates the world. It criticizes the world and it affirms the world.
It understands the world in this time and at all times as its providentially
imposed partner, the arena with which and in which it lives and moves
in faithfulness to the one God who always stands in relation to all. The
church is the society of those who recognize that God's way in Jesus
Christ discloses itself only by setting us entirely in the world, and that
when we participate faithfully in the world, it is always already the world
created, sustained, judged, and reconciled in the reality of God. "This,"
to borrow a sentence from Dietrich Bonhoeffer, "is the inner meaning of
the revelation of God in the man Jesus Christ."[10]

The community and institution of those who explicitly acknowledge
this inner meaning is a community and institution with a particular purpose and direction. It has a calling or vocation, and with this fundamental observation our preliminary definition is completed. The church is the
association of those who acknowledge God's transformative way with the
world in Jesus Christ, and whose purpose it is to increase love of God and
neighbor.

It may seem odd to say that the church has *a* purpose, since it is clear
that the church does many things. It assembles persons for public worship
and prayer. It preaches the gospel and administers the sacraments. It trains
people in the scriptures and in the wisdom of Christian piety. It cultivates
the Christian life. It builds up corporate life and structures. It maintains a
fellowship of mutual services and care. It goes out to all peoples and nations, witnessing to God-in-Christ with words and deeds of reconciliation and renewal. Nonetheless there *is* a single, overarching goal, a basic
purpose, unifying task or direction. There is no community in Christ that

does not lead directly to a community of vocation. Following H. Richard Niebuhr's suggestion, and in a reforming perspective, we designate that purpose with Jesus' language of love of God and neighbor. *The purpose of the church is to increase love of God and neighbor.*

At this point, it is important not to divide our preliminary definition into two separate parts. By God's grace, and in and through traditions, structures, and ministries, the church does not *first* acknowledge God's transforming way with the world in Jesus Christ and *then* (sometime later) take on the vocation and direction signaled by love of God and neighbor. These really are two dimensions or aspects of the same thing. Indeed, there is no genuine acknowledgment of God's transformative way with the world in Jesus Christ without activity directed toward increasing love of God and neighbor. Luther was right to say that faith is active in love. So one perhaps may come across an association of people who claim to acknowledge God's transformative way with the world in Jesus Christ but who either are not yet committed to increasing the love of God and neighbor or are still debating whether to act on this commitment. In that case, one simply has come across an association of people who do not yet truly and *fully* acknowledge God's transformative way with the world.

The church is the community and institution of those who recognize and appropriate the increase of love of God and neighbor as "the patriotism of the universal commonwealth."[11] Caught up in the messianic event of Jesus Christ, the church is guided by this transformative standard and empowered to pursue this transformative possibility.

Indeed, the church acknowledges that the two loves are inseparable. It recognizes that they are law: the summary requirement of the good and abundant life for which we are fitted, sustained, and redeemed; and the demand to turn away from sin's brokenness and constriction. It recognizes that they are gospel: the gift given by the costly demonstration in Jesus Christ, the Word of grace that God is faithful; and that therefore, persons, communities, and institutions encounter possibilities for new attentiveness, new devotion, and new responsiveness.

The church recognizes that love of God, "the conviction that there is faithfulness at the heart of things," ineluctably leads and directs us to love of neighbor.[12] This is so because, for the community and institution of those who acknowledge God's transformative way with the world in Jesus Christ, love of God is rejoicing over the presence of the faithful God-for-others. It is thankfulness for God's faithful companionship. It is a reverence for the integrity of the faithful God-for-others that refuses to manipulate God for one's own advancement. It is loyalty to God and God's cause, a willingness to serve God's universal commonwealth. Precisely within the frame of love for the faithful God-for-others, then, all of the many others become neighbors. They become companions in God's great and inclusive community, over whose presence we rejoice, for whose company we are thankful, of whose integrity we are reverent, and to whose good we are loyal.

The increase and promotion of these two inseparable and interconnected loves is the purpose of the community and institution called church: in worship and in prayer, in preaching and in sacrament, in training, in building up corporate structures, in mutual service and care, and in going out to all peoples and nations with words and deeds of reconciliation and renewal. Pursuing this distinctive calling, the community and institution called church is critical, ever mindful of the summary requirement in Jesus Christ, ever resisting temptations to turn in on itself and so betray the messianic event on which it depends. It is constructive, ever testifying to God's inclusive and beloved community by crossing boundaries, remaining in communion with all of the many other communities, and so holding up an alternative in a fragmented and broken world. It is the community and institution whose spirit is one of faithful participation in God's universal commonwealth, a gift given by God's transformative way with the world in Jesus Christ.

A Multivalent Relationship

Let the church be the church! This declaration both has been and remains genuinely important.[13] It means that the church should be itself rather than something else. The church should be itself rather than the guardian of western culture or of one or another political ideology; it should be itself rather than merely a social club or a therapeutic community aimed at individual fulfillment; it should be itself rather than merely a nondescript religious society or another social service agency. It should be itself and so resist loyalties and practices that are alien to its integrity in Jesus Christ.

Reforming Protestants in America today have every reason to repeat and reaffirm these things. We live in a time and place where the integrity of particular communities and traditions, including our own, is profoundly threatened. Precisely because this is the case, however, and in order to avoid confusion, we should also recognize that the dictum, "Let the church be the church," is actually only a formal statement and summary. Its fuller meaning waits for some further definition or specification of what the church is. Having explored such a definition, we now are in a position to suggest this fuller meaning and content. Let the church be the church means this. Let the church be the association of those who acknowledge God's transformative way with the world in Jesus Christ, and whose purpose it is to increase love of God and neighbor. Let it be that rather than something else. Let it be that with integrity, dynamism, and faithfulness. Let it be that without compromise and without dilution.

The basic point of this chapter, then, is that the church cannot be the church without standing in a dynamic relationship with the world. Let the church be the church! Understood in a reforming perspective, this slogan affirms the integrity of the church rather than either its capitulation or its isolation, an integrity that requires a passionate, intentional, and critical engagement. Let the church be the church. If we do, then we shall find that, in being itself rather than something else, the church is caught up in a multivalent relationship with the world.

The association of those who acknowledge God's transformative way with the world in Jesus Christ and whose purpose it is to increase love of God and neighbor is in, with, against, and for the world. This means that, among other things, the question of church and world is not fundamentally a matter of choosing or endorsing just one of these prepositions as normative and invariant. It is, rather, a matter of understanding how, in conjunction with the others, each appropriately comes into play, and how now one, now another receives special emphasis. Moreover, in this regard we will do well to recognize that each aspect, valency, or dimension of the tensive relationship between church and world has a rich and important history.

The Church *in* the World

The church is *in* the world. As a matter of historical fact, where else could it be? As a matter of faithfulness, where else would it be? The church does not reject God's good creation. It does not separate or remove itself from a fallen world of fragmentation and conflict. On the contrary, it affirms, celebrates, embraces, and endures God's world.

The church is sent to all peoples and nations, and, therefore, is intentionally mixed into the world. It refuses to give up on what the faithful God refuses to give up on. It honors the dynamic, intention, and pattern of the Word incarnate. It does not shrink from either the command or the gift of communion with God in community with others. All of which says that this world, God's world, is neither alien nor strange for the church, but is partner, companion, and neighbor. Indeed, we can speak of the solidarity of the church with the world, a solidarity that consists in the recognition that, since Jesus Christ is God's transformative way with the world, the church too should be in the world, not unwillingly nor with a bad conscience, but willingly and with a good and faithful conscience. Therefore, the church does not refrain from active involvement in the world. It is the community and institution whose dynamic spirit is that of faithful participation in God's inclusive commonwealth. It is the church precisely as it reaches into the world.[14]

That the church is in the world in this sense is a matter of fundamental importance, because it means that the church intentionally is mixed into a world of variability and plurality, of distinct communities, institutions, and groups, and therefore of distinctive interests, visions, and practices. So one way that the church resists temptations to turn in on itself and so inappropriately diminish or curtail the meaning of its loyalty to God and God's universal commonwealth, is to remain in conversation and dialogue with the varied and plural perspectives and reflections of others. Again, one way that the church resists temptations to exchange loyalty to God and God's commonwealth for the partial cause of one or another ethnic group, political community, or economic class is by remaining in dialogue and conversation with many such groups, communities, and classes.

Precisely because it is *in* the world, the church may endeavor to measure its faults by attempting to see itself as others see it. Obviously, it may also fail to do so. There are no guarantees. Nonetheless, the intentional and faithful presence of the church in the world is an indispensable condition for a church that reflects on its presence and action in the world from beyond the visible boundaries of the church, for a church that is able to learn from others and respond to changing currents. Gustavo Gutiérrez notes that this intentional and faithful presence "implies an openness to the world, gathering the questions it poses, being attentive to its historical transformations."[15]

To be in the world in this way requires fidelity, energy, attention, and grace, but it need not always require that the church journey far. In some sense, the church need not journey at all, since precisely because it is intentionally and faithfully in the world, the world is also in the church. The world is in the church in the form of selected practices, insights, and attitudes that it borrows from its surrounding environment, such as one or another political form, educational strategy, or perspective on human development. Primarily, though, the world is in the church in the persons of those whose sensibilities and abilities, ideas, tendencies, possibilities, and limits are shaped by mundane constellations of conditions, communities, traditions, institutions, and practices. It is in the church in the persons of Christians who are shaped by genotypes and phenotypes, kinship ties and ethnic groups, apprenticeships and educations, nationalities, friendships, rivalries, and animosities. The world is in the church in the persons of Christians who are shaped by their lives in the world, and whose many roles and identities are not simply lost or blotted out in the church.[16]

This means that within the church there are male and female, black, brown, white, red, and yellow, parent and child, laborer and executive, poor and wealthy, mechanic, teacher, governor, musician, Korean, Brazilian, American, German, and so on. There is in the church a melange of memories, hopes, tragedies, experiences, triumphs, failures, and sufferings. There is a world of ideas, commitments, expectations, customs, languages, and gestures. There is a world of worldly activities, perspectives, and identities. And, let us repeat, this is not just a sociological and historical fact, a circumstance that cannot be avoided. It is an intentional occurrence, a dynamic that the church embraces in faithfulness as a faithful participant in God's world.

So, the world is in the church, and this too is a matter of fundamental consequence, for it means that the church confronts within itself a significant and worldly variability and plurality. This is why it often need not journey far in order to attend to the perspectives, insights, and interests of diverse communities and groups. Indeed, this is one way the church celebrates and embraces the world, even as, by the effort to hold together in a single communion of faithful participants diverse groups, communities, and identities, it endeavors to cross boundaries and so witness to an alternative to a world of fragmentation, conflict, and division. Again, diverse communities, groups, and interests within the church may justifiably criticize the inordinately partial loyalties, visions, and practices that often corrupt and captivate the church.[17] Attending to these criticisms is one way the church attends to the world for the sake of the gospel, one way it endeavors to determine whether it has allowed one or another inappropriately constricted and exclusionary orientation to displace genuine devotion to God and God's commonwealth, one way the church resists the temptation simply to turn in on itself.

"Go therefore and make disciples of all nations . . . " (Matt. 28:19). The church in the world, responding to and learning from changing currents and conditions, has a history that stretches back as far as the missionary thrust of early communities into the Hellenistic culture of the Mediterranean basin. Indeed, this broad and initial refusal to leave the world continues to have profound consequences for virtually every branch of the Christian movement.[18]

A more recent history of which reforming Protestants should be particularly aware concerns the decisive emergence of their current ecclesiastical forms in the accommodations of Calvinism, especially its free churches, Puritans, and congregationalists, to the emergence of modern, democratic states. Calvinists in England, the Netherlands, and North America, often under pressure and certainly not without struggle, finally relinquished the ideal of a state church in favor of the legal separation of church and state. Their communities, therefore, took on the form of voluntary associations where membership is a matter of individual choice, a development that accorded with democratic more than monarchic impulses and that implied at least some toleration of religious diversity.[19]

Again, during the twentieth century, a number of Protestant churches in North America have altered long-standing traditions that excluded women from ordained leadership. These changes, at least in part, have been made in response to broader social and cultural currents. Where women are educated participants in professions, business corporations, and civil government, it becomes increasingly difficult to argue that ministry ought to be restricted to men. Moreover, the broader influence of feminism and the women's movement on the ethos of American society continues to push many institutions, including churches, toward the inclusion of women in positions of leadership. Many of the more profound consequences of these changes, for almost every aspect of Christian life and theology, are only now beginning to be seen, not least among them a fuller appreciation for the deleterious consequences of sexism and abuse, as well as a revised appropriation of the contributions of women to our own traditions.[20]

It is obvious, however, if the worldly variability and plurality within the church enables the church to attend to the world for the sake of the gospel, it also creates significant tensions, conflicts, and brokenness among disparate interests and factions. For example, we cannot deny that within the church there are racists and sexists, oppressors and oppressed, opposing nationalists, and the like. Neither can we deny the persistent alignment of specific churches with the inordinately partial regional, racial, political, and economic interests of their constituents. This, indeed, is one of the ways in which the church bears and suffers the world for the sake of the gospel.

The Church *with* the World

In a reforming perspective, this is one of the reasons it is never enough simply to observe that the church is in the world and the world is in the church. It is never enough to say that the church is in the world, responding to and learning from changing currents and conditions. We must also say that the church is *with* the world, confessing our common faults and sins. This should not surprise us because, as we have seen, the church is a community and institution of those who recognize the radicality and universality of sin's corruption. "There is no one who is righteous, not even one" (Rom. 3:10; Ps. 14:3; 53:3). Precisely because it acknowledges God's transformative way with the world in Jesus Christ, the church knows that no human capacity, no person, movement, or institution is sin-free. It knows that all are subject to criticism, all are called to repentance, and all stand in need of reformation and transformation.

The church certainly has every means and reason at its disposal to apply this insight to itself. Aided by the many questions and criticisms posed by the world both beyond and within the church, the church measures itself by the critical corollary of divine sovereignty that God alone is God and we should have no other. It measures itself by the constructive corollary that God always stands in relation to all and, therefore, nothing is godless and nothing profane. It measures itself against the summary requirement and demand of good and abundant life given with the messianic event.

When the church does these things, then, it finds itself wanting, accused, and threatened because it has been infiltrated by lesser worldly faiths and devotions to humanity for its own sake, to race or country as the ultimately worthwhile reality, to the redemptive powers of wealth and economic production, to salvific claims made for science and technology, and so on. It finds itself captivated by lesser ecclesiastical faiths and devotions to the church for its own sake, to Christians as the exclusive community of concern, to the redemptive powers of the church, and to salvific claims made for its tradition or its practices. That is, when the church measures itself by its own first and theocentric principles, it finds itself threatened by, and sometimes in bondage to, alien pieties that bring with them a train of myopic visions and practices. It finds itself skewed by orientations that finally are unresponsive to God and God's all-inclusive commonwealth. Too often, therefore, it finds itself inattentive to important dimensions of the interpersonal and social relations of interdependence in which we stand with one another and with our natural environments, inattentive to and unmoved by the sufferings of innocents, as well as other terrible costs of inordinate constriction. It finds itself infiltrated and captivated by idolatrous devotions, corrupt rationalities, and disobedient patterns of responsibility, and so it confesses its sin.

Consequently, the church is *with* the world, confessing sin in two related senses. On the one hand, the church confesses that it often is in bondage to a corrupted world—corrupted cultures and societies. It confesses that it is captivated by forms of worldliness that infiltrate the church, so that the idolatrous devotions, disordered loves, and sins that plague the world often are duplicated in the church and religiously sanctified with a few stray Christian sentiments.[21] On the other hand, the church also confesses that it often succumbs to the constricting tendencies of the human fault, to the inordinate narrowing and dimunition of the human spirit, in distinctly and explicitly ecclesiastical forms. Here again, we have to do with corrupted devotion, vision, and responsibility. Here again, we have to do with a corrupting dynamic that Christians share with all people and that Christian communities share with all communities. Only here, the church is captivated not by forms of worldliness but by forms of "church-liness." The church is with the world confessing sin in the sense that it too often shares particular forms of inordinate constriction with the world, and also in the sense that, too often, radical and universal tendencies toward corruption take particular and distinctive forms within the church.

The history of the church *with* the world, confessing sin, is no less important than the history of the church *in* the world responding to and learning from changing currents and conditions. For example, the protean evils of racism furnish compelling occasions for many churches to confess that they too often have been captivated by corrupted devotions and commitments that typically plague the world. Obviously, such occasions ought to be recognized around the globe, as is apparent from the holocaust of the Jews, the South African experience, and recent developments in central and eastern Europe. Even so, here we do well to note that white Protestants in the United States bear an especially heavy burden in virtue of their participation in a particular history of violent, unjust, and prejudicial treatment of nonwhite persons and communities. Thus, part of the point of continued concerns and statements about race relations by predominately white Protestant churches in America is, and ought to be, a kind of repentant self-examination, a confession of the powers of sin in the lives of Christians and their communities. These churches know, or ought to know, that our common involvement in the sins of racial loyalty and prejudice is evidence that all fall short of the summary requirement of the good and abundant life. They ought to know that the corrupting powers of sin are more terrible and persistent than mere ignorance; that the question of race is one that they had best approach with a genuine and repentant humility. And, as James Cone and others have pointed out, they ought to know that theological discussions need to be approached with a willingness to learn insights into the meaning of the gospel from others who remain genuinely "other."[22]

The efforts of some Christians and their communities to correct past judgments about and attitudes toward scientific inquiries and inquirers furnish examples of churches confessing that they too often have been captivated by distinctly ecclesiastical forms of corrupting constriction. For, in part, these are exercises in self-criticism, attempts to expunge myopic visions and corrupt rationalities that result from wrong-headed, if not idolatrous, conceptions of and commitments to ecclesiastical dogma. Because of this a number of churches have moved from authoritarian and biblicistic condemnations of evolutionary biology and critical historiog-

raphy toward sponsoring more open inquiries into the relationship between theology and the sciences and supporting critical methods of biblical scholarship at church-related educational institutions. Of particular
interest too are statements made by Pope John Paul II about "the Galileo
case." In 1983, the pontiff spoke before a meeting of scientists at Rome
to commemorate the 350th anniversary of the publication of *Dialogue on
the Two Chief World Systems,* the book that led to Galileo's infamous trial.
There he acknowledged that "the Church's experience during the Galileo
affair and after has led to a more mature attitude and to a more accurate
grasp of the authority proper to her."[23] Nine years later, the pope made a
speech vindicating Galileo and restoring the Renaissance scientist as a
faithful Christian.

I must also add a hope for the future. I believe that my own church, as
well as most others, is wrong in its predominant approach to homosexuality. Here, as with our experiences of other races, we have found it especially difficult to acknowledge the integrity of others who remain truly
"other." We often have become obsessed, and our obsession frequently
has led us to demonize those whose sexuality differs from our own. This
helps to explain why, proportionately speaking, we have spent so much
energy decrying the corruptions of a gay minority and comparatively little exposing the corruptions of heterosexuals and their relationships (corruptions that often have been supported by Christian traditions).

Confessing our long-time constriction in this regard would be a step
toward health. It might help move discussions of gay sexuality, morality,
and ordination away from a handful of exclusionary norms and biblical
texts toward a biblically informed, "positive vision and communal practice that is compassionate and egalitarian." If so, there may also be
prospects for refocusing conversations away from lists of prohibited acts
toward "what is commonly upbuilding and what is not."[24] We may find
ourselves addressing questions concerning covenantal qualities of mutual
commitment, companionship, and responsibility in marriage and family
(including same sex unions and gay households).[25]

It is a significant sign of health whenever the church recognizes that it
stands with the world confessing sin, because the confession of sin, corruption, and disorder is essential for *metanoia,* conversion, transformation,
and renewal.[26] It is basic to the recognition that all of our partial and selective commitments, fields of attention, and patterns of responsibility
stand in need of continual correction toward the expansive compass of
God's universal commonwealth. It is essential for the faithful reforming
and reordering of Christian communities. It is no coincidence that it is
also a check against the hubris of holiness, a hubris that may lead the
church falsely to distinguish itself from the world. Indeed, such false

distinctions rear their heads wherever the church is described as nothing else than the locus of all truth, the fountain of all goodness, the source of all light, and so on, while the world is portrayed as nothing else than error, evil, and darkness. In that case, the church subtly testifies to and acknowledges itself rather than God's transformative way with the world, recommending itself rather than the God-in-Christ who reconciles the world; holding itself up as the exclusive object of God's grace. Then, in effect, it rewrites John 3:16 to read "For God so loved the church . . ."

The principle of confession and repentance, then, is the reforming principle of self-criticism. God alone is God and we should have no others. God always stands in relation to all, and so nothing is godless, nothing profane. Measured by these plumb lines and the commitment to God and God's universal commonwealth that they entail, all are found wanting and all are called to confession and repentance. The church is the community and institution that recognizes this, and its confession of sin, therefore, facilitates a further recognition of its solidarity with the world.

The Church *against* the World

If it is to be at all genuine, the church's solidarity with the world must also be prophetic. The church is *in* the world and the world is in the church. The church is *with* the world, confessing our common faults. But it is no easy friend of the world (James 4:4). Precisely as the association that acknowledges God's transformative way with the world in Jesus Christ, the church is also *against* the world, criticizing idols and corrupting constrictions.

This is so because the spirit of faithful participation in God's all-inclusive commonwealth is no simple affirmation or endorsement of things as they are. Instead, it presses toward another possibility. This, indeed, is part of the meaning of confessing common faults and sins. Again and again the theocentric stance of faithful participation, its radical devotion, capacious eye, and disposition toward universal responsibility, come into conflict with other, more constricted orientations and their inordinately partial devotions, visions, and patterns of responsibility. Reforming piety therefore issues in an indispensable dimension of prophetic criticism. It denounces the inordinate and destructive narrowness that inevitably accompanies interactive orientations centered on the isolated causes and interests of individuals and groups.

Genuinely reforming churches will not shrink from the prophetic task. For example, they will denounce the persistent scourges of racism, sexism, and homophobia. They will point to severe economic disparities among communities linked in a single garment of global interdependence.

They will attest to destructive failures of political responsibility in the midst of dispersed and interdependent powers and point to the potentially perilous consequences of many of our present actions and practices for future generations and conditions. They will testify that the fates of many are increasingly in the hands of many and that this, in turn, magnifies the issue of human responsibility. They will focus attention on the suffering of innocents as well as other terrible costs of inordinate constriction.

Prophetic criticism raises the possibility that the world, both within and beyond the church, will feel menaced or threatened. This obviously need not mean that the church will be cursed and accused or come under any sort of direct pressure. A menaced world may respond with benign neglect by dismissing the nuisance and refusing to take the church at all seriously.[27] It may choose to leave the church alone and pursue its own aims in reliance on the lesser gods of race, nation, and wealth, and on the salvific promises of political might, economic production, technical and scientific advance. In that case, prophetic churches have all the more reason to remain in the world, refusing to leave *it* alone. Among other things, they have reason to be pests and persistent nuisances, calling into question life and business as usual.

On the other hand, we ought not discount the possibility of significant conflict, particularly if the church remains prophetic, retains its saltness, and refuses to retreat. There have been, are, and will be situations and circumstances in which the prophetic task of denouncing corruption carries with it unusual costs and burdens. The task of faithfully objecting to the forfeiture of the good and abundant life for which we are fitted may place the church in direct opposition to principalities, powers, and climates of opinion. It may lead others to question the church's good sense and prudence. It, therefore, may demand the patient endurance of private and public refusals to cooperate with severely corrupted attitudes, institutions, and practices. It may demand an active resistance and struggle against injustice that works for change even as it eschews violence. In extreme instances, it may lead the church into a *status confessionis,* and therefore into intentional and fundamental noncompliance with civil policies and governments.

By the faithful logic of theocentric devotion, none of these possibilities constitutes a reason to relinquish or attenuate the critical and prophetic attitude. Instead, the costs, tensions, and risks largely serve to confirm the underlying and undying commitment. God alone is God, and we should have no others. Reforming churches have to remain true to the first commandment. They have to proclaim the gospel even in severely corrupted circumstances dominated by plainly demonic powers, but not under these powers or in their spirit.[28] In criticism and denunciation, the church is the association of those who rejoice in having no other Lord. It is the community and institution of those who pray for the faith, the discernment, and the courage to recognize and seize the opportunity to witness to God's glory. Therefore, the church that intentionally and faithfully mixes into the world, that embraces the world in itself, and that is with the world confessing sin, is also the church that declares its sole dependence on God and God's commonwealth and so its independence from the world. It is the community and institution of those who say yes to God-in-Christ, even on those occasions and in those situations where genuine faithfulness requires that it say no to a world of idolatrous and corrupted practices.

As is well known, the church *against* the world has a passionate history that stretches back to the earliest Christian communities. More than a few followers of Christ have suffered explicitly for the sake of upholding a good Christian confession. Consider, for example, the persecutions of Christians at the hands of imperial power in ancient Rome: apostles imprisoned, Polycarp, Bishop of Smyrna, burned for refusing to curse Christ and say "Caesar is Lord." John Fox noted in his *Universal History* that early martyrs, both celebrated and obscure, often took Jesus to be their example, as well as their comforter and Savior.[29] Moreover, there are many similar instances during the twentieth century such as the struggles of some "confessing Christians" under Hitler, or the trials of a number of churches under communist rule. In almost every case, the willingness of governments to engage in systemic and violent persecutions points to a corrupt politics, if not also to simple political idolatry.

Let me mention here a less-publicized circumstance. Following the death of King Kojong in 1919, Korean Christians, especially the Presbyterians, were active in the movement for independence from Japanese rule. The government retaliated by closing churches and arresting thousands of worshipers. On April 15, Japanese troops gathered all of the male Christians in the village of Cheam-ni (about 30) into their church, massacred them, set fire to the building, and then left. Before the end of the year, "forty-one Presbyterian leaders were shot; six were beaten to death; twelve Presbyterian churches were destroyed."[30] Persecutions intensified again during World War II, as Korean loyalty became an increasingly urgent Japanese concern. The Japanese administration this time urged all Koreans to participate in Shinto ceremonies. Many Christians refused, believing that such participation violated the first and second commandments. The Presbyterians, in particular, called it idolatry. Repressive measures followed that eventually forced the larger Christian denominations to officially approve shrine attendance.[31]

Christians also have suffered because of both their refusals to cooperate with and their protests against grossly unjust attitudes, institutions, and practices. Some of the most impressive contemporary examples come from Latin America. One recalls, for example, the murder of Archbishop Oscar Romero in San Salvador, as well as the widespread imprisonment, killing, and expulsion of Jesuits and other priests by totalitarian regimes. In many of these instances, there emerges a pattern not unlike the one associated with more purely religious persecutions. Protests against human suffering caused by corrupt economics uncover a corrupt politics that stands behind the corrupt economics.[32] Indeed, the beating and killing of those who protest is one of the things that finally drives home to others just how grossly corrupt a given regime has become. The moral legitimacy of the regime is called into question when it becomes apparent that its leaders are willing to do literally anything to suppress protest and to preserve their own power. The following words of Archbishop Romero, from a sermon he preached only days before being fatally shot while celebrating evening Mass, give eloquent expression to this pattern.

> Brothers . . . You are killing your own brothers and sisters. No soldier is obliged to obey an order that is contrary to the law of God. Nobody has to fulfill an immoral law. . . . In the name of God, and in the name of this suffering people whose cries rise to heaven each day more despairingly, I beg you, I plead with you, I order you in the name of God: cease the repression.[33]

The church *against* the world denounces. As the community and institution that acknowledges God-in-Christ and whose purpose it is to increase the love of God and neighbor, it criticizes and resists corrupted powers, declaring its independence from severely corrupted institutions and practices. In doing so, it testifies to the excellence of the good and abundant life for which we are fitted, sustained, and redeemed. It testifies to the excellence of God's all-inclusive commonwealth or city.

The Church *for* the World

This means, of course, that the reforming spirit of faithful participation cannot come to rest only in denunciations and in resistance. In a world of fragmentation and conflict, its genuinely prophetic vision of a new and changed order always has a constructive side. Its passionate witnesses always press toward new possibilities. They envision a new heaven and a new earth (Rev. 21:1). Romero's eloquent appeal actually presupposes this. That is why he addresses the government's soldiers as "brothers," and why he can tell them that they are killing their own brothers and sisters.

Thus, in the midst of myopic and exclusionary societies, the prophetic association that acknowledges God's transformative way in Jesus Christ structures itself for inclusion. Amid nations where particular persons and groups are systemically disenfranchised, it enfranchises the disenfranchised as participants in its life and mission. In circumstances where persons and groups are threatened with hatred and violence, it strives to protect the threatened. It remembers the forgotten, hides the hunted, and feeds the hungry. By its polity and its practice, then, it witnesses to God's all-inclusive commonwealth. It says no to a world of myopic and quite possibly demonic corruption, and yet precisely in uttering this no it says yes to a renewed world, one that the present world rejects and perhaps also refuses to see.

With these observations, yet another valency of the dynamic relationship between church and world comes into view. The church intentionally and faithfully mixes into the world, and it intentionally and faithfully embraces the world in itself. It is with the world, confessing common faults and sins, and it is against the world in prophetic denunciations and resistance. Yet in all these things it is also and fundamentally true that the church is *for* the world.

This follows from the affirmation that God is faithful. The church affirms that God refuses to abandon creatures to sinful corruption. In Jesus Christ, it recognizes that the great faithfulness of God extends even and especially to sinners, to those who betray the fundamental vocation and chief end for which they are fitted and sustained. Thus, the church is the community and institution of those who announce that God is faithful and that the faithful God is the God of grace and glory. It proclaims the gospel, and informed by that good news it recognizes that sin is never the only or the last word. It recognizes that there is also and decisively a Word of grace, and so it believes that ultimate reality is graceful, that the world is finally God's commonwealth of grace.

This is why the church is a community of hope, which believes that if sin means derangement, then grace means rearrangement. If sin means inordinate constriction, then grace means enlargement. If sin means the brokenness of human relationships with one another and with God, then grace means the transforming divine power and initiative that elicits a new responsiveness to God and neighbor. The church believes that grace means the conversion, restoration, and rehabilitation of faithful participants in the divine commonwealth, and from this belief there arises hope for the renewal of genuine communion.

The church recognizes and affirms these things partly because it knows itself to be a tattered, imperfect, but nonetheless promising, expression of the great faithfulness, grace, and community-forming power of God's transformative way in Jesus Christ. Reflecting on its own experience of gratuitousness, it cannot help but also recognize and affirm promising possibilities for other persons, communities, and institutions. It announces that God is faithful and, therefore, that corrupted persons, groups, and institutions do not lie beyond hope for regeneration and renewal. It hopes for the renewal of the world.

Within the frame of reforming piety, then, this is what it means to say that the God disclosed in the histories of Israel and of Jesus Christ is sovereign. The arc of the universe is God's arc, and this arc, although we cannot always make out its curvature, bends toward God's universal commonwealth, kingdom, or city. Finally, not without confessing sins, not apart from judgments, prophetic criticisms, chastening defeats, and passionate sufferings, reforming piety supports a truly cosmic optimism. The God of grace and glory, the power of goodness made perfect in weakness, is greater than the powers of evil.[34] This is why the church is *in* the world and why it embraces the world with true loyalty, commitment, and a good conscience. It is why the church is *with* the world, confessing common faults and sins. This is why it is *against* the world for God's sake and for the sake of a world renewed. The church recognizes that God is *for* the universal commonwealth, *for* a world transformed, *for* human beings, as well as all creatures, in their appropriate interrelations to God and to one another. This is why the church is a community of hope. This is why it is *for* the world.

From the beginning, against long odds and in the midst of unlikely circumstances, Christian communities have pointed to and embodied new possibilities for a more genuine life together. One thinks of antihierarchical teachings about mutual service, as well as emphases on hospitality and charitable distributions to the poor in the earliest communities. New possibilities certainly were presented, at least by implication, in early communities where there was neither Jew nor Greek, slave nor free, male nor female. What might it have meant for Philemon to receive Onesimus "no longer as a slave but more than a slave, a beloved brother . . . both in the flesh and in the Lord" (Philemon v. 16)?[35]

We do not lack more recent examples. One of the most impressive has been the reformist posture of black churches in America from the underground railroad to the civil rights movement. In this case, the efforts of a minority to obtain freedom and economic opportunity for itself also have meant announcing new possibilities for many of the most basic and influential institutions of American culture.[36] It is interesting that Martin Luther King Jr.'s realistic strategy of nonviolent pressure and resistance also tried to win over opponents in friendship and understanding. It was a strategy borne by hope, because it was informed by the christological

confidence that unearned suffering is redemptive. It was a strategy borne
by hope because it was informed by the conviction that God is for the
beloved community, or that the divine and creative force in this universe
"works to bring the disconnected aspects of reality into a harmonious
whole."[37] We should not fail to recognize as well that the involvements
of the poor in Christian base communities in Latin America often point
toward and prepare for a new possibility for society at large by "developing a vision of faith that encourages people to participate politically."[38]
Gustavo Gutiérrez says that precisely this is the new and hopeful thing that
those who suffer see "germinating in this universe of unmerited afflic-
tions."[39]

This, of course, is not all. Precisely because they are communities of
hope, churches that are for the world point to the costs to ourselves and
others of gross inattention, costs that prompt strategies of restraint, as well
as timely reconsiderations of wider and interdependent contexts. They
testify to a broader and more genuine attentiveness suggested and embodied by persons, communities, and institutions that refuse to let others
drop out of their fields of vision. They point to the bad consequences of
idolatrous devotions and misdirected desires that call for strategies of con-
tainment and balances of power even as they prompt passionate criticisms
of our untrue virtues. They testify to more genuine patterns of loyalty and
love suggested and embodied by persons and groups who order their ends
and causes in ways that point to more varied and inclusive societies of concern and mutual service. They point to lies and broken promises, as well
as to experiences of malice, injustice, and oppression that call for checks
and limits even as they lead us to criticize our deceptive and deficient patterns of interaction. They testify to promises, trusts, and obligations splendidly kept that suggest possibilities for redemptive reconfigurations of human responsibility.

The Faithful Formation of the People of God

The church is the association of those who acknowledge God's transformative way with the world in Jesus Christ and whose purpose it is to increase the love of God and neighbor. It is a community and an institution
in the service of God and God's all-inclusive commonwealth or city. Precisely as it attempts to embody this acknowledgment, purpose, and service, the church finds itself caught up in a multivalent relationship with
the world. It finds itself *in, with, against,* and *for* the world.

An additional practical significance of these statements becomes apparent as soon as we realize that a basic aim of the church and its ministry is
the faithful formation of the people of God. Thus, pastoral ministry is the

attempt to build up the community in genuine faith and love, or to help the congregation more truly embody its belief. Pastoral care contributes to this attempt by faithfully tending to the needs of people in the light of Christian believing. Preaching comprises the regular and formal opportunity in the context of worship to interpret the religious message in a manner that is responsive to the congregation's concerns. In these and other ways, Christian leadership tries to shape the congregation in accord with a good confession. It tries to help the congregation live to God.[40]

The everyday lives of believers take place in a variety of social locations, and so their needs and concerns often emerge from their experiences in communities and associations other than the congregation. This is why the faithful formation of the congregation takes place within a social context broader than the congregation itself. It takes place in a wider context that includes interactions with city hall, forests, families, schools, armies, the arts, businesses, and more. This, in turn, is why pastoral ministry inevitably raises the question of church and world. For, among other things, *different understandings of church and world amount to different specifications of the wider context for the pastoral formation of the people of God.*

What ought to be the relationship between the community of those who consciously live to God and other communities and institutions? What ought to be the relationship between our formation in the community and institution whose purpose it is to increase love of God and neighbor and our involvements in communities and institutions ordered and designed to serve other immediate ends? Should pastoral leadership try to nurture the congregation in a way of life that dissociates itself from the wider society? Should it equip persons to participate in the wider society primarily as an inevitable, and perhaps also tiresome, necessity? Should it attempt to form them in a manner of living that simply legitimates and endorses the wider society and its primary values and institutions?

Answers to questions such as these inescapably involve the concrete experiences and decisions of actual ministers and laypeople. Moreover, in the concrete situation, it becomes apparent that Christians attempt to guide and build up their faithful communities in the midst of circumstances that often lie largely beyond their control. This is one reason we are not surprised to find significantly different statements about the church-world relationship being made in seventeenth-century New England, in Germany during the 1930s, and in contemporary Brazil. Again, the question of church and world very often is posed with reference to the participation of Christians in quite particular insitutions. Should we at Grace Covenant Church strongly support and participate in the Richmond City public schools? Should we support alternative private or

church-sponsored schools? Both?[41] Concrete determinations about issues
such as these cannot be preempted. Neither should we think and write as
if, by some gross intellectualist mutation of scholastic Calvinist doctrine,
they were theologically predetermined. Our specific practical experiences
and decisions often lead us to revise and refine our theological understandings of the church-world relationship.

Nevertheless, if the basic thrust of this chapter is correct, then our concrete decisions about relationships and interactions between our Christian
communities and insititutions and other communities and institutions
ought to be informed by certain generalizations. Within the frame of reforming piety, the wider context for the pastoral formation of the people
of God ought to be defined by a variable and dynamic relationship rather
than one that is uniform or static. The relationship between reforming
churches and the world ought to be neither complete opposition nor
complete acceptance. Instead, reforming churches are *in, with, against,* and
for the world, so that now one, now another quality of interaction comes
to the fore. Indeed, it is by the interplay of these varied qualities that the
church truly bears the reforming spirit of faithful participation, at the same
time that it also orders the wider context for the pastoral formation of the
people of God in a manner favorable for the formation and equipment of
faithful participants in God's all-inclusive commonwealth or city.

In other words, reforming churches are caught up into a ministry of
reconciliation that understands the world in this time and place, and at all
times and places, as its providentially imposed partner. Therefore, they attend to the world, love the world, and are responsible to the world. They
interpret the world, suffer the world, and celebrate the world. They criticize and affirm the world. Reforming churches do not dissociate themselves from God's world; neither do they simply embrace a world of sin,
fragmentation, and conflict. They recognize and lament the constricting
powers of sin, even as they acknowledge and celebrate regenerating powers of grace. They refuse to give up on what God refuses to give up on.
That is how they embody the theocentric spirit of faithful participation.
That is how they support a Christian commitment in the world, and that
also is how they help to form and equip persons as faithful participants.

6

The Sanctification of the Ordinary

A major thrust of this book is that the spirit of reforming Protestantism is a theocentric piety. Reforming piety means a life reordered and reformed by devotion to God and God's commonwealth, a stance of faithful participation. If I am correct, then reforming theology is faithful reflection, an intellectual enterprise in the service of this particular spirit or bias. Reforming theology is a critical and constructive reflection whose fundamental aim is to explicate, promote, deepen, and extend the faithfully participatory and theocentric orientation of reforming piety. It emerges from and also endeavors to support the life of a community that, however slightly and surprisingly, has begun to be reordered and reformed by godly devotion. It tries to further true enlargement or a form of human faithfulness as broad as the divine commonwealth. It serves a definite Christian commitment *in* the world.

Understood theologically, our current circumstance raises the critical question of whether and how reforming Protestants will continue to support a theocentric piety and its "worldly" bias toward faithful participation. Will they succumb to narrower therapeutic, moralistic, and communitarian commitments? Will they be co-opted by opposing conservative and progressive culture-Protestantisms? In this circumstance, and under the pressure of these questions, I have argued that the dynamic of sin and grace combines attitudes of pessimism and optimism in such a way as to lend to the stance of faithful participation the twin qualities of responsible realism and creative responsibility. I have claimed too that the multivalent relationship between church and world specifies a politics of

117

reconciliation and renewal as a context for the pastoral formation of faithful participants.

The Question of Calling and Vocation[1]

Having considered these things, we now go a step further. How does reforming piety endow the manifold tasks of everyday life with passionate meaning and significance, and how do the manifold tasks and involvements of everyday life enliven and enrich reforming piety? At this point, we approach a subject of immense practical concern to Protestants ever since Martin Luther left the cloister to recommend the responsibilities of married life and the Reformation theologies definitively rejected an exceptional monastic life isolated from family and other ordinary demands in the world.[2] Here we confront a basic issue for faithful participants. How can the ordinary life of production, reproduction, and statecraft, the world of work, family, and civil government, become the main locus of faithfulness and the good life? In short, we confront the question of calling and vocation in its distinctly Protestant form.[3]

What we should notice here is an impetus toward the sanctification of the ordinary and a correspondent, mundane disciplining of the spiritual. The spiritual is not a life apart, but rather, a quality of all living that both forms ordinary life and comes to expression in it. Ordinary life is not spiritually inert. Actually, our everyday converse with others in the world draws out and forms the spiritual quality of all living. Properly understood and properly reformed, the ordinary is spiritual and the spiritual is ordinary. The spiritual sanctifies the ordinary and the ordinary disciplines the spiritual. "There is no such thing as a profane or merely secular order from which God is absent, and in which God is not to be served."[4]

Genuine faithfulness and the good life, then, are not defined by an exalted occupation, office, or activity, but by the way in which one lives in any and all occupations, offices, and activities. This really is as antielitist a notion of the Christian life as it first appears, one that contains the seeds for a discipleship of equals. What is done in the spirit of faith, even the most daily and ordinary sufferings and tasks, is pleasing to God and glorifies God's name. The Puritan theologian William Perkins insisted some four hundred years ago:

> . . . if we compare worke to worke, there is a difference betwixt washing of dishes, and preaching the word of God: but as touching to please God none at all . . . whatsoever is done within the lawes of God though it be wrought by the body, as the wipings of shoes and such like, howsoever grosse they appear outwardly, yet are they sanctified.[5]

No doubt such insistences both have been and can be misused to reenforce false stereotypes and hierarchies. Who, we may ask, is most likely to be washing most of the dishes and wiping most of the shoes? Might not the sanctified worth of outwardly "grosse" works be taken as an argument for keeping some people at them? I want, however, to focus attention elsewhere: the sanctification of the ordinary and the mundane disciplining of the spiritual.

Embedded in these ideas is a drive toward unity, toward the integration of all of life in a religious vision. Embedded in these ideas is a rejection of church-world dichotomy, as well as a rejection of the limitation of faith and religious practice to a merely private sphere. To emphasize these points, a reforming theological exploration of the theme of calling and vocation will point to the coherent complexity of the basic path, journey, or pilgrimage of faithful participation in the world. It will emphasize that there are different ways of living ordinary life and that genuine faithfulness entails a particular manner of living. It will concern a sense of purpose amid purposes and a sense of direction amid directions. It will suggest a living unity amid plurality, a dynamic continuity of faithfulness in the midst of our many involvements.

Reforming piety poses the compelling question of calling and vocation in a rather specific way. What is the relationship between our chief end and our many other ends? What is the relationship between our basic responsibility and our many other responsibilities? What is the relationship between our fundamental role and our many other roles? In each instance, reforming piety tries to hold together two things: the common calling of every believer to be a Christian, and the manifold callings or specific lines of responsibility of particular persons in everyday life. It fears that the former without the latter will degenerate into a mere formula, convention, or ceremony of godliness apart from the motility of actual living in God's world. And it fears that the latter without the former will degenerate into just so many disconnected, confused, and faithless bits of posture and activity at crossed purposes. Reforming piety, therefore, insists that the only way to avoid these dangers is to show how we may praise and glorify God in and through the multiple relationships, responsibilities, and aims of ordinary life.

Faithfulness and Worship

The spirit of reforming Protestantism is a theocentric piety characterized by devotion to God and God's purposes; an imaginative vision of the world in which we live and move as God's commonwealth or city; and an active tendency or disposition of universal regard, benevolence, or responsibility. In this tradition, therefore, piety is an attitude of reverence and love of God that entails duties and responsibilities. It does not refer to a segregated portion of life labeled "spiritual" or "religious" but to all our actions and to all parts of our life. Reforming piety has to do with life as a whole. For this reason it insists on the sanctification of the ordinary and the mundane disciplining of the spiritual. This is also why, in the authentic practice of reforming piety, liturgy and life, worship and work are inextricably connected.

To understand how this is the case, we need to begin with the insistence that the purpose of reforming worship is worship. As the Westminster Directory states, the congregation assembles "in all reverence and humility acknowledging the incomprehensible greatness and majesty of the Lord."[6] Reforming worship is doxological. It acknowledges the holiness and excellence of God and divine things; it glorifies and praises the God who creates, sustains, and renews creatures for an abundant and good life together in relation with God. It therefore is the heart of a community of praise.

It follows, then, that reforming worship ought not be reduced to a means to some other end such as personal growth, the health of the nation, or the success of the church. Authentically pursued, it may or may not contribute to these things as they are presently understood. Certainly, it may help put them into a proper perspective. But the purpose of reforming worship is to worship God, and we are not God, the nation is not God, and the church is not God. In reforming worship, then, we witness to the one God. We affirm that first and foremost, we belong to God, and that we should have no others. God's first. Therefore, we assemble corporately, publically, and willingly to worship our creator, sustainer, and redeemer.

But this is not all. Reforming worship aims to glorify and to praise God and so direct human life toward its authentic and chief end. Precisely to the extent that God is first, reforming worship fulfills this aim. Authentic reforming worship therefore insinuates and suggests a master purpose amid our many purposes, a basic responsibility amid our many responsibilities, a fundamental role amid our many roles. Reforming worship directs those who acknowledge God's transformative way with the world in Jesus Christ toward the good and abundant life. It directs them toward a communion with God in community with others that both qualifies and informs the manifold tasks and involvements of ordinary life.

This should be clearly understood from the variety of emotional responses and sensibilities that reforming worship may call forth in the worshiper.[7] Calls to worship, hymns of praise, and prayers of adoration evoke sensibilities of mystery, awe, wonder, and reverence at the One who alone

is holy, who alone holds all things in existence, and who alone is the fountain of mercy and grace.[8] These elements of worship make sure that, from
the very outset, the worship service directs us toward the glorification and
praise of God. Sorrow and humility at our faults and our shortcomings—
our forfeitures of the good and abundant life in relation to God and neighbor for which we are fitted, sustained, and renewed—come to expression
in prayers of confession. Assurances of pardon evoke confidence that God
is gracious, and so they also help sustain a hope for renewed possibilities
for abundant and good life. Scripture readings and sermons call forth a
wide range of pious sensibilities in response to the One who always stands
in relation to all, who delivered Israel from captivity, whose grace is decisively disclosed in Jesus Christ, and to whom all things, therefore, fundamentally and finally belong. Prayers of thanksgiving voice gratitude to
the One "from whom cometh every good and perfect gift," whose goodness creates us, whose bounty sustains us, whose discipline corrects us, and
whose love redeems us.[9]

What often goes unnoticed is that the *reach* of these and other doxological sensibilities clearly extends well beyond the sanctuary. Indeed, the
explicit concern for linking worship with the contexts and activities of ordinary life is evident in a number of Protestant prayerbooks and hymnals.
Thus, we find litanies for those who serve as laborers, rulers, teachers, and
ministers, for travelers, and for captives. We also find prayers for the natural order, families, courts of law, countries, all those in positions of public authority, schools, social justice, armed forces, people at work, those
in need, and responsible citizenship.[10]

Consider too the practice of including the Ten Commandments
within services of worship. John Calvin's Strassburg Liturgy (1545) directed the congregation to sing both tables of the Law following a prayer
of confession and an asssurance of pardon. In *The Book of Common Prayer*
(1552), Thomas Cranmer placed the Commandments near the beginning
of the Order for the Administration of the Lord's Supper, and so introduced a potent liturgical expression of the relationship between ordinary
life and the chief end of communion with God in community with others. Richard Baxter's Puritan-inspired Savoy Liturgy (1661) allowed for
the Commandments to be read before the confession of sin.[11] According
to *The Book of Common Worship* of the United Presbyterian Church in the
United States of America (1946), the "Order of the Commandments"
may stand as an independent service, an introduction to Holy Communion, or within morning or evening worship. It begins with a short litany
and a prayer by the pastor asking God to cleanse our hearts. Then all Ten
Commandments are read, the people responding to each with "Lord have
mercy upon us, and incline our hearts to keep this law." Following a read-

ing of Jesus' summary of the Law from the Gospel of Matthew, the order concludes with a Prayer of Confession and an Assurance of Pardon.[12]

The point I wish to make is that the inclusion of the Commandments in services of worship inevitably connects worship, or the praise and glorification of God, with manifold contexts, ends, and relationships in the life of production, reproduction, and civil law because the Commandments themselves insist on this same connection. When combined with an acknowledgment of sin, the Commandments make it clear that our corrupted devotions, visions, and patterns of responsibility skew the many ends and relationships of ordinary life. When combined with assurances of mercy and requests for assistance in upholding the Law, they make it clear that only the regenerating and renewing grace of God can save us from ruin and set us on the way toward the good and abundant life, a way that will qualify and inform all of the tasks and responsibilities of ordinary life as well. The use of the Commandments in worship joins worship to life. It is a liturgical form that both expresses and engenders the sanctification of the ordinary and the mundane disciplining of the spiritual. It points to a participatory faithfulness equally at home in worship and work, in sanctuaries, in commercial transactions, in courtrooms, and in family relationships.

The central idea, then, is that reforming worship praises God, and in doing so it directs us toward our authentic and chief end, an end toward which we are to live in *all* parts of our life. This stands in marked contrast to the persistent tendency to think of religion as essentially a series of intensely private experiences, as well as to the equally common assumption that the sum total of religion amounts to churchgoing and prayer saying. From a reforming perspective, then, popular understandings of spirituality as the search for interior wholeness are seriously flawed, and one ought to be very concerned to know what Sunday morning has to do with the rest of the week. The normal accompaniment of worship is not some specially holy compartment of life but a faithfulness that has its place in midstream, and genuine faithfulness is the joyful, realistic, and creative overfowing of a community of praise.[13]

Calling, Vocation, and the Public Good

Genuinely reforming piety, whether it comes to expression in sanctuaries or anywhere else, acknowledges that the glorification of God, or the good and abundant life in relation with God and others, is the chief end of human existence. To put this same point another way, reforming Protestants historically have believed that God orders human life in and through God's universal reign, and that Jesus Christ marks off a manner of living characterized by love of God and neighbor that corresponds to God's reign. To be a Christian, to believe in Jesus Christ with the early communities, is also to follow him in this manner of living, and to follow him is to actively commit oneself to increase the love of God and neighbor, or to the well-being of God's universal commonwealth. Reforming followers or disciples of Jesus Christ respond to God's reign—they participate in it—by loving and serving God in their relationships with others. In Pauline terms, faithful followers of Jesus Christ ought to do what is helpful and what builds up (1 Cor. 10:23). We ought to look not only to our own interests but also to the interests of others (Phil. 2:4). Near the center of the devout life, there should be a posture of attentiveness to the neighbor. The Christ-formed disposition of reforming piety is to glorify God in the midst of things by attending to the welfare of others.

As a rendering of the true depth of human life, this christoform pattern or disposition is inexhaustible, and so it cannot be reduced to a single set of concepts, ideas, or rules. That, indeed, is one reason why reforming Christians continually return to worship, to the narratives of the Gospels (Word) and the symbolic true communion of the Supper (Sacrament). Nonetheless, the idea of calling and vocation may be understood as an attempt to underscore this basic disposition or pattern and to lend it a certain direction and definition in the world. Thus, in extending the idea of calling or vocation to all social stations, Luther's claim was that persons who are in the world always stand in relation with others. A calling or vocation (*Beruf, vocatio*) is any station or office-in-relationship that is by nature helpful to others.[14] It is an attempt within ordinary life to enter into the self-offering pattern of Jesus Christ that stands at the heart of genuine communion between humanity and God.

The New England divine, John Cotton, declared that "not only my spiritual life but even my civil life in the world, all the life I live, is by the faith of the Son of God." A true Christian, he said, "exempts no life from the agency of his faith," so that faith draws the Christian to live in a calling. Indeed, wrote Cotton, "we live by faith in our vocations, in that faith, in serving God, serves men, and in serving men, serves God."[15] Perkins in old England, ever concerned that theology or the science of living well should help to integrate every aspect of life under God, furnished the following definition: "a vocation or calling is a certain kind of life ordained and imposed on man by God for the common good."[16] We might say that the idea of calling and vocation is an attempt to redirect ordinary life toward the good and abundant life of true communion with God in community with others. It is an attempt to form persons in their relationships as faithful participants, or to plot a part of the pattern of a renewed, enlarged, and participatory person.

A calling or vocation, then, is a certain manner of living, abiding, and conversing in the world, yet not just any manner of living will do. Perkins therefore noted that many persons, although they may persuade themselves otherwise, actually have no calling, "as for example such as live by usury, by carding and dicing, by maintaining houses of gaming." Indeed, God is the author of lawful callings, and an unlawful calling is really no calling at all.[17]

The point is basic: there is a critical dimension to the idea of calling and vocation. Luther, therefore, rejected the duties defined by his office as a monk in the Roman Catholic Church of his time. Not all stations are legitimate, and as Calvin notes, "there is no vocation in which a great deal of abuse is not committed."[18] This is the import of the phrase "for the common good" in Perkins's definition.

> The common good of men stands in this; not only that they live, but that they live well, in righteousness and holiness and consequently in true happiness. . . . Here then we must in general know, that he abuseth his calling whosoever he be that, against the end thereof, employs it for himself, seeking his own and not the common good. And that common saying, Every man for himself and God for us all, is wicked and is directly against the end of every calling or honest kind of life.[19]

Cotton had similar concerns. He insisted that a "warrantable" calling is one that we enter on by legitimate means rather than by deceit or the undermining of persons. It is one for which God's providence has prepared us with appropriate gifts of body and mind. And it is one

> wherein we may not only aim at our own, but at the public good. This is a warrantable calling: "Seek not every man his own things, but every man the good of his brother" (1 Cor. 10:24); (Phil. 2:4) "Seek one another's welfare"; "Faith works all by love" (Gal. 5:6).[20]

What, then, is the source of the consistent bias in these writers toward the claim that a true calling aims not only at one's own but at the common good or the public good? How shall we "in general know" what constitutes the gross abuse of a calling or even no legitimate calling at all? The fundamental answer actually amounts to a restatement of the essential substance of reforming piety and the practical stance of faithful participation that it supports. Faithful Christians are persons caught up in a life reordered and reformed by devotion to God and the well-being of God's all-inclusive commonwealth. The most expansive common or public good is finally the good of that commonwealth. Or we could say, what authorizes appeals to the common good and the public good in Perkins's and Cotton's understandings of calling and vocation are the convictions that we are fitted and sustained for a good and abundant life, that sin means the dimunition of that life, and that grace means an enlarging regeneration and renewal toward the community of all things in relation to God and one another. These convictions, in turn, are authorized by interpretations of the sweeping epic of the scriptures and especially the cruciform pattern of love of God and neighbor that reforming Christians find decisively displayed and disclosed in Jesus Christ.

Mingling Practices

With this in mind, we return to our basic question. How does the idea of calling or vocation help us understand the ordinary world of work, family, and civil government as the main locus of faithfulness? How does it help us understand the relationship between our chief end and our many other ends, our basic responsibility and our many other responsibilities?

The answer to these questions points to a kind of a transformation, to the reordering and reformation of ordinary life, or to "ordinary-life-with-a-difference." This will be clarified if we note a basic distinction. For Perkins, there are two kinds of vocations—general and particular. The calling of Christianity, or as we might say, the calling to be a Christian is the general calling "common to all in the church of God." Particular callings, by contrast, belong only to some members of the community and institution called church. Thus, some Christians rather than others have the particular callings of a magistrate, a mother, a teacher, a student, a friend and so on.[21]

According to Perkins, there are four main duties of the calling to be a Christian. The first is worship, the invocation of the name of God in Christ, or prayer and thanksgiving in the name of Jesus Christ. The second is to further the good estate of the church by means of prayer, edification, and the appropriate use of our gifts and blessings. Third, by the duties of love, Perkins says, "every man should become a servant . . . unto every man . . . as occasion shall be offered, and that for the common good of all men (1 Cor. 9:19; Gal. 5:13)." The fourth and last general duty is that Christians should live in a manner that is worthy of their calling in Christ Jesus; they should walk as those renewed by God's mercy and love (Eph. 4:1–2).[22]

Because he believed that God wills persons to be social creatures whose converse with others takes place in civil society, church, and family, Perkins also maintained that "every person of every degree, state, sex, or condition . . . must have some personal and particular calling." Indeed, each basic social context is a body in which different, interdependent parts perform certain functions and discharge particular roles. Each is a community, association, or institution in which the responsible exercise of different callings tends to "the happy and good estate of the rest," and even of all persons everywhere.[23]

For reforming piety and its participatory faithfulness, the relationship between the calling to be a Christian and particular callings is crucial. Here again, Perkins makes a trustworthy guide: "every man must join the practice of his personal calling with the practice of the general calling of Christianity . . . more plainly, every particular calling must be practiced in and with the general calling of a Christian."[24] In this sense, the sanctification of the ordinary and the mundane disciplining of the spiritual may be understood as a mingling of practices.

One of Perkins's basic points was simply that a Christian magistrate, wife, student, soldier, or cobbler should combine or join the practice of his or her personal calling with the four main duties of the general calling to be a Christian. This is part of what it means to reorder and reform ordinary life. The ordinary life of the Christian is "ordinary-with-a-difference." A Christian school teacher, for example, should worship in the name of Jesus Christ and also use his or her gifts to further the good of the church. He or she ought to envision the specific lines of responsibility involved in teaching children as occasions to serve others and to further the common good of all. At school and elsewhere, he or she ought to live in a manner worthy of our calling in Christ Jesus: oriented by one faith, one hope, and one baptism; walking in humility, gentleness, and patience; and forebearing others in love (Eph. 4:1–7).

We might say that a Christian school teacher who participates in the main duties or practices of the Christian calling is one whose dominant devotion, vision, and pattern of interaction are responsive to the divine commonwealth, to the chief end of human existence decisively disclosed in Jesus Christ. A Christian teacher is one whose character, commitments, and dispositions are shaped by the practice of public worship in the name of Jesus Christ and by building up the community and institution whose purpose it is to increase the love of God and neighbor. That teacher's everyday practices at school and elsewhere are informed by the manner of living (the devotion, vision, and patterns of interaction) worthy of redemption in Jesus Christ. He or she is oriented by an abiding passion to participate in the most expansive common or public good, a commitment to the abundant and good life of true communion with God and neighbor that is the deep meaning of the divine commonwealth or city.

This is why the calling to be a Christian may be said to sanctify our more particular and personal callings. Indeed, Perkins was convinced that, when severed from the calling of Christianity, the duties and activities of a particular calling would be transmuted into "a practice of injustice and profaneness" by the astringent of human sinfulness.[25] Apart from practices that orient us toward the chief end of human life, we chronically abuse our particular callings. We subvert their true excellence or promise by turning them toward inordinately partial and isolated goods rather than toward the public good.

However, the mingling of practices also means that our specific lines of responsibiity in the world appropriately shape and inform the calling to be a Christian. This is one reason why reforming churches should reject the contemporary notion that someone is "just a school teacher." Teaching first-graders at Mary Scott School in Richmond, Virginia (or anywhere else), is a particular calling of high worth and good purpose. Indeed, the responsibilities, practices, and experiences of teaching children may enrich and inform the Christian community's understanding of what it is to truly worship and praise God. Teaching school conscientiously and compassionately is one way that the calling to be a Christian becomes incarnate in concrete life, society, and history. It is the mundane disciplining of the spiritual, and Perkins put it this way: "the general calling of Christianity without the practice of some particular calling is nothing else but the form of godliness without the power thereof."[26] In short, just as the reforming bias toward faithful participation includes the reformation of the ordinary or the "ordinary-with-a-difference," it also includes the reformation of the spiritual or the "spiritual-with-a-difference."

When the calling to be a Christian becomes detached from the practices of particular callings in the ordinary world, then, the astringent of human sinfulness often transmutes Christian practice into something else. Christian practice becomes a cover for inordinately constricted interests rather than an expression of devotion to communion with God in community with others. Our religious practices become priestly and cultic in a negative sense, matters of mystic withdrawal and the noise of solemn assemblies that may perhaps legitimate but certainly do not challenge current understandings of everyday life. Perhaps one pursues a spirituality centered on an interior wholeness entirely separated from politics and business. Perhaps one orders life piously and exclusively around the church. In any case, the calling to be a Christian remains largely unincarnate. The ordinary is not sanctified; neither is the spiritual truly disciplined by mundane practice.

Among reforming Protestants Cotton's insistence that "all the life I live, is by the faith of the Son of God" has the ring of what's axiomatic. The bias of reforming piety, even in the midst of services of worship, is to encounter without illusion a world of sin, fragmentation, and conflict; to engage with genuine hope God's commonwealth of grace and possi-

bility. Within this frame of reference, the genuine practices entailed by
the calling to be a Christian necessarily push toward particular practices in
the world, undertaken in responsibile realism and creative responsibility.
Apart from engaging in mundane practices, the congregation's religious
life and piety is more likely to turn in upon itself precisely because it is no
longer so definitely pulled into the world beyond itself. Apart from mundane practices, the Christian does not experience concretely what it is to
attend to the welfare of others in family, church, civil society, and so on.
Apart from mundane practices, the inherent dynamic and integrity of
Christian faithfulness in the reforming stream is cut short. Obviously, in
some sense, one continues to worship and also to participate in a community and institution called church. Only now, these signal practices are
in danger of becoming merely cultic exercises, the rote motions of a sleep-
ing church. Now they lack the realistic and hopeful resolve, the living
spirit, that emerge only where worship and ecclesiastical participation are
joined with the other main practices of a Christian: concrete actions of
love to neighbor and a concrete manner of living that is worthy of redemption.

We may note here some of the significant checks against clericalism
that are connected with reforming understandings of calling and vocation.
First, as Perkins points out, the calling to be a pastor is one particular calling among many, and its basic tasks and functions are not to be ranked
more highly than the functions and tasks of any other. Second, the particular calling to be a pastor or a minister entails responsibilities in the
midst of things rather than a life apart. This is a continuing constructive
meaning of Luther's rejection of the cloister. It is as if Luther had said that
the Christian community benefits in its worship and its life together (in
its spirit) when its ministers must worry about educating their own children as well as the children of others. It also benefits when they must man-
age budgets in order to pay for food, housing, and retirements. Finally,
the reforming ministry is a particular calling exercised in the midst of communities where (1) the bills are paid by the voluntary contributions of
laypeople, and (2) the laypeople who pay the bills are participants in a
melange of worldly responsibilities in virtue of their own particular callings. A net effect of this arrangement is that pastors are encouraged to be
responsive to needs and concerns of laypeople that often emerge from experiences in communities and institutions other than the congregation.
This is yet another sense in which pastors are encouraged to attend to the
world.

Faithful participants are persons whose devotion, vision, and responsibility (heart, mind, and will) are tempered in the crucibles of mundane interdependencies. They are persons who, in loving God and neighbor,

strive to be responsive to the practices, possibilities, and limits of particular callings. They are persons whose patterns of participation in God's universal commonwealth are concretized by particular responsibilities within and among particular communities and institutions.

We should also observe that, where it is properly practiced and understood, where it has not degenerated into a cover for inordinately constricted interests, the calling to be a Christian takes priority. Genuine faithfulness takes priority. The orientation toward communion with God in community with others takes priority. The glorification and praise of God takes priority. Finally, the chief end of human existence is the criterion of our many other ends. Our basic responsibility is the criterion of our many other responsibiities, and our fundamental role the criterion of our many roles.

Perkins understood this too. "A particular calling must give place to the general calling of a Christian when they cannot both stand together . . . because we are bound unto God in the first place and unto man, under God."[27] This is so because a particular calling that cannot stand together with the general calling of a Christian is one that does not allow for the increase of love of God and neighbor, but instead furthers some inordinately constricted interest. It is an activity or a role that fails genuinely to restrain evil and pursue good. It is a practice out of accord with the dynamic movement beyond resignation toward reconciliation and renewal. By structure, design, or intractable circumstance, a calling or practice that cannot stand with the calling of a Christian seeks an end contrary to the public good and well-being of God's all-inclusive commonwealth. By Cotton's reckoning it is unwarrantable, and by Perkins's it really is no calling at all.

Consequently, Perkins's rule that a particular calling must give place to the calling of a Christian when the two cannot stand together amounts to a practical restatement of the critical corollary of reforming piety. God alone is God and we should have no others. Apart from the glorification of God, there is no true communion in community for when we fail to uphold the first commandment, then we have gods other than God, with the result that our lives become oriented by constricted devotions to lesser realities such as self, race, nation, or church. We turn our backs on the project of being faithful persons-for-others, and instead become persons who are for only *some* others. We forfeit the good and abundant life for which we are fitted, sustained, and redeemed, so that communion with God is broken, as is community with those others who do not share our partial relations to ourselves and our isolated groups. Then the ordinary is not sanctified, and then our worldly practices do indeed become unjust and profane.

Spouses, Parents, Congregants, Doctors, and Soldiers

Few thinkers have understood better than did Richard Baxter that much
of the proof of these ideas lies in specifics. Published in 1673, his *Christian Directory or a Sum of Practical Theology, and Cases of Conscience* was a
massive work that aimed to advance the pastoral formation of believers by
advising them on the "skilful exercise" of "Christian practice" in their
"ecclesiastical, civil, and family relations."[28] In it, Baxter attempted to relate much of life both critically and constructively to God and neighbor,
and he made extensive use of what I have called the mingling of practices.

Thus, the heart of Part I of the *Directory* on "Christian Ethics" was a
chapter on "The General Grand Directions for Walking with God, in a
Life of Faith and Holiness." Baxter there directed believers "in that exercise of grace which is common to all Christians," or to those who, having access to God in Christ, live to God as their chief end.[29] He then
turned to more particular social contexts and relations, treating "Christian
Economics" or family relations in Part II, "Christian Ecclesiastics" or directions to pastors and people in Part III, and "Christian Politics (or Duties to Our Rulers and Neighbors)" in Part IV.[30]

From the outset of Part II on "Christian Economics," Baxter regarded
the family as an interdependent society that is structured by a contract or
covenant of marriage and that tends toward the public good of God's
commonwealth. He recognized that not everyone is called to marry, there
sometimes being advantages for serving God in a single state, especially
among persecuted Christians. People are called by God to marry, said
Baxter, only when it is clear that they will better serve God and do good
to others in a married state that involves weighty, sometimes wearisome
duties to spouse, and (should one be so blessed) also to children.[31]

For Baxter, then, marriage and family indicate a particular community
and institution that may help those who are suited, as well as their children, to order a life of true communion with God in community with
others. It is (or it may become) a covenantal society that embodies a genuine mutuality and Christian practice in the midst of a variety of specific
aims, roles, and responsibilities. This is why he introduced his discussion
of the mutual duties of husband and wife to one another with a general
principle that well accords with reforming apprehensions of sin, or the
constricting human fault, and grace, or the enlargement of persons toward
God and neighbor.

> It is the pernicious subversion of all societies, and so of the world that
> . . . ungodly persons enter into all relations with a desire to serve them-
> selves . . . but without any sense of the duty of their relation. . . . They are
> very sensible what others should do to them; but not what they should be

and do to others. Thus it is with magistrates, and with people, with too many pastors and their flocks, with husbands and wives, with parents and children, with masters and servants, and all other relations . . .[32]

Baxter then listed twenty-two directions for marital companionship. These included mutual duties to "a true entire, conjugal love"; cohabitation; helping one another in the knowledge of God, the rearing of children, worldly business, and works of hospitality. Then, in a particularly touching sentence, he said, "Lastly, it is a great part of the duty of husbands and wives to be helpers and comforters of each other in order to a safe and happy death."[33]

Nonetheless, Baxter's insistence on mutuality stands in tension with his endorsement of a traditional hierarchy of authority. Baxter understood it to be a special duty of the husband to "undertake the principal part of the government of the whole family, and even of the wife herself." And, although he found circumstances in which a wife might lawfully depart from her husband, he believed it a special duty of wives to "live in voluntary subjection and obedience." At the same time, however, the husband's government must always be consistent with marital love, a principle that limited what Baxter believed to be otherwise allowed in the name of hierarchy alone.

> Divines used to say, that it is unlawful for a man to beat his wife: but the reason is not, that he wanteth authority to do it; but, 1. Because he is by his relation obliged to a life of love with her; and therefore must so rule as tendeth not to destroy love: and, 2. Because it may often do otherwise more hurt to herself and the family, than good.[34]

Duties of parents to children included the dedication of children to God in the sacred covenant (or baptism), their holy education, their training in obedience, their encouragement in appropriate sports and recreations, and the choice of an appropriate calling. Baxter counseled that parental discipline be neither too lax nor too stringent, and he obviously judged that the relationship between parents and children adheres to a definite hierarchy of authority. Even so, he wrote that parents should make children "perceive that you dearly love them, and that all your commands, restraints, and correction are for their good, and not merely because you will."[35]

Part III on "Christian Ecclesiastics" had to do with the calling to be a Christian and participation in the community and institution called church. Baxter began with the practice of worship, an order for which he also exposited in his "Reformed Liturgy."[36] First, he counseled congregants to understand aright what it is to praise God, namely to acknowledge to God's honor God's being and perfections. He claimed that, indirectly, all of holy living acknowledges God, and so there is a sense in which all is worship.[37] Baxter also advised the people to know the true ground and nature of the ministerial office, as well as their duties to their pastors; to escape heresy; to avoid schism; and to behave well in public services of worship. These directives he followed with a lengthy section on "Ecclesiastical Cases of Conscience" concerning everything from whether a papist may be saved (Yes, if he or she is more convinced of true Christian faith than of papist errors.), to the sacraments and the true canon of Scripture, and including the lawfulness of church music and the use of catechisms.

Part IV of the *Directory* began with an account of rules for upright living in public society. Baxter insisted that Christians generally are to keep in union with the church, love God and neighbor, take notice of relevant circumstances, and so on. With these benchmarks of Christian practice established, he then offered additional directions concerning particulars. First, he addressed civil rulers and subjects. Next, he turned to the duties of lawyers, physicians, and schoolmasters, where his concern was to show how certain professions may be sanctified by serving God. Then came a comparatively lengthy set of directions to soldiers.[38]

Baxter's directions to physicians were relatively untroubled, because it was abundantly clear to him that the particular calling to be a physician entailed practices and aims that stand together with the calling to be a Christian. At the outset, Baxter said he had no intention of intermeddling in the subtleties of medical art. The disclaimer was calculated to ease any offence physicians might take at receiving directions from a theologian. Clearly, however, it also recognized the relative independence and integrity of the medical profession and its practice. The pastor's purpose was neither to practice medicine nor to pretend that he knew more about it than physicians do. Baxter only intended to tell physicians "very briefly, what God and conscience will expect from them."

Baxter's claim was that the particular line of service in which a physician stands has "the saving of men's lives and health" as its chief responsibility. As Cotton might have said, this means that the practice of medicine is a warrantable calling since it clearly is a particular way of attending to the welfare of others that serves the public good under God. Thus, as Perkins would have insisted, it also indicates that a physician abuses his or her calling whenever this particular line of responsibility is diminished or displaced by some contrary interest or end. Said Baxter: Where personal gain and professional honor become the physician's first intention, the physician serves not God and the public good but an isolated personal interest. Personal gain and professional honor are two ways that sin's constricting tendencies typically threaten to corrupt professionals. "Take heed lest you here deceive yourselves . . . for God and the public good are not every man's end, that can speak highly of them, and say they should be so."

For Baxter, then, a primary test of faithfulness was whether a physician helps the poor as well as those who are able to pay. Another test had to do with referrals: Where physicians reach the limits of their skills, pride should not prevent them from advising their patients "to use the help of other, abler physicians, if there be any to be had." Finally, said Baxter, due to the "abstruse and conjectural" character of the medical profession, only those possessed of natural strength of intellect and wisdom, significant reading, a great deal of acquaintance with the techniques of able physicians, and considerable experience of their own should venture to practice medicine.[39]

The basic point, I think, is one that we do well to ponder today. Whether we are physicians, parents, or plumbers, faithful participation means an attempt to glorify God in the midst of our many interrelations with others by joining Christian practice and the practices of particular callings. This is why we should take the time to understand exactly how a particular practice or profession contributes to the public good of God's inclusive commonwealth. Again, we should take care to see that we are adequately prepared and equipped for the particular line of service in question. Care also must be taken that our labors do not degenerate into a sinful striving after self-aggrandizement. Given, then, the specific skills and reponsibilities of a particular calling—in this case medicine—certain relatively specific directives follow. For example, "Be ready to commit yourself to long hours of study with able physicians" and "Provide medical care for the poor." By doing these things, we sanctify the ordinary and we discipline the spiritual.

For our purposes here, the primary significance of Baxter's directions for soldiers is that soldiering represents a hard case. Due to certain practices closely associated with the particular office or profession of soldiering, it is less clear that the ordinary is susceptible to genuine sanctification. Baxter himself well understood the difficulty, as is reflected in a persistent unease in what he wrote. The dissenting pastor, whose activities were restricted and who often found himself threatened with imprisonment, noted that civil governors might be displeased if he wrote in detail. Moreover, although he would "not omit them as some do, as if they were a hopeless sort of men," he also believed soldiers liable to mutiny, rebellion, thieving, plundering, oppression, and excessive drink.

Baxter could not share in Luther's boast that "not since the time of the apostles have the temporal sword and temporal government been . . . so highly praised as by me."[40] Not that he was a pacifist. Baxter nowhere agreed with the judgment of radical reformers, such as Peter Rideman, that "a Christian neither wages war nor wields the worldly sword."[41] Instead, he counseled civil rulers to "remember that, under God, your end is the public good." To this end, said Baxter, rulers should preserve the country and its peace. Indeed, he explicitly affirmed the theory of lawful, limited, or just war, and he, therefore, believed that soliders have a clear line of responsibility in preventing harm to the innocent, whether from anarchy or some rival country.

Nevertheless, Baxter also thought it a matter of utmost importance that soldiers determine whether they have a good cause and call. Because, in a bad cause "if you conquer, you are a murderer of all that you kill; if you are conquered and die in the prosecution of your sin, I need not tell you what you may expect." Indeed, he said, in a directive certainly not calculated to win the favor of civil authorities and military commanders, "when you are doubtful . . . it (ordinarily) is safest to sit still, and not to venture in so dangerous a case."[42] Here he also differed from Luther, who counseled soldiers to obey their lords unless they were sure and certain that their lords were wrong.[43]

The fundamental source of Baxter's uneasiness was his judgment that the military life gives "great opportunity to the tempter . . . both to errors in judgment, and viciousness of heart and life." Indeed, he found it "to be much more desireable to serve God in prison, than in the army . . . [since] the condition of a prisoner hath far less in it to tempt the foolish, or to afflict the wise, than a military." Or again,

> I am not simply against the lawfulness of war . . . but it must be a very extraordinary army, that is not unto common honesty and piety the same that a stews or whorehouse is to chastity. And oh how much sweeter is the work of an honest physician that saveth men's lives, than of a soldier, whose virtue is shown in destroying them! or in a carpenter's, or mason's, that adorneth cities with comely buildings, than a soldier's that consumeth them by fire.[44]

Baxter, in short, believed that it would not be easy to join military service with the calling to be a Christian. In large part, this was because he understood the practice of killing to be integral to soldiering.

> It is the skill and glory of a soldier, when he can kill. . . . He studieth it; he maketh it the matter of his greatest care, and valour, and endeavour; he goeth through very great difficulty to accomplish it; this is not like a sudden or involuntary act.[45]

That is, the soldier is equipped to be the sort of person who is adept at killing; his training and practice have their inherent end in a premeditated act of violence and destruction. One therefore needs to be more than a little concerned that military training may render persons morally numb, perhaps even disposed to trespass against fundamental moral norms and boundaries. Again, armies necessarily mean the institutionalization and stockpiling of deadly force. As it is notoriously difficult to hold in check, such a concentration of lethal power seems especially subject to abuse by those in authority or command. Moreover, where armies and the practice of soldiering are abused, the consequences are often both horrible and massive.

In the final analysis, then, the mingling of practices drove an uneasy reforming pastor to reject unbridled militarism as well as uncritical obedience to king and country. Baxter wanted a practice of soldiering that fit with his understanding of the legitimate aims and responsibilities of civil government. He wanted a military service under God and for the public good, and he believed that type of service could not be had apart from training people in the practice of killing. However, he also had a nagging sense that, too often if not ordinarily, military service develops a kind of warrior mentality, temperament, or ethic that is contrary to "reason, religion, righteousness, professions, vows, and all obligations to God and man."[46] As if to underscore the point, he followed his directions to soldiers with these words in his chapter against murder.

> The greatest cause of the cruellest murders is unlawful wars. All that a man killeth in an unlawful war, he murdereth; and all that the army killeth, he that setteth them at work by command or counsel, is guilty of himself. And therefore, how dreadful a thing is an unrighteous war! . . . Thieves and robbers kill single persons; but soldiers murder thousands at a time: and because there is none at present to judge them for it, they wash their hands as if they were innocent, and sleep as quietly as if the avenger of blood would never come. Oh what devils are those counsellors and incendiaries to princes and states, who stir them up to unlawful wars.[47]

Four Things to Say Today

The value of these reflections on the theme of calling and vocation, its Puritan and other purveyors, is that they put us in a position to say four rather important things in our own place and time. (1) For many people today, the basic question of calling and vocation has become particularly pressing. (2) A reforming theology of calling and vocation points toward a genuinely participatory self who is in the world of structured practices, institutions, and responsibilities as a matter of faithfulness and with a good conscience. (3) A reforming theology supports a resolutely critical stance that recognizes important tensions between the general calling to be a Christian and certain structures, practices, and particular callings. (4) A reforming theology of calling and vocation affirms that God works to form faithful participants not only in and through the church, but also in and through the wider world of particular callings, associations, and institutions.

1. For many people today, the basic question of calling and vocation has become particularly pressing. How can ordinary life—the world of work, family, and civil government—become the main locus of faithfulness and the good life? This is certainly one way to understand current concerns about ethics and the professions.[48] Another reason this question and its attendant issues have become so pressing is that contemporary, mobile participants in American society often find themselves having to negotiate a variety of changing roles and lines of responsibility. To be more specific, many people experience increasing pressures regarding their roles and responsibilities in the arenas of work and family.[49]

This is especially true among women who find themselves with more options than their mothers had. Middle-class women with careers try to juggle the roles of wife, mother, and work (as well as the PTA board and church membership). Those not working outside of the home often are made to feel guilty by a society that places high value on remunerative employment. Many times women in contemporary America feel pulled in different directions, and the experience of juggling roles in the midst of divided cultural expectations raises questions such as: Are there interconnections among my many relations and responsibilities and, if so, how can I understand them? How can I pull it all together? What is really important, and what should I really put myself into?

Many women today confront these and other questions without previous role models to emulate. Jobs and careers, families, children, husbands, and more—all may be sources of values and identity. The sociologist, Wade Clark Roof, claims that women today are "on society's frontier, having to redefine their roles and forge new identities."[50] How can ordinary life, the world of work, family, and civil government, become the main locus of faithfulness and the good life? Just because they are on society's frontier, contemporary American women raise the basic question of calling and vocation every bit as compellingly as Martin Luther did when he left the cloister.

Among other things, women's questioning points toward a restructuring of family life in the direction of greater mutuality and equality with respect to domestic roles and tasks. Evidence suggests that contemporary American men don't do nearly as much domestic work when they get home as working women do. Nonetheless, there have been more than a few attempts to redefine what it is to be a husband and a father. For example, one commentator hopes that "in a transformed society, men can articulate their identities in support of and in relation to the new ways of living that have rightly developed out of the women's movement." He also wishes that "men would radically change the way they parent so that when little boys and girls individuate from their mothers, there really is a father to turn to."[51] Sentiments such as these may not be universally accepted, but they enjoy an impressively broad currency. Indeed, expectations and divisions of labor and responsibility that seemed stable or even "natural" to many Americans only decades ago, now routinely come in for considerable discussion and revision. Individual and structural accommodations to the changing patterns of work and family responsibilities and their contributions to gender equality have become major issues.[52]

There are additional circumstances and pressures that also point toward significant reconceptualizations of basic family relationships. How should single parents understand and negotiate their many roles and responsibilities? What are the responsibilities of divorced parents and spouses? To their children? To each other? What is the relationship between a single-parent family and the parents of an ex-spouse (the children's grandparents)? Then there is the question of whether some persons are called to live within single-sex partnerships that entail specifiable roles and responsibilities.[53]

All of this has rather important implications for voluntary associations, businesses, and government. How shall we structure churches, corporations, and government policies so that they are genuinely supportive of families at a time when families themselves are undergoing significant change?[54] From working mothers, to fathers who take on significant domestic responsibilities, to single parents, to gay couples, Americans today discharge basic callings and responsibilities in ways that demand greater flexibility in patterns of voluntary participation, employment, and government services.[55] This is one reason why, if we do not want the calling to be a Christian to become detached from the actual world, we need to see that it is informed and disciplined by genuine engagements with current practices.[56] Within a reforming theological frame of reference, contemporary questions about our particular callings as spouses, mothers, fathers, and professionals sometimes signal important shifts in the textures of Christian faithfulness.

The sanctification of the ordinary and the mundane disciplining of the spiritual. Without attempting to say even a fraction of what needs to be said, we should also note that, in our current circumstance, traditional reforming conceptions bear helpful resources. For one thing, a reforming theology of calling and vocation encourages us to ask about the interconnections between our responsibilities and roles in the arenas of family and work. It encourages us to search for a living unity in the midst of plurality, a dynamic continuity of faithfulness in the midst of our many involvements. In fact, the interplay between the calling to be a Christian and our particular callings assumes that faithful participants glorify God, that they serve the public good of true communion with God in community with others, in and through both their domestic and their professional roles and responsibilities. Again, the very idea of calling and vocation presents an alternative to sexist stereotyping by its insistence that all Christians share a fundamental and general calling. A drive toward the restructuring of gender relations might take root in the conviction that, in Christ, a person is defined neither by career track nor domestic role. *All* are called to use their gifts and talents to glorify God in service to neighbor.[57] Finally, a reforming understanding of calling and vocation will not encourage the devaluation of domestic roles, although it is compatible with their reconfiguration and redistribution. For, by considering domestic roles as vocations, reforming Protestantism furnishes a basis for serious appeals to men about their opportunities and responsibilities as husbands and fathers.

This brings us to a spate of critical concerns that are being raised by women's experiences in families. For many women, home itself is a dangerous place. Some statistics indicate that nearly 40 percent of rapes happen within heterosexual marriage.[58] Marie M. Fortune writes that "violence against women is a fact of life in the United States. It is the common thread of women's existence which binds us together across race, age, class, sexual orientation and religious preference." Indeed, "statistically, we are most likely to be assaulted by a family member or acquaintance."[59] To these statements, we should also add our increased awareness of the appalling incidence of the neglect, domestic molestation, and abuse of children.

In this context, a reforming theology of calling and vocation needs to say something very definite about faithfulness within one's callings as husband and father. It needs to uphold positive images and statements of men's domestic roles as avenues by which persons may contribute to the well-being of God's commonwealth. It needs to underscore a husband's appropriate respect and care for his wife, as well as a father's appropriate respect and care for his children. It also needs to say something quite strict about the gross corruptions and abuses that too often take place; these corruptions and abuses are unholy, and they subvert the glorification of God in a man's callings. It needs to say that abusive husbands and fathers do not serve but, instead, seriously and hideously injure the welfare of God's inclusive commonwealth. It needs to contend that they harm and oppress neighbor and that they do not live in a manner worthy of their calling in Jesus Christ to be a Christian. It needs to say that they attack the abundant and good life of true communion with God in community with others for which we are fitted and sustained. It needs to declare that violently abusive men fail to practice their particular domestic callings in and with the calling to be a Christian. Reforming theology needs to encourage abusers and their victims to seek appropriate care. But it also needs to say that abusive men are less than they ought to be, that they are diminished in the sense that they are not suited for the excellent and enlarging exercises of human capacity and ability that are elicited by our joys and responsibilities as husbands and fathers.

Finally, a reforming theology of calling and vocation also needs to critique sexist social images and constructions that contribute to the violent corruption and abuse of the callings of husbands and fathers. Specifically, it should critique the romanticization of violence, as well as the construction of heterosexual sexuality in terms of patterns of dominance and submission where men are expected to be dominant and women submissive.[60] So not only with respect to family and work but in other contexts as well, a reforming theology of calling and vocation ought to press for a continuing reformation of our social attitudes, practices, and depictions.

2. A reforming theology of calling and vocation points toward a genuinely participatory self who is in the world of structured practices, institutions, and responsibilities as a matter of faithfulness and with a good conscience. Strictly speaking, this statement parallels much that was said about the church in chapter 5. With the church, in the church, as the church, and like the church, reforming Christians are sent and intentionally mixed into the world. They do not shrink from either the command or the gift of communion with God in community with others. They are reforming Christians precisely as they reach into the world of practices and institutions, affirm it, celebrate it, criticize it, embrace it, suffer it, and reform it.

As we have seen, the idea of calling and vocation points toward an apprehension of life in its many interconnections. It joins faith's inward experience and outward commitment in a manner that endows all of life with spiritual and religious significance. It helps to show how the chief end of human being, in sanctuaries as well as outside of them, is to glorify God in community with others. It therefore supports a participatory activism as at home among institutional patterns as it is in the midst of personal relations. This is why the reforming idea of calling and vocation stands against mistaken modernist notions that true religion has nothing to do with politics and business. It stands against every privatistic reduction of faith and faithfulness that robs our institutional lives, our everyday

roles and structured responsibilities, of their appropriate religious significance. This, then, is part of what it means to say with Cotton, "not only
my spiritual life but even my civil life in the world, all the life I live, is by
the faith of the Son of God."

Thus, amid the therapeutic spiritualities, the emphases on personal
growth, self-help, self-improvement, and self-esteem that often define the
religious quests of contemporary Americans, a reforming theology of calling and vocation will underscore the importance of appropriate organization, structure, association, and institution. It will point to the indispens-
ability and positive value of institutions. It will stand against any excessive
devaluation of the routine. And it will aim to support the stability and dependability of fair routinizations that represent mutual and reciprocal expectations that are basic to our lives as persons in societies.[61]

A genuinely reforming theology will not be surprised to learn of persistent corruptions that render organizations hurtful of persons and their
potentialities, and it will be indebted to therapeutic sensibilities, practices,
and analyses that underscore and attack these corruptions. This, after all,
is a part of what it means to say that sin's contagion spares no individual,
institution, or society. Where a reforming theology parts company with
Howard Clinebell, M. Scott Peck, and other advocates of reductively
therapeutic.stances is when they advocate personal wholeness, "the spiritual growth of the individual," or "growth toward greater wholeness in
individuals and intimate relationships" as the *primary* criterion by which
to measure the worth of institutions.[62] Precisely here it discerns a privatistic reduction of both genuine faithfulness and human life. It suspects
that indispensable dimensions of genuine participation, necessary aspects
of both responsible realism and creative responsibility, have been neglected and left out of account. An adequate reforming theology at the
minimum wants to add that an individual's contributions to productive,
relatively just, and participatory associations, movements, and institutions
that help to restrain evil and pursue good is also an important criterion for
genuine personal wholeness.

A reforming theology of calling and vocation points toward an interactive and social conception of persons that does not picture the abundant
and good life apart from institutional structures. It acknowledges that humans are associational and institutional beings and that the history of human beings is in large part the history of their associations and institutions.[63] It recognizes that sin's corruptions are expressed in the rigidity of
institutions that are unresponsive to individual persons and their needs.
But it also insists that narrowness, constriction, diminution, and implosion are expressed in the unwillingness of persons to be formed, and perhaps even transformed, in their dispositions and patterns of interaction by

the discipline of faithful participation in institutional structures. It acknowledges that sin's corruption is also at work in the indifference of persons toward participation in organizations, associations, and institutions for the sake of the public good and for the sake of becoming a responsible self.[64]

This last point indicates why the reforming idea of calling and vocation does not deny the importance of appropriate self-fulfillment and self-concern. Instead, it tries to channel impulses toward fulfillment of self and concern for self into a particular direction. Genuine faithfulness is a living-for-others, a life reordered and reformed by the messianic pattern of devotion to God and God's all-inclusive commonwealth. A particular calling or vocation is a specific way of attending to neighbor and of contributing to the general welfare. Reforming piety and theology, then, do not advise persons to love and to care for themselves alone. The practical stance of faithful participation stands against the narcissistic preoccupation with self that trivializes and retreats from any subordination of self to purposes and causes beyond self, supports a truncated ethic of psychic satisfaction, and seems rooted in subjective experiences of acquisitive isolation and emptiness.[65] However, reforming piety and theology *do* encourage persons to look after themselves within the context of vocational service. They *do* advise people to develop their own capacities and to care for themselves for the sake of effectiveness in their callings.[66] And they *do* support institutional and social orders that will enable persons to develop needed potentialities and capacities.

Indeed, the idea that we pursue our general calling to love God and neighbor in the midst of our many particular callings is part of a wider attempt to plot a pattern for the emergence of a new and true self. Reforming theology points to the emergence of an expanded and faithful self, one whose constriction, diminishment, and implosion have been disturbed by a heartfelt and disciplined enlargement toward a meaningful and genuine quality of participation in the good and abundant life of true communion with God in community with others. It points toward the true fulfillment of self in community or toward a self engaged in the excellent exercise of human capacity and ability in service to neighbors and to the common welfare. In this sense, the reforming conception of calling and vocation joins appropriate concern for self and the development of personal ability and capacity with commitment to both community and institution at home, at church, in the marketplace, the nation, and more. This is a part of the meaning of Baxter's Puritan insistence that persons be well-prepared and equipped by experience and learning for their particular callings. We might say that, by this preparation and equipment, they are *empowered* to participate. They are *empowered* to participate faithfully in associational and institutional structures on which both they themselves and others depend and which contribute to the public good. In this manner, a reforming theology of vocation points toward a genuinely participatory self meaningfully engaged in the true life of God's all-inclusive commonwealth.

3. A reforming theology supports a resolutely critical stance that recognizes important tensions between the general calling to be a Christian and certain structures, practices, and particular callings. This is a part of the socially critical dimension of faithful participation, and its importance should be apparent from what we have said about the restructuring of family and work in contemporary American society. Reforming Christians are sent into the world not only to affirm and to celebrate structured practices and institutions but also to criticize and reform them. Thus, the historic bias of reforming Protestantism toward representative and participatory institutional structures may be understood as an attempt to guard against the tendency of human associations to develop power elites focused on their own partial interests. In a similar way, classical Puritan conceptions of calling and vocation attempted to criticize institutionalized practices, roles, and objectives that did not contribute to the "public good." Earlier in the twentieth century, reforming theology was especially mindful of the demonic consequences of totalitarianism, as well as the dehumanizing and depersonalizing disfunctions of industrialization and bureaucratization.[67] Today, it also stands against rigid and limiting institutional orders that enforce stereotypical interactions or encode patterns of abusive power and dominance.

A genuinely reforming theology, therefore, supports a vigilant and, at times, even suspicious attitude toward organizations and institutions and their routinized practices, roles, and expectations. This is a part of what Perkins meant when he insisted that "a particular calling must give place to the general calling of a Christian when they cannot stand together." It is also part of the meaning of Baxter's uneasiness about military service. To say that soldiering may be a warrantable calling does not mean that all possible military practices and stratagies are legitimate. Neither does it mean that Christians may participate in any and every army. It means only (but significantly) that the calling to be a Christian and the particular calling to military service *may* stand together and that it is the duty of a Christian to determine whether, in any actual instance, they really do stand together. This same sort of determination needs to be made about any other particular calling as well.

This is why, in response to the social ethics espoused by some evangelicals, reforming theology will underscore the need to criticize too-easy identifications of the calling to be a Christian with certain particular practices and callings. True, from the vantage point of reforming theology, we can appreciate that many evangelicals continue to raise the question of calling and vocation in a manner that encourages sustained attention to family, work, and citizenship, and that also recognizes the importance of organization, association, and institution. We also can appreciate the notes of critical caution sounded by some evangelicals in response to the deluge of therapeutic spiritualities and techniques. Nonetheless, pointed parallels to Baxter's centuries-old appreciation for the typical corruptions of physicians and other professionals seem altogether too rare. The primary point of evangelical discussions of calling and vocation frequently reduces to yet another endorsement of industriousness and the work ethic. Again, we search in vain for anything approaching the profound tensions that Baxter discerned between the calling to be a Christian and military service.[68]

Nowhere is this moralistic flight from serious social criticism more apparent than when it comes to some evangelical estimates of our responsibilities as Christians and as Americans. Consider Pat Robertson's basic understanding of our current circumstance. The noted televangelist from Virginia Beach accuses leftist liberals (and others) of promoting a homogenized world and working for the dissolution of the American society and nation, as well as for the destruction of Bible-based Christianity.[69] Poised between two destinies, he claims that we now are in the midst of "an epic struggle for the future."[70] Robertson recommends that true Christians join the fight, take all the territory that is available with minimal struggle, and "surround and isolate each stronghold and prepare to blast the [radical liberal] enemy out of its positions." For, if present conditions and tendencies continue "this nation will have passed the point of no return."[71]

Robertson's interpretation of circumstances is dramatic, and his "Christian agenda" to "rebuild the foundation of a free, sovereign America from the grassroots" includes a number of well-known electoral and legislative objectives.[72] For our purposes, however, the important point is that his reading of current circumstances has a deep theological backing. Robertson learns from Deuteronomy that God set before the people of Israel two contrasting destinies. Wonderful blessings were promised, among them international primacy, productive agriculture, the defeat of Israel's enemies, and financial prosperity, all if the nation would diligently obey God and keep the commandments. Grave consequences were threatened if Israel was disobedient. Again, Robertson learns from Kings and Chronicles that when the leaders of Israel and Judah follow the way of the Lord, both they and their nations are blessed; when they depart, the leaders and their nations are judged.[73]

According to Robertson, these same blessings and curses hold true for the United States. Good things have happened to America—for example, material prosperity and victory in battle—"because those men and women who founded this land made a solemn covenant that they would be the people of God and that this would be a Christian nation." However, in response to recent apostasy, America has been visited by Deuteronomic curses. These include the defeat of our armed forces in Vietnam, economic woes, the assassination of one president and the driving from office of still another in disgrace, and the humiliation of still another "by an old cleric in a Third World power." In addition, our children have been victimized by drugs, unbridled sex, "a pop music culture that has destroyed their minds," and more. By Robertson's covenantal logic, then, the nation's divine "Friend and Protector" has become its "Judge." Indeed, he says that the only thing "holding back even worse wrath on the nation is the sizable body of faithful believers," as well as ministries such as his own that are reaping an unprecedented spiritual harvest.[74]

The fundamental conclusion is clear. If we are genuine Christians and support traditional values and practices, then America will be blessed. Otherwise, "we can witness the imminent collapse of our culture."[75] If America recaptures its standing in God's sight as a Christian nation, then it will thrive; if it does not, then it will be judged. The net effect of this theo-logic is that the particular calling to American citizenship, to a political and cultural responsibility for the well-being of the American society and nation, is at the same time the general calling to be a Christian. The calling to be a Christian, to take up a way of life in obedience to God and God's purposes, is at the same time the particular calling to be a patriotic American. There is little or no tension between the two, as they are virtually collapsed by Robertson's plainly utilitarian covenant.

Where is Reinhold Niebuhr with his Christian realism when we really need it? From the perspective of reforming piety and theology, Robertson's virtual identification of the calling to be a Christian with the calling to American citizenship is simply and dangerously naive. Moreover, it thwarts the movement toward the enlargement of human vision, devotion, and responsibility that is a basic mark of redeeming grace. The well-being of the American nation that Robertson seeks to further and protect is an almost entirely isolated one. Robertson casts the other (whether Soviet Communist or radical liberal) as mythical enemy and monster, at the same time that he fails to appreciate the ambiguities of American patriotism.

A genuinely responsible realism with respect to the nation, or anything else, is not possible apart from a realistic understanding of sin or the human fault. Sin is radical, so that even our best achievements both as individuals and groups (including our patriotic ones) are corrupted by sin's constriction. Sin is universal; there is no person or aspect of human society that is exempted from sin's effects, and there is no sin-free society. Our lives as individuals and in families, in voluntary associations and in nations, are all infected by sin's corrupting tendency. Again, a genuinely creative responsibility with respect to the nation, or anything else, is not possible apart from the optimistic sense that persons and communities can be enlarged beyond the constricted bounds of merely isolated interests. These, then, are the deep theological backings for the socially critical dimensions of reforming piety and the practical stance of faithful participation. It is why reforming theology recognizes that abuses abound in every calling, that there are important tensions between the calling to be a Christian and certain particular callings, and that the two do not always stand together.

4. **A reforming theology of calling and vocation affirms that God works to form faithful participants not only in and through the church, but also in and through the wider world of particular callings, associations, and institutions.** Faithful participants are formed by the structured life and practices of the association of those who consciously acknowledge God's way with the world in Jesus Christ and whose purpose it is to increase the love of God and neighbor. They are formed in worship, fellowship, study, and mission; they are formed by their participation in the church. We saw in chapter 5 that a basic purpose of reforming ministry is to help the church to form faithful participants, to build up the community in genuine faith and love, and to help the congregation and its members to embody their beliefs more truly. It is not just anyone and everyone who attempts to sanctify the ordinary; it is those who are formed into a good faith and confession. Or, in Puritan terms, apart from the calling to be a Christian and its main practices and duties, our particular callings as parents, plumbers, physicians, citizens, and so forth, degenerate into disconnected, confused, and faithless bits of activity.

But the corresponding point also needs making, and this is what I mean to emphasize here. The reforming idea of calling and vocation proposes that the manifold tasks, practices, and involvements of everyday life enliven and enrich genuine faithfulness. It suggests that faithful participants are formed by their taking part in the world of communities, associations, and institutions, that our entering into the structured responsibilities, practices, and roles of everyday life draws out and informs the qualities of faithful living. Indeed, it is not just anyone and everyone who attempts the mundane disciplining of the spiritual; it is those who have been shaped by particular patterns and lines of responsibility in the world. Apart from participation in particular callings, their main duties and practices, the calling to be a Christian degenerates into mere formula, convention, or ceremony apart from the motility of actual living in God's world.

Faithful participants are formed in and through their participation in Christian communities. They are also formed in and through their participation in other communities, associations, and institutions. Put these two points together, and you have the mingling of practices endorsed by Perkins's classical insistence that the two callings—the general calling to be a Christian and particular callings—are mutually necessary.

Now it is just this mutual necessity, or mingling of practices, that needs to be emphasized in response to the Christian communitarianism advocated by Stanley Hauerwas, John Howard Yoder, and others. True, from the vantage point of reforming theology, we can appreciate Hauerwas's insistence that faithful Christians are formed by their participation in the story-formed community called church, as well as his persistent criticism of Protestant tendencies to equate Christian faithfulness with American patriotism.[76] We can also appreciate his creative discussions of "being a parent" as "an office of the community for the well-being of children," and of medicine as a practice concerned with patients' well-being.[77] Yet nowhere does Hauerwas expound a theory of particular callings, and he understands work as little more than a way to survive and earn a living that becomes idolatrous when we attribute to it too great a significance.[78] Yoder, who stands in the tradition of Peter Rideman, takes explicit aim at Lutheran and Calvinist understandings of vocation. Endorsing the way of radical discipleship, he regards the idea of particular callings as a compromise with alien moral directives, a feature of an inauthentic morality of conformity that amounts to "a divine rubber stamp for the present social order."[79]

In effect, then, both Hauerwas and Yoder uphold the calling to be a Christian apart from particular callings. They fear that the idea of particular callings lends work a significance it ought not have, and that it threatens the formation of faithful Christians by giving them over to alien practices and standards. By contrast, reforming theology tries to integrate all of life into a holistic vision of love of God and neighbor. Rather than uphold the strict imitation of Christ that lies behind the ethics of radical discipleship, it emphasizes a broader approximation of Christ as our pattern, which forms the deep meaning of the classical insistence that a warrantable calling serve the public good of the divine commonwealth.

Reforming theology acknowledges that we participate in God's commonwealth of grace—in the world as doxology of divine presence, power, and goodness. It therefore affirms that, however partially and ambiguously, we may participate in God's provident and redemptive care. It affirms that, by grace, we may become mirrors of God's glory. This, in turn, is precisely what we are called to be and to do in and through the many mundane lines of interrelationship and responsibility in which we are involved.

Faithful participants attempt to exercise a creative responsibility that aims at possibilities for renewed attentiveness and enlarged devotion to the well-being of God's universal community. They try to respond to the needs of crying infants, anxious friends, aging parents, the homeless, inner-city children learning to read and succeed, customers who rely on safe and effective products, patients who depend on practiced and sensitive care, employees whose livelihoods depend on the continued profitability of a corporation, populations caught in cycles of economic stagnation, the victims of political violence, and so on. As they do so, they come to recognize that "God's care is a *mediated* care." They come to recognize that God's care can be mediated in and through our faithful participation in the world of associations, institutions, and roles. Put another way, they come to recognize that there is no higher calling than the call to be a Christian, and that this high calling is lived out amid our many particular callings. That is why "under vocation's sacred canopy, all experiences of life take on a sacramental quality."[80]

As this book has pointed out again and again, this optimistic note is not the only one. Reforming theology also acknowledges that the venture of faithful participation is fraught with tensions and ambiguities. It knows and confesses that there is no sin-free person, institution, or society. It therefore knows and confesses that there is no sin-free calling, and so it supports the continuing criticism, reordering, and reformation of all persons, institutions, societies, and roles. But this is not the same thing as pronouncing alien or inauthentic the relatively independent practices, aims, and standards that necessarily accompany our particular callings. Rather, it is to acknowledge that wherever we participate in God's provident and redemptive care, we do so in the midst of sin's multifaceted, radical, universal, inevitable, and destructive corruption of the entire human project. We do so in a world of fragmentation and conflict.

That is why faithful participants are responsible realists who understand that in all of their attempts to restrain evil and to pursue good by means of their callings and vocations, they are enmeshed in a world of relative evils and goods. That is why they know that not every calling can stand together with the calling to be a Christian; that even their best accomplishments are corrupted and deserving of criticism. But that is why they also know that complete purity and righteousness are unavailable, and that lesser evils must sometimes be tolerated in order to avoid greater ones. There is almost no thoughtful and faithful parent, friend, teacher, trade unionist, executive, minister, physician, citizen, or politician who is entirely unaware of this. And it was just this awareness that led Baxter not only to note the extraordinary moral perils of military service and to criticize its terrible abuses, but also (and nevertheless) to regard it as a warrantable calling.

All of which brings us at last to a further disagreement, one that goes to the very heart of reforming theology and ethics and the practical stance of faithful participation. Hauerwas's communitarianism emphasizes the formation of faithful Christians by their participation in the ethos and practices of the story-formed community called church. This is not only because he favors an ethics of character, but also because, like Yoder, he remains suspicious of other communities and institutions. Like Yoder, Hauerwas believes that many of the institutions and roles in the wider society remain alien and that they work against the faithful formation of persons. He therefore envisions a confessing church as "a beachhead, an outpost, an island of one culture in the middle of another." Indeed, this is a normative image, not only for specially trying and demonic circumstances. "It is the nature of the church, at any time and in any situation, to be a colony" that rejects the dominant culture with a few exceptions and that forms Christians as resident aliens.[81]

By contrast, reforming piety believes that faithful persons are formed not only in and through their participation in Christian communities, but also in and through their participation in other communities, associations, and institutions. It does not believe that Christian faithfulness is doomed to fatal erosion where persons are formed by their participation in the ethos and practices of other communities and institutions. It believes, instead, that such worldly participation often helps to complete and extend the faithful formation of persons. Indeed, it believes that faithfulness to God and neighbor actually and positively calls for the formation of Christians by the church but also in other social settings as well. Reforming piety points toward both the "ordinary with a difference" and the "spiritual with a difference." It believes that faithful participants are persons whose devotion, vision, and responsibility are tempered in the crucibles of mundane interdependencies that have been concretized within particular communities and institutions.

In our society, as in any other, this belief represents something of a wager. Every particular social setting and institution has its own relatively independent aims, offices, and powerfully forming practices. Will these dilute and subvert genuine faithfulness, or will they help enrich and empower it? Reforming theology does not give its answer lightly. It does not answer apart from a keen sense for sin's radical, universal, and inevitable corruption of the human project. It recognizes that some offices cannot stand together with the calling to be a Christian. It recognizes that, at any specific place and time, fundamental subversions of basic moral principles, as well as gross harm to the public good, may require that we refuse to participate in one or another community, institution, or role. It also recognizes that our social histories are replete with tragedies, ambiguities, and confusions.

Nevertheless, it answers that, on balance, participation in the world's many institutions, roles, and responsibilities is a good thing. It offers this answer in theocentric confidence. It takes this risk confident that, despite sin's radical corruption and despite persistent ambiguities, God has been, is now, and will continue to be active in and through the many differentiated social contexts, roles, and forming powers. It takes this risk confident that this is *God's* world, and that in and through its many communities, histories, movements, and institutions, God's provident and redemptive care works to form a faithful society of love and praise.

Conclusion

The sanctification of the ordinary and the mundane disciplining of the spiritual—these are complementary dimensions of the spirit of reforming Protestantism, of a theocentric piety disposed to reorder and reform all of life in devotion to God and God's all-inclusive commonwealth. This basic disposition entails the leading conviction that first and foremost we belong to God. It entails the conviction that we are created good, equipped for an abundant and good life together in God's encompassing reign, fitted and sustained for conscious and responsible relations with God and others. It also entails the further conviction that sin is a radical corruption of this creative possibility, a turning away from God and God's interdependent commonwealth. Sin means the diminution and fragmentation of the good life that befits us, and so the recognition of sin calls for a realistic assessment of the persistently destructive tendencies of persons, communities, and institutions. But grace is the good news of the gospel that the great God who creates all things good and also sustains them refuses to abandon creatures to corruption and destruction. Grace means rearrangement, enlargement, regeneration, renewal, conversion, restoration, and rehabilitation. Grace means recreative possibility, and grace is God's transformative way with the world in Jesus Christ. God is faithful, and the purpose of the faithful God is new and renewed life. Reforming piety, therefore, calls for a hopeful recognition of the promise of persons, communities, and institutions in God's world.

This is cosmic optimism, a piety that strains to see the kingdom. It looks for a history of fragmentation and conflict transfigured by regenerative possibility. It believes that the steadfast God is not absent from any part of the human project and that this is the faithful God's good world. It is the reason why reforming Protestants envision a church in, with, against, and for the world that helps to form faithful participants. It is the reason why reforming faithfulness risks a definite Christian commitment *in* the world. For the spirit of reforming Protestantism must finally say to both your and my anxiety, as also to every defensive posture that fears its participatory wager, "I do not believe you. The great God of glory is the good God of grace."

Notes

Chapter 1. The Spirit of Reforming Protestantism

1. Robert Wuthnow, *The Struggle for America's Soul: Evangelicals, Liberals, and Secularism* (Grand Rapids, Mich.: William B. Eerdmans Pub. Co., 1989), 22–23; James Davison Hunter, *Culture Wars: The Struggle to Define America* (New York: Basic Books, 1991).

2. Wade Clark Roof and William McKinney, *American Mainline Religion: Its Changing Shape and Future* (New Brunswick: Rutgers University Press, 1987), 72–105; Wade Clark Roof, *A Generation of Seekers: The Spiritual Journeys of the Baby Boom Generation* (San Francisco: HarperSan Francisco, 1993), 61–148.

3. Hunter, *Culture Wars*, 34.

4. Allan Boesak, *Black and Reformed: Apartheid, Liberation and the Calvinist Tradition* (Maryknoll, N.Y.: Orbis Books, 1984), 88.

5. See H. Richard Niebuhr, *The Kingdom of God in America* (New York: Harper & Row, 1937), 17–44.

6. Quoted in Sidney E. Ahlstrom, *A Religious History of the American People* (New Haven, Conn.: Yale University Press, 1972), 136–37.

7. Irwin H. Polishook, ed. *Roger Williams, John Cotton, and Religious Freedom: A Controversy in New and Old England* (Englewood Cliffs, N.J.: Prentice-Hall, 1967), 65.

8. *The Correspondence of Roger Williams, Volume I (1629–1653),* ed. Glenn W. LaFantasie (Hanover: University Press of New England; London: Brown University Press, 1988), 57–65; Edmund S. Morgan, *Roger Williams: The Church and the State* (New York: Harcourt, Brace & World, 1967), 137.

9. Amanda Porterfield, *Female Piety in Puritan New England: The Emergence of Religious Humanism* (New York: Oxford University Press, 1992), 95–106.

10. Ahlstrom, *A Religious History of the American People,* 376. See also David

Little, "The Reformed Tradition and the First Amendment," *Affirmation* 2, no. 2 (fall 1989): 1–19.

11. So, for example, by 1860, there were more than two hundred chapters of the YMCA and the YWCA in North America, with a combined membership of about twenty-five thousand. See James Luther Adams, "The Voluntary Principle in the Forming of American Religion," in *Voluntary Associations: Socio-cultural Analyses and Theological Interpretation,* ed. J. Ronald Engel (Chicago: Exploration Press, 1986), 180–83; Ahlstrom, *A Religious History of the American People,* 640–68.

12. Ahlstrom, *A Religious History of the American People,* 635. I like the phrase, but do not see how the nation's "first truly fundamental moral encounter" can fail to include its attitudes and policies toward the native inhabitants of North America.

13. On the activities and statements of the Grimke sisters, see Rosemary Radford Reuther and Rosemary Skinner Keller, eds. *Women and Religion in America, Volume 1: The Nineteenth Century, A Documentary History* (San Francisco: Harper & Row, 1981), 294–95, 312–15.

14. Ahlstrom, *A Religious History of the American People,* 657.

15. Ibid., 635. The most extended defense of slavery offered by a faculty member at Union Theological Seminary in Virginia was Robert Lewis Dabney's *A Defence of Virginia [and Through Her of the South] in Recent and Pending Contests Against the Sectional Party* (Harrisonburg, Va.: Sprinkle Publications, 1977). It was originally published in 1867. Dabney was also a vigorous opponent of women's rights, immigration, and trade unions.

16. Reuther and Keller, eds. *Women and Religion in America, 217.*

17. See J. Philip Wogaman, *Christian Ethics: A Historical Introduction* (Louisville: Westminster/John Knox Press, 1993), 186–90.

18. See, for example, Horace Bushnell, *Building Eras in Religion* (New York: Charles Scribner's Sons, 1903), 71–105, 360–85; Barbara M. Cross, *Horace Bushnell: Minister to a Changing America* (Chicago: University of Chicago Press, 1958), 77–78, 81–82; Howard A. Barnes, *Horace Bushnell and the Virtuous Republic* (Metuchen, N.J. and London: The Scarecrow Press, 1991), 70–71.

19. Walter Rauschenbusch, *Christianity and the Social Crisis* (Louisville: Westminster/John Knox Press, 1991), 143. See also Harlan Beckley's very helpful account of Rauschenbusch's discovery of the centrality of the kingdom of God in *Passion for Justice: Retrieving the Legacies of Walter Rauschenbusch, John A. Ryan, and Reinhold Niebuhr* (Louisville: Westminster/John Knox Press, 1992), 27–56.

20. William McGuire King, "The Reform Establishment and the Ambiguities of Influence," in *Between the Times: The Travail of the Protestant Establishment in America, 1900–1960,* ed. William R. Hutchison (Cambridge: Cambridge University Press, 1989), 124–25.

21. For example, the Federal Council sponsored joint studies of industry and labor with the Central Conference of American Rabbis and the National Catholic Welfare Conference. It also established a Committee on Goodwill between Christians and Jews. See Benny Kraut, "A Wary Collaboration: Jews, Catholics, and the Protestant Goodwill Movement," in *Between the Times,* 179–82.

22. Roof and McKinney, *American Mainline Religion,* 80.

23. See Walter Marshall Horton, *Realistic Theology* (New York: Harper & Brothers Publishers, 1934), ix–x, 1–40, 41, 78. We should not assume that all of the realists always had a careful and highly developed understanding of the liberal thinkers they criticized. For instance, Beckley notes that Reinhold Niebuhr never "carefully read or completely understood Rauschenbusch." See his *Passion for Justice,* 18, 190.

24. David W. Wills, "An Enduring Distance: Black Americans and the Establishment," in *Between the Times,* 179–82.

25. David Tracy, *Dialogue with the Other: The Inter-Religious Dialogue* (Louvain: Peeters Press; Grand Rapids, Mich.: William B. Eerdmans Publishing Co., 1990), 5–6.

26. Alan Heimert, "Puritanism, the Wilderness, and the Frontier," in *Puritanism and the American Experience,* ed. Michael McGiffert (Reading, Mass.: Addison-Wesley Publishing Co., 1969), 169.

27. Voluntary societies continued to furnish women with their most regular opportunities for faithful participation and leadership through much of the twentieth century. As Virginia L. Brereton notes, "Excluded from the centers of authority and education in the churches in the early twentieth century, women continued to be most active and successful in the separate and parallel organizations they had established during the nineteenth century." See "United and Slighted: Women as Subordinated Insiders," in *Between the Times,* 146.

28. William Lee Miller, *The First Liberty: Religion and the American Republic* (New York: Alfred A. Knopf, 1986), 266–67.

29. John M. Mulder, "Introduction" to Horace Bushnell, *Christian Nurture* (Grand Rapids, Mich.: Baker Book House, 1979), xix–xx, xxv–xxvi; Horace Bushnell, *Building Eras in Religion,* 75–77, 380; Barbara M. Cross, *Horace Bushnell,* 40–41, 77–78, 81–82; Howard A. Barnes, *Horace Bushnell and the Virtuous Republic,* 33–34, 53–55, 128, 134, 160.

30. Barnes, *Horace Bushnell and the Virtuous Republic,* 36–40.

31. Walter Rauschenbusch, *A Theology for the Social Gospel* (Nashville: Abingdon Press, 1987), 28, 230–31, 240–79; idem, *Christianity and the Social Crisis,* 207; idem, *Christianizing the Social Order* (New York: MacMillan Co., 1912), 278, 442.

32. H. Richard Niebuhr, *The Social Sources of Denominationalism* (New York: World Publishing Co., 1972).

33. William M. King, "The Reform Establishment and the Ambiguities of Influence," in *Between the Times,* 138.

34. See, for example, Reinhold Niebuhr, *Moral Man and Immoral Society: A Study in Ethics and Politics* (New York: Charles Scribner's Sons, 1932), 83–112, 252–56; H. Richard Niebuhr, "War as the Judgment of God," *The Christian Century* 59 (1942): 630–33; idem, "Is God in the War," *The Christian Century,* 59 (1942): 953–55; idem, "War as Crucifixion," *The Christian Century,* 60 (1943): 513–15.

35. Howard J. Clinebell, Jr., *Growth Counseling: Hope-Centered Methods of Actualizing Human Wholeness* (Nashville: Abingdon Press, 1979), 35–36.

36. Howard J. Clinebell, Jr., *Basic Types of Pastoral Counseling: New Resources for Ministering to the Troubled* (Nashville: Abingdon Press, 1966), 15, 18–20; idem,

Mental Health Through Christian Community: The Local Church's Ministry of Growth and Healing (Nashville: Abingdon Press, 1965), 45; idem, *Growth Groups* (Nashville: Abingdon Press, 1972, 1977), 13.

37. M. Scott Peck, M.D., *The Road Less Traveled: A New Psychology of Love, Traditional Values and Spiritual Growth* (New York: Simon & Schuster, 1978), 32, 167–68, 260, 311.

38. Howard J. Clinebell, Jr., *Contemporary Growth Therapies: Resources for Actualizing Human Wholeness* (Nashville: Abingdon Press, 1981), 229. This fits the profile of a theology "absorbed into the categories of contemporary psychology" mentioned by Robert N. Bellah, et al., *Habits of the Heart: Individualism and Commitment in American Life* (New York: Harper & Row, 1985), 239.

39. Clinebell, *Growth Counseling*, 32–34.

40. Jerry Falwell, *Listen, America!* (Garden City, N.Y.: Doubleday & Co., 1980), 13, 70–71, 73, 74, 77–78, 244, 266. See also Falwell, *Finding Inner Peace and Strength* (Garden City, N.Y.: Doubleday & Co., 1982), 126; Pat Robertson, *The Turning Tide: The Fall of Liberalism and the Rise of Common Sense* (Dallas: Word Publishing, 1993), 170, 185.

41. Clinebell, *Basic Types of Pastoral Counseling*, 18–20.

42. A cautionary note. Hauerwas rejects the communitarian label. He says that we need "much thicker accounts of the different positions embraced" by the terms "liberal" and "communitarian." He also says he does not want community to be an end in itself. See Stanley Hauerwas, *Dispatches from the Front: Theological Engagements with the Secular* (Durham, N.C.: Duke University Press, 1994), 157–58.

I agree. By calling him a radical Christian communitarian I do not mean that he does not mean what he says. And I don't mean simply to resurrect the charge that he is sectarian. I mean that he places an emphasis on the faithful formation of Christians by their participation in the distinct practices of the Christian community that basically precludes their faithful formation in and through participation in other communities, institutions, and practices as well. Christians, for Hauerwas, are not only significantly and inescapably dependent on participation in the Christian community for their faithful formation; they are radically and rather exclusively dependent on it. This leads to a different style or quality of Christian commitment in the world of extra-ecclesiastical institutions, roles, and practices than is supported by reforming Protestantism. It specifically leads to genuine differences over what has often been called the doctrine of calling and vocation. More on that in Chapter 6.

43. Stanley Hauerwas and William H. Willimon, *Resident Aliens: Life in the Christian Colony* (Nashville: Abingdon Press, 1989), 17, 12.

44. Stanley Hauerwas, *After Christendom: How the Church Is to Behave if Freedom, Justice, and a Christian Nation Are Bad Ideas* (Nashville: Abingdon Press, 1991), 78, 85–86, 122, 124, 127, 147, 150; idem, *Against the Nations: War and Survival in a Liberal Society* (Minneapolis: Winston Press, 1985), 122–31; idem, *A Community of Character: Toward a Constructive Christian Social Ethic* (Notre Dame, Ind.: University of Notre Dame Press, 1981), 169–70.

45. See Julian Hartt, "Theological Investments in Story: Some Comments on Recent Developments and Some Proposals," in *Why Narrative? Readings in Nar-*

rative Theology, ed. Stanley Hauerwas and L. Gregory Jones (Grand Rapids, Mich.: William B. Eerdmans Publishing Co., 1989), 279–92.

46. Hunter, *Culture Wars,* 322–25.

47. See James F. Childress, *Civil Disobedience and Political Obligation: A Study in Christian Social Ethics* (New Haven, Conn.: Yale University Press, 1971), 149–64.

48. It is clear that the mere presence of democratic institutions does not guarantee genuine political participation and responsiveness. On the other hand, subversion of the promise of democratic politics at the hands of racial loyalties, economic interests, bureaucratic inertia, or what have you does not necessarily justify a rejection of democratic forms or their replacement by other political forms. Consider, for example, William Greider's recent claims of a "civic breakdown" in contemporary America and a failure of formal electoral politics. Greider's criticisms of the present state of affairs do not signify a readiness to throw constitutional democracy overboard. Instead, he calls for a revitalization of voluntary and mediating institutions, as well as of the civic or "social faith in the promise of democracy" and its "self-correcting mechanisms" to adjust to changing conditions. See his *Who Will Tell the People: The Betrayal of American Democracy* (New York: Simon & Schuster, 1992), 11, 13, 15, 23, 413.

49. To estabish these points firmly would require considerable additional argument about current circumstances. At this point, let me merely note that contributing to wider conversations is not the only faithfully participatory strategy under every circumstance. For example, revolution is another possibility, and under certain circumstances, reforming Protestants both have been and ought to be willing to adopt explicitly revolutionary stances that include genuine rejections of many dominant institutions and also resistance and active rebellion against political authorities. Even then, however, revolution is a phase of a broader strategy that also pursues renewed possibilities for construction.

50. "The Christian Witness in the Social and National Order," *The Essential Reinhold Niebuhr: Selected Essays and Addresses,* edited and introduced by Robert McAfee Brown (New Haven, Conn.: Yale University Press, 1986), 100.

51. Stephen L. Carter points out that in America today many are suspicious of any religious element in public moral discourse and even of the religious motivations of some public-spirited people. I agree and would only add that some of those who remain suspicious of religious motivations for "public-spiritedness" are themselves theologians. Like Carter, I also believe that attempts to expunge all religious terms and commitments from American public culture are misguided. However, my reasons for believing this are explicitly theological and theocentric, and not because I regard the well-being of the nation as the ultimate standard of meaning and value. See Carter's *The Culture of Disbelief: How American Law and Politics Trivialize Religious Devotion* (New York: Basic Books, 1993), 4, 9, 277.

Chapter 2. Reforming Protestantism: Identity and Relevance

1. The terms are Davison Hunter's, from his *Culture Wars: The Struggle to Define America* (New York: Basic Books, 1991), 115. See also Robert Wuthnow,

The Struggle for America's Soul: Evangelicals, Liberals, and Secularism (Grand Rapids, Mich.: William B. Eerdmans Publishing Co., 1989), 23.

2. Wade Clark Roof and William McKinney, *American Mainline Religion: Its Changing Shape and Future* (New Brunswick, N.J.: Rutgers University Press, 1987), 186–228.

3. Wade Clark Roof, "The Third Disestablishment and Beyond," *Mainstream Ministry in the Twentieth Century,* the Council on Theological Education, Presbyterian Church (U.S.A.), 27–37; idem, *Community and Commitment: Religious Plausibility in a Liberal Protestant Church* (New York: Pilgrim Press, 1978), 204.

4. Robert W. Lynn, "Sprunt Lectures, 1989," no. 5, audiotape in Spence Library, Union Theological Seminary, in Richmond, Virginia.

5. Foster Freeman, "Spiritual Direction for Seminarians," *Theological Education* 24, no. 1 (autumn, 1987): 44, 55.

6. Allan Jones, "Are We Lovers Anymore? (Spiritual Formation in Seminaries)," *Theological Education* 24, no. 1 (autumn, 1987): 11.

7. See, for example, Joseph Hough and John Cobb, *Christian Identity and Theological Education* (Chico, Calif.: Scholars Press, 1985); Max L. Stackhouse, *Apologia: Contextualization, Globalization, and Mission in Theological Education* (Grand Rapids, Mich.: William B. Eerdmans Publishing Co., 1988).

8. Don S. Browning, "Globalization and the Task of Theological Education in North America," *Theological Education* 23, no. 1 (Autumn, 1986): 48.

9. See Francis Cardinal Arinze, "Globalization of Theological Education," *Theological Education* 23, no. 1 (autumn, 1986): 14–16.

10. Marsha Hewitt, et al., "Education for a Global Theology," *Theological Education* 26, Suppl. 1 (1990): 110. Most of these "new subjects" are elements of a liberal arts education to which candidates for ministry are increasingly less likely to be exposed as college and university studies become increasingly specialized and more focused on professional preparation.

11. John R. Meyer and James M. Gustafson, eds., *The U.S. Business Corporation: An Instituton in Transition* (Cambridge, Mass.: Ballinger Publishing Co., 1988), xiii, 11–20, 79.

12. Roland Robertson, "Church-State Relations and the World System," in Thomas Robbins and Roland Robertson, eds., *Church-State Relations: Tensions and Transitions* (New Brunswick, N.J.: Transition Books, 1987), 45; Roland Robertson and Joann Chirico, "Humanity, Globalization, and Worldwide Religious Resurgence: A Theoretical Exploration," *Sociological Analysis: A Journal in the Sociology of Religion* 46, no. 3 (fall, 1985): 227.

13. See Gordon D. Kaufman, *Theology for a Nuclear Age* (Manchester: Manchester University Press; Philadelphia: Westminster Press, 1985), 16–17.

14. Richard R. Niebuhr, *Experiential Religion* (New York: Harper & Row, 1972), xii–xiii, 1–14.

15. Stackhouse, *Apologia: Contextualization, Globalization, and Mission in Theological Education,* 22.

16. Niklas Luhmann, *The Differentiation of Society,* trans. Stephen Holmes and Charles Larmore (New York: Columbia University Press, 1982), 197.

17. Talcott Parsons, *The System of Societies* (Englewood Cliffs, N.J.: Prentice-Hall, 1971), 12–13.

18. Robert N. Bellah, et al., *Habits of the Heart: Individualism and Commitment in American Life* (New York: Harper & Row, 1986), 55–84.

19. Wade Clark Roof, *Community and Commitment: Religious Plausibility in a Liberal Protestant Church* (New York: Pilgrim Press, 1978), 212.

20. Similar effects come with the differentiation of other social roles, including political ones. Thus, Niklas Luhmann writes in *The Differentiation of Society*, 141, "Whether politicians or civil servants are rich or poor, into which families they marry, to which gods they pray, which circles they frequent, with whom they are friends or neighbors, with whom they have been prisoners of war, and to whom they owe money—all this is not supposed to be of any structural importance."

21. The same or similar skills are also necessary for modern secular civil service. See note 13 above.

22. Ernest Gellner, *Nations and Nationalism* (Ithaca, N.Y.: Cornell University Press, 1983), 12, 35–38, 110.

23. Robertson, "Church-State Relations and the World System," 45–46.

24. Charles Taylor, *Sources of the Self: The Making of Modern Identity* (Cambridge, Mass.: Harvard University Press, 1989), 12.

25. I think this fits with what B. A. Gerrish calls the Reformed habit of mind. Gerrish distinguishes five notes of that habit, among them an appropriate deference or respect for the past tradition, as well as an openness to wisdom and insight wherever it may be found. "Tradition in the Modern World: The Reformed Habit of Mind," T. V. Moore Lecture at San Francisco Theological Seminary on April 20, 1990.

26. A sign of hope in this regard is the response to a number of resolutions concerning the "Re-Imagining . . . God, the Community, the Church . . ." conference in the report of the Assembly Committee on General Assembly Council Review of the 206th General Assembly (1994), Presbyterian Church (U.S.A.). The "Re-Imagining Conference," as it has come to be called in Presbyterian circles, was an ecumenical gathering held in Minneapolis, November 4–7, 1993. The majority who attended were women. The conference included dialogue and discussion around the theme of re-imagining. Some statements made by persons in attendance, as well as some of the worship rituals, pressed the limits of the Reformed theological tradition. There followed a rather fierce controversy between conservative and progressive elements in the Presbyterian Church. In response, the report affirms that "theology matters." It affirms the historic commitments of the Presbyterian Church to ecumenical, cross-cultural, and interfaith conversations in which our theologies may be challenged and stretched. It also affirms Presbyterian confessional standards, as well as "the use of imagination as a part of our theological task" (12-12, 12-14 to 12-15).

27. See Ronald F. Theimann, *Constructing a Public Theology: The Church in a Pluralistic Culture* (Louisville: Westminster/John Knox Press, 1991), 41–42.

Chapter 3. A Theology for Reforming Protestantism

1. Gordon D. Kaufman, *Theology for a Nuclear Age* (Manchester: Manchester University Press; Philadelphia: Westminster Press, 1985), 54–55.

2. H. Richard Niebuhr, *Radical Monotheism and Western Culture with Supplementary Essays* (New York: Harper & Row, 1960), 32–33.

3. Dietrich Bonhoeffer, *Ethics,* ed. Eberhard Bethge, trans. Neville Horton Smith (New York: The Macmillan Co., 1955), 188–95.

4. There obviously are important biblical passages where some persons and communities are indeed regarded as alien or foreign, for example, Deut. 12:2–3, Prov. 1–9, 1 John 3:10. Reforming theology learns much from these passages concerning faith in God, idolatry, true wisdom, and sin. However, its universalistic bias has roots in other passages that depict one world in relation to God. This certainly is the sense one gets from the creation story in Genesis 1:1–2:3 and Psalm 24:1, the idea that all things come into being through the Word of God (John 1:3), and the claim that, in Christ, all things hold together (Col. 1:17). It also comes through in certain Pauline ideas about the unity of all humanity in Christ, for example, Rom. 5:18, Gal. 3:28 "There is no longer Jew or Greek, there is no longer slave or free, there is no longer male and female; for all of you are one in Christ Jesus." There surely is little theological reason to insist that some others are ultimately foreign after that.

Again, that God is the power at work in all of the interdependent interrelations of things is part of the point of God's speeches from the whirlwind in Job 38:1–42:6. It becomes apparent there that God is concerned not only with humans but with all creatures. God's interrelatedness with all things in their interrelations constitutes an all-encompassing ecology. Carol A. Newsom says things like this in her comments on Job in *The Women's Bible Commentary,* ed. Carol A. Newsom and Sharon H. Ringe (Louisville: Westminster/John Knox Press, 1992), 135–36. Similar themes are prominent in Psalm 104.

5. George Rupp tries to combine an incarnational motif that affirms this world as the locus of God's presence, power, and goodness with an apocalyptic motif that points toward a continuing tension between redemption and the present shape of things and so the need for the criticism and reshaping of historical life. George Rupp, *Commitment and Community* (Minneapolis: Fortress Press, 1989), 38–39. Paul D. Hanson argues that tension between the visionary and the real, as well as a drive toward criticism and the reordering of life are important features of apocalyptic. Paul D. Hanson, *The Dawn of Apocalyptic: The Historical and Sociological Roots of Jewish Apocalyptic Eschatology* (Philadelphia: Fortress Press, 1975), 30–31, 412–13.

6. William Ames, *The Marrow of Theology,* trans. and ed. John Dykstra Eusden (Boston: Pilgrim Press, 1968), 77.

7. See Mary Douglas, *Natural Symbols: Explorations in Cosmology* (New York: Vintage Books, Random House, 1973), 139–52.

8. R. Jeffrey Smith and John Goshko, "Ill-Fated Iraq Policy Originated Shortly after Bush Took Office," *The Washington Post* (27 June 1992) sec. A, p. 7.

9. Robert Hughes, "The Fraying of America," *Time Magazine* 139, no. 5 (3 February 1992): 44–45.

10. See, for example, George A. Lindbeck, *The Nature of Doctrine: Religion and Theology in a Postliberal Age* (Philadelphia: Westminster Press, 1984), 117–18, 131. Much of my argument in this section amounts to an attempt to restate Lindbeck's notion of intelligibility as "skill" in terms of my own proposal. I am also indebted

to work done in the philosophy of science. See Richard J. Bernstein, *Beyond Objectivism and Relativism: Science, Hermeneutics, and Praxis* (Philadelphia: University of Pennsylvania Press, 1988); and Harold I. Brown, *Perception, Theory, and Commitment: The New Philosophy of Science* (Chicago: University of Chicago Press, 1977). I discuss these matters directly in "Between Foundationalism and Nonfoundationalism," *Affirmation* 4, no. 2 (fall 1991): 27–47.

11. Jon D. Levenson, *Sinai and Zion: An Entry into the Jewish Bible* (Minneapolis: Winston Press, 1985), 206–9, notes the subtle and mutually correcting interplay between Sinaitic and Zionistic traditions concerning the covenant in Psalm 50 and in Jeremiah 7:1–15. Among other things, he shows that the universalistic dimension of the covenant is enhanced when Sinaitic traditions are translated into Zion, whereas in Jeremiah's temple speech, Sinai undermines the priestly tendency of the Zion traditions to an otherworldliness that evades responsibility.

12. Jonathan Edwards, *Charity and Its Fruits: Christian Love as Manifested in the Heart and Life,* ed. Tryon Edwards (Edinburgh and Carlisle, Pa.: The Banner of Truth Trust, 1982), 18–19.

13. H. Richard Niebuhr, *Christ and Culture* (New York: Harper & Row, 1951), 15–29.

14. H. Richard Niebuhr, *Radical Monotheism and Western Culture,* 42.

15. James M. Gustafson, *Ethics from a Theocentric Perspective,* vol. 1, *Theology and Ethics* (Chicago: University of Chicago Press, 1981), 276.

16. Paul Lewis, "Right Affections: Pointers from Thomas Aquinas and Jonathan Edwards," a paper delivered at the annual meeting of The Society of Christian Ethics (1992), 34 pages.

17. *The Works of Jonathan Edwards,* revised and corrected by Edward Hickman (Edinburgh and Carlisle, Pa.: The Banner of Truth Trust, 1974), 1: 122, 126 (The Nature of True Virtue); 1: 281–82 (Treatise on Religious Affections).

18. *The Journal of John Woolman and a Plea for the Poor* (Gloucester, Mass.: Peter Smith, 1971), 235.

19. H. Richard Niebuhr, *The Responsible Self: An Essay in Christian Moral Philosophy* (New York: Harper & Row, 1963), 86–89, 101, 106–7; *Christian Ethics: Sources of the Living Tradition,* ed. Waldo Beach and H. Richard Niebuhr, 2d ed. (New York: Wiley & Sons, 1973), 34–35.

20. Richard R. Niebuhr, *Experiential Religion* (New York: Harper & Row, 1972), 58–65, 105; idem, *Streams of Grace: Studies of Jonathan Edwards, Samuel Taylor Coleridge and William James* (Kyoto: Doshisha University Press, 1983), 9–10, 119.

21. Gordon D. Kaufman, *Theology for a Nuclear Age,* 61.

22. *A Testament of Hope: The Essential Writings of Martin Luther King Jr.,* ed. James Melvin Washington (San Francisco: Harper & Row, 1986), 12, 87, 122.

23. *The Works of Jonathan Edwards,* ed. E. Hickman, 1: 122 (The Nature of True Virtue); *The Journal of John Woolman, and a Plea for the Poor,* 235; H. Richard Niebuhr, *The Kingdom of God in America* (New York: Harper & Row, 1959), 156; idem, *Radical Monotheism and Western Culture,* 34; idem, *The Responsible Self,* 87–88.

24. Gustafson, *Ethics from a Theocentric Perspective,* vol. 1, *Theology and Ethics,* 158–59.

25. Julian N. Hartt, *Theological Method and Imagination* (New York: Seabury Press, 1977), 77, 10.

Chapter 4. Responsible Realism and Creative Responsibility

1. John Calvin, *Institutes of the Christian Religion*, ed. John T. McNeill, trans. Ford Lewis Battles (Philadelphia: Westminster Press, 1960), II, i, 10.

2. Paul Tillich, *Systematic Theology*, vol. 2, *Existence and the Christ* (Chicago: University of Chicago Press, 1957), 47.

3. Gustavo Gutiérrez, *A Theology of Liberation: History, Politics, and Salvation*, 15th Anniv. Ed., rev., with a new introduction, trans. Sister Caridad Inda and John Eagleson (Maryknoll, N.Y.: Orbis Books, 1988), 100–101, 103.

4. Leonardo Boff, *Liberating Grace*, trans. John Drury (Maryknoll, N.Y.: Orbis Books, 1979), 4–5.

5. Mary Potter Engel, "Evil, Sin, and Violation of the Vulnerable," in *Lift Every Voice: Constructing Theologies from the Underside*, ed. Susan Brooks Thistlethwaite and Mary Potter Engel (San Francisco: Harper & Row, 1990), 164. See also Susan Brooks Thistlethwaite's reflections on the differences that both gender and race make in understanding sin and its characteristic forms in her *Sex, Race, and God: Christian Feminism in Black and White* (New York: Crossroad Publishing Co., 1989), 77–91.

6. James M. Gustafson, *Ethics from a Theocentric Perspective*, vol. 1, *Theology and Ethics* (Chicago: University of Chicago Press, 1981), 293–306.

7. Jonathan Edwards, *The Works of Jonathan Edwards*, ed. E. Hickman, 2 vols. (Carlisle: Banner of Truth Trust, 1974), 1:149–51.

8. I agree with Reinhold Niebuhr that Christianity is mythologically profound. See his *Reflections on the End of an Era* (New York: Charles Scribner's Sons, 1934), 290. On Niebuhr's understanding and use of myth, see Dennis P. McCann, *Christian Realism and Liberation Theology: Practical Theologies in Creative Conflict* (Maryknoll, N.Y.: Orbis Books, 1981), 37–50; and Harlan Beckley, *Passion for Justice: Retrieving the Legacies of Walter Rauschenbusch, John A. Ryan, and Reinhold Niebuhr* (Louisville: Westminster/John Knox Press, 1992), 256–64. On original sin, see Reinhold Niebuhr, *The Nature and Destiny of Man: A Christian Interpretation*, vol. 1, *Human Nature* (New York: Charles Scribner's Sons, 1964), 251–64. Years earlier, Niebuhr wrote that "original sin is not an inherited corruption, but it is an inevitable fact of human existence, the inevitability of which is given by the nature of man's spirituality." *An Interpretation of Christian Ethics* (New York: Seabury Press, A Crossroad Book, 1979), 55.

9. Even, and perhaps especially, if we do not read it literally, this is part of the point of Genesis 2–11. Here, the sin of Adam and Eve is presented as the first in a series that not even the deluge can bring to an end. At Babel, God, therefore, is driven to confuse humanity in order to hold their ineradicable tendency in check.

10. Reinhold Niebuhr, *Reflections on the End of an Era*, 290.

11. Leonardo Boff, *Liberating Grace*, 4.

12. *The Works of Jonathan Edwards*, 1:275, 122.

13. Ibid., 1:283.

14. Ibid., 1:xiii. See also H. Richard Niebuhr, *The Kingdom of God in America* (New York: Harper & Row, 1959), 116.

15. *Christian Ethics: Sources of the Living Tradition,* ed. Waldo Beach and H. Richard Niebuhr, 2d ed. (New York: Wiley & Sons, 1973), 34–35.

16. Richard R. Niebuhr, *Streams of Grace: Studies of Jonathan Edwards, Samuel Taylor Coleridge and William James* (Kyoto: Doshisha University Press, 1983), 117.

17. A fuller discussion of Jesus Christ as the one who teaches the truth, embodies the way, and empowers the life can be found in my previous book, *Jesus Christ and Christian Vision* (Minneapolis: Fortress Press, 1989), 73–95.

18. Richard R. Niebuhr, *Streams of Grace,* 119.

19. Horace Bushnell, *The New Life* (London: Richard D. Dickinson, 1885), 69.

20. Reinhold Niebuhr, *Beyond Tragedy: Essays on the Christian Interpretation of History* (New York: Charles Scribner's Sons, 1937), 169.

21. The reference is to the French village of Le Chambon-Sur-Lignon that took in and sheltered 5,000 Jews from the Nazis during World War II. The story is documented in the powerful film, *Weapons of the Spirit,* directed by Pierre Sauvage, Pierre Sauvage Productions, 1988, color, 91 minutes. For information, write to Friends of Le Chambon, 8033 W. Sunset Blvd., Los Angeles, Calif. 90046.

22. Richard R. Niebuhr, *Experiential Religion* (New York: Harper & Row, 1972), 112–13.

23. John Calvin, *Institutes of the Christian Religion,* III, vii, 6.

24. *The Constitution of the Presbyterian Church (U.S.A.), Part I Book of Confessions* (Louisville: Office of the General Assembly, 1991), 4.086.

25. The term is used by Perry Miller to describe elements of Puritan piety in *The New England Mind: The Seventeenth Century* (Boston: Beacon Press, 1961), 18. "Also in the interests of consistency, the Puritans were led to a further deduction: if the creation is ruled by God's will, and His will is itself the norm of justice and equity, the universe must be essentially good. They may be described as cosmic optimists."

26. Jonathan Edwards, *A History of the Work of Redemption,* ed. John F. Wilson, vol. 9, *The Works of Jonathan Edwards,* John E. Smith, gen. ed. (New Haven, Conn.: Yale University Press, 1989), 513, 113, 515.

27. John Calvin, *Institutes of the Christian Religion,* I, xiv, 3.

28. Frederick Denison Maurice, *Theological Essays* (London: James Clarke & Co.,1957), 323.

29. H. Richard Niebuhr, *Faith on Earth: An Enquiry into the Structure of Human Faith,* ed. Richard R. Niebuhr (New Haven, Conn.: Yale University Press, 1989), 100.

30. H. Richard Niebuhr, *The Responsible Self: An Essay in Christian Moral Philosophy* (New York: Harper & Row, 1963), 177, 142. See also, idem, *Faith on Earth,* 97. "This is the resurrection of Christ which we can experience. In and through his betrayal, denial and forsakenness, we are given the assurance that God keeps his promises. In and through and despite this we hear him, we read him, we accept him as God's word to us that God is faithful and true, that he does not

desire the death of the sinner, that he is leading his kingdom to victory over all evil, that we shall not die but live, that the last word to us is not death without ending, but life everlasting."

31. Consider the following from John Calvin, *Institutes,* III, ii, 2 (p. 545). "We do not obtain salvation either because we are prepared to embrace as true whatever the church has prescribed, or because we turn over to it the task of inquiring and knowing. But we do so when we know that God is our merciful Father because of reconciliation effected through Christ. . . ." See also *Institutes,* III, ii, 7; and *The Consitution of the Presbyterian Church (U.S.A.): Part I Book of Confessions,* 4.026.

32. *A Testament of Hope: The Essential Writings of Martin Luther King Jr.,* ed. James Melvin Washington (San Francisco: Harper & Row, 1986), 122, 254, 290.

33. King, *A Testament of Hope,* 88.

34. Gordon D. Kaufman, *Theology for a Nuclear Age* (Philadelphia: Westminster Press, 1985), 5.

Chapter 5. The Church In, With, Against, and For the World

1. This is the fundamental respect in which one may speak, as does Juan Luis Segundo, of "Church–World Interdependence." Juan Luis Segundo, S.J., in collaboration with the staff of the Peter Faber Center in Montevideo, Uruguay, *The Community Called Church,* trans. John Drury (Maryknoll, N.Y.: Orbis Books, 1973), 98–112.

2. James Luther Adams, *An Examined Faith: Social Context and Religious Commitment,* edited and introduced by George K. Beach (Boston: Beacon Press, 1991), 187.

3. Wayne A. Meeks, *The First Urban Christians: The Social World of the Apostle Paul* (New Haven, Conn.: Yale University Press, 1983), 79; Martin Hengel, *Property and Riches in the Early Church: Aspects of a Social History of Early Christianity* (Philadelphia: Fortress Press, 1974), 37, 42–46, 65–69. See also Walter Rauschenbusch, *Christianity and the Social Crisis* (Louisville: Westminster/John Knox Press, 1991), 116, 139; James Luther Adams, *On Being Human Religiously: Selected Essays in Religion and Society,* ed. Max L. Stackhouse (Boston: Beacon Press, 1976), 64.

4. John Calvin, *Institutes of the Christian Religion,* trans. Ford Lewis Battles, ed. John T. McNeill (Philadelphia: Westminster Press, 1960), 4.1.3.

5. *John Wesley,* ed. Albert C. Outler (New York: Oxford University Press, 1964), 312, 315.

6. Thus, when Calvin turned to the church, he not only called it the communion of saints, he also discussed "its government, orders, and power." *Institutes,* 4.1.3.

I think the basic point is also biblically noncontroversial. Without it, surely one would have difficulty making sense of passages like Acts 7; 1 Cor. 12:27–31; 2 Cor. 8–9; and Titus 1:5–9. Joseph A. Fitzmyer points out that the word *ekklesia* is used in ways that refer both to local congregations and a church that transcends local barriers. "Pauline Theology," *The New Jerome Biblical Commentary,* ed. Raymond E. Brown, S.S., Joseph A. Fitzmyer, S.J., and Roland E. Murphy,

O. Carm. (Englewood Cliffs, N.J.: Prentice-Hall, 1990), 79: 149–56. An important passage is Eph. 2:19–22. After claiming that Christ is the head of the *ekklesia*, the passage reads as follows:

> So then you are no longer strangers and aliens, but you are citizens with the saints and also members of the household of God, built upon the foundation of the apostles and prophets, with Christ Jesus himself as the cornerstone. In him the whole structure is joined together and grows into a holy temple in the Lord; in whom you also are built together spiritually into a dwelling place for God.

See also Ernest Best, *Ephesians* (Sheffield: Sheffield Academic Press, 1993), 65–73. Raymond Brown notes uses of *ekklesia* in the late New Testament ecclesiology that move in the direction of a more regularized church structure. See "Early Church," in *The New Jerome Biblical Commentary*, 80:27–29. On the church as a building, see Eberhard Faust, *Pax Christi et Pax Caesaris: Religiongeschichtliche, traditionsgeschichtliche und sozialgeschichtliche Studien zum Epheserbrief* (Freiburg, Gottingen: Universitatsverlag Freiburg, Vandenhoeck & Ruprecht, 1993), s.197–207.

7. H. Richard Niebuhr, *The Purpose of the Church and Its Ministry* (New York: Harper & Row, 1956), 21–22.

8. See Karl Barth, *Church Dogmatics*, trans. G. W. Bromiley (Edinburgh: T. & T. Clark, 1956), 4/1: 79, 82, 157.

9. In a similar manner, Leonardo Boff notes that "the reality of the Kingdom is that which defines both the world and the church." *Church: Charism and Power, Liberation Theology and the Institutional Church*, trans. John W. Diercksmeier (New York: Crossroad Publishing Company, 1985), 1.

10. Dietrich Bonhoeffer, *Ethics*, ed. Eberhard Bethge (New York: The Macmillan Co., 1955), 195.

11. H. Richard Niebuhr, *The Purpose of the Church*, 37.

12. Ibid.

13. See, for example, *The Churches Survey Their Task: The Report of the Conference at Oxford, July 1937, on Church, Community, and State,* (London: George Alen & Unwin Ltd., 1937), 82, 204.

14. See Karl Barth, *Church Dogmatics*, ed. G.W. Bromiley and T. F. Torrance (Edinburgh: T. & T. Clark, 1962), 4/3.2: 774, 779.

15. Gustavo Gutiérrez, *A Theology of Liberation: History, Politics, and Salvation*, 15th Anniv. Ed. (Maryknoll, N.Y.: Orbis Books, 1988), 9.

16. James B. Nelson, *Moral Nexus: Ethics of Christian Identity and Community* (Philadephia: Westminster Press, 1971), 217–19.

17. So, for example, one may hope that an ethnically diverse and truly "world church" will find it more difficult simply to align itself and its interpretations of the gospel with the inordinately partial interests of one particular group or region.

18. See Martin Hengel, *Between Jesus and Paul: Studies in the Earliest History of Christianity* (Philadelphia: Fortress Press, 1983), 48–64. Hengel writes that "The irresistible expansion of Christian faith in the Mediterranean world during the

first 150 years is the scarlet thread running through any history of primitive Christianity" (48).

19. The basic story was outlined by Ernst Troeltsch in *The Social Teaching of the Christian Churches,* trans. Olive Wyon (Louisville: Westminster/John Knox Press, 1992), 656–91.

20. Barbara Brown Zikmund, "Winning Ordination for Women in Mainstream Protestant Churches," *Women and Religion in America, Volume 3: 1900–1968,* ed. Rosemary Radford Ruether and Rosemary Skinner Keller (San Francisco: Harper & Row, 1986), 339–348. On economic, educational, and political conditions that have helped make the women's movement possible, see Janet Saltzman Chafetz and Anthony Gary Dworkin, *Female Revolt: Women's Movements in World and Historical Perspective* (Totowa, N.J.: Rowman & Allanheld, Publishers, 1986), 101–104. On retrieving the participation of women in our own traditions, see *Women and Religion in America, Volume 1: The Nineteenth Century Background,* ed. Rosemary Radford Ruether and Rosemary Skinner Keller (San Francisco: Harper & Row, 1981), viii–x.

21. Reinhold Niebuhr, *Love and Justice: Selections from the Shorter Writings of Reinhold Niebuhr,* ed. D. B. Robertson (Louisville: Westminster/John Knox Press, 1992), 97.

22. See *Black Theology: A Documentary History, 1966–1979,* ed. Gayraud S. Wilmore and James H. Cone (Maryknoll, N.Y.: Orbis Books, 1979), 135; Major J. Jones, *The Color of God: The Concept of God in Afro-American Thought* (Macon, Ga.: Mercer University Press, 1987), 2. On the need for repentant self-examination with respect to race, see also Reinhold Niebuhr, *Love and Justice,* 128–29, 153. A troubling feature of Niebuhr's call for repentance in this regard is that he connects it with an unsatisfying gradualism.

23. Robert L. Spaeth, "Trial and Error: Galileo and the Church," *This World: A Journal of Religion and Public Life* 20 (winter 1988): 104–113.

24. See Lisa Sowle Cahill, "Sexual Ethics: A Feminist Perspective," *Interpretation* 49, no. 1 (January 1995): 14–15.

25. These are among the sorts of questions often underscored by an older Puritan theology of practical divinity. See Chapter 6. See also the emphasis on mutuality, reciprocity, and relationship in Gary David Comstock, *Gay Theology without Apology* (Cleveland: Pilgrim Press, 1993), 127–40.

26. Martin Luther regarded repentance and knowledge of sin as the beginning of salvation. *Luther's Works,* vol. 26, *Lectures on Galatians 1535,* ed. Jaroslav Pelikan and Walter A. Hansen, trans. Jaroslav Pelikan (St. Louis: Concordia Publishing House, 1963), 131–32.

27. Hans Küng, *The Church,* trans. Ray and Rosaleen Ockender (New York: Sheed and Ward, 1967), 99–100.

28. Eberhard Busch, *Karl Barth: His Life from Letters and Autobiographical Texts,* trans. John Bowden (Philadelphia: Fortress Press, 1976), 226.

29. Robert M. Grant, *From Augustine to Constantine: The Thrust of the Christian Movement into the Roman World* (New York: Harper & Row, 1970), 86; John Fox, *A Universal History of Christian Martyrdom: From the Birth of Our Blessed Saviour to the Latest Periods of Persecution* (Philadelphia: Key, Meilke & Biddle, 1832), 5. See also W. H. C. Frend, *Martyrdom and Persecution in the Early Church: A Study*

of a Conflict from the Maccabees to Donatus (Oxford: Basil Blackwell, 1965), 268–302.

30. Wi Jo Kang, *Religion and Politics in Korea under Japanese Rule,* Studies in Asian Thought and Religion 5 (Lewiston, N.Y.: The Edwin Mellen Press, 1987), 25.

31. Ibid., 35–39. See also Donald N. Clark, *Christianity in Modern Korea* (Lanham, Md.: University Press of America, 1986), 13–14.

32. See Brian H. Smith, "Churches and Human Rights in Latin America," in *Churches and Politics in Latin America,* ed. Daniel H. Levine (Beverly Hills, Calif.: Sage Publications, 1979, 1980), 156, 183–84.

33. Mary Craig, *Candles in the Dark: Six Modern Martyrs* (London: Hodder and Stoughton, 1984), 203.

34. I think we always have to ask whether, under certain circumstances, we have not misused this affirmation in order to support inappropriate hopes or even overly optimistic hopes. Surely, however, even a robust account of Christian hope need not deny both the actuality and the further possibility of massive suffering. Consider the following exhortation in "A Letter to the Catholics of Chile" (17 December 1982) by the Chilean bishops. "Despite all the negative signs, we urge you to hope. Hope is an essentially Christian virtue. It is grounded in our certainty that in the death of Jesus Christ God has assumed all our sufferings and failures and that in the resurrection of Jesus God has overcome all evil. In God's hands life is mightier than death." Quoted by Gustavo Gutiérrez, *We Drink from Our Own Wells: The Spiritual Journey of a People,* trans. Matthew J. O'Connell (Maryknoll, N.Y.: Orbis Books, 1984), 120.

35. See Martin Hengel, *Property and Riches in the Early Church: Aspects of a Social History of Early Christianity* (Philadelphia: Fortress Press, 1974), 42–43; Wayne A. Meeks, *The First Urban Christians: The Social World of the Apostle Paul* (New Haven, Conn.: Yale University Press, 1983), 63–64, 81, 161; *The Moral World of the First Christians* (Philadelphia: Westminster Press, 1986), 113. See Elisabeth Schussler-Fiorenza, *In Memory of Her: A Feminist Reconstruction of Christian Origins* (New York: Crossroad Publishing Co., 1984), 205–18. If Schussler-Fiorenza is correct about the earliest Jesus movement as a "discipleship of equals," then this will be another important instance of the church embodying new possibilities.

36. C. Eric Lincoln and Lawrence H. Mamiya, *The Black Church in the African American Experience* (Durham, N.C.: Duke University Press, 1990), 212. The civil rights struggle during the 1960s was, among other things, the fight of a minority movement, closely tied to black churches, for a new American society. That seems abundantly clear to me, anyway, when I read things like Chapter 11, "Baptism on Wheels," and Chapter 12, "The Summer of Freedom Rides," in Taylor Branch, *The Parting of the Waters: America in the King Years, 1954–1963* (New York: Simon and Schuster, 1988), 413–91.

37. *A Testament of Hope: The Essential Writings of Martin Luther King Jr.,* ed. James Melvin Washington (San Francisco: Harper & Row, 1986), 5–9, 12, 18, 20, 41–42.

38. Scott Mainwaring, "Brazil: The Catholic Church and the Popular Movement in Noya Iguacu, 1974–1985," in *Religion and Political Conflict in Latin Amer-*

ica, ed. Daniel H. Levine (Chapel Hill: University of North Carolina Press, 1986), 148.

39. Gustavo Gutiérrez, *We Drink from Our Own Wells,* 115.

40. Richard Baxter, *Gildas Salvianus: The Reformed Pastor,* edited and introduced by John T. Wilkenson (London: The Epworth Press, 1950), 16, 71–73, 172.

41. These are difficult and complicated questions that are intertwined with virtually every aspect of society in Richmond, Virginia. They confront me, as well as many of my colleagues and friends, and I will not attempt to resolve them in an endnote.

In general, however, we note that congregations can respond to many of the difficulties surrounding public education in the United States today in many different ways. Some may respond with complete silence; others by dissociating themselves from the public schools. Still others may endeavor to lift up the goal of high quality education for every student, help parents impart to their children a love of learning as an expression of service to God, restore a sense of calling to teaching as a profession, and encourage public involvement in education. In short, they may find "a communal role to play in grounding and building a fellowship whose ethos supports education and learning." Raymond R. Roberts, "A Pastor's View: Is Public Education Hopeless?" *The Presbyterian Outlook* (26 April 1993): 8.

Chapter 6. The Sanctification of the Ordinary

1. I have also discussed some of these themes in "Recovering Faithfulness in Our Callings," *Spiritual Traditions for the Contemporary Church,* ed. Robin Maas and Gabriel O'Donnell, O.P. (Nashville: Abingdon Press, 1990), 222–34.

2. Luther tended to view marriage as a divine estate to be contrasted with the often false spirituality of the monastic estate. See "The Order of Marriage for Common Pastors," *Luther's Works,* vol. 53, *Liturgy and Hymns,* ed. Ulrich S. Leupold, Helmut T. Lehmann, gen. ed. (Philadephia: Fortress Press, 1965), 112. He wrote that "when a father goes ahead and washes diapers or performs some other mean task for his child . . . God with all his angels is smiling—not because he is doing diapers, but because he is doing so in Christian faith." Again, the estate of marriage "together with all its works, however insignificant, is pleasing to God and precious in his sight. These works are indeed insignificant and mean; yet it is from them that we all trace our origin, we have all had need of them. Without them no man would exist. For this reason they are pleasing to God, who has so ordained them and thereby graciously cares for us like a kind and loving mother." "The Estate of Marriage," *Luther's Works,* vol. 45, *The Christian in Society,* ed. Walther I. Brandt, Helmut T. Lehmann, gen. ed. (Philadelphia: Muhlenberg Press, 1962), 40, 42–43.

3. On the general importance of these developments, see Charles Taylor, *Sources of the Self: The Making of the Modern Identity* (Cambridge, Mass.: Harvard University Press, 1989), 20–23, 216–18. On Luther's understanding of vocation, see Gustaf Wingren, *Luther on Vocation,* trans. Carl C. Rasmussen (Philadelphia: Muhlenberg Press, 1957), viii–ix; and on his judgments about marriage and

celibacy, see Lisa Sowle Cahill, *Between the Sexes: Foundations for a Christian Ethics of Sexuality* (Philadelphia: Fortress Press and New York: Paulist Press, 1985), 128–31. On the importance of Luther's conception of vocation for understanding work and labor in Western society, see Emil Brunner, *Christianity and Civilization, Second Part: Specific Problems* (New York: Charles Scribner's Sons, 1949), 61–63. See also Paul Ramsey, *Basic Christian Ethics* (Louisville: Westminster/John Knox Press, 1993), 153–54. Ramsey's chapter on "Christian Vocation" is a particularly important discussion of that theme by a noted Protestant ethicist.

4. Robert L. Calhoun, "Work and Vocation in Christian History," in *Work and Vocation: A Christian Discussion,* edited and introduced by John Oliver Nelson (New York: Harper & Brothers, 1954), 108.

5. Quoted from William Perkins, *Works,* in Charles H. George and Katherine George, *The Protestant Mind of the English Reformation* (Princeton: Princeton University Press, 1961), 139. See Charles Taylor, *Sources of the Self,* 224, where the quotation is put to much the same use as I have made of it here.

6. *The Westminster Directory,* edited with an introduction and notes by Thomas Leishman (Edinburgh: William Blackwood and Sons, 1901), 16. See also the opening prayers in Richard Baxter's Reformed Liturgy, *The Practical Works of Richard Baxter,* vol. 1 (Ligonier, Pa.: Soli Deo Gloria, 1990), 922.

7. James M. Gustafson discusses the senses of dependence, gratitude, repentance, obligation, possibility, and direction in *Can Ethics Be Christian?* (Chicago: University of Chicago Press, 1975), 91–114.

8. See, for example, *Venite Adoremus II: Prayers and Services for Students* (Geneva: World Student Christian Federation, n.d.), 12–16.

9. *The Book of Common Worship* (Philadelphia: The Board of Christian Education of the United Presbyterian Church in the United States of America, 1946), 11–15.

10. See, for example, *The Book of Common Prayer and Administration of the Sacraments and Other Rites and Ceremonies of the Church According to the Use of the Protestant Episcopal Church in the United States of America* (New York: Harper & Brothers, 1952), 17–18, 32, 35–46, 55–57; *The Hymnal of the United Church of Christ* (Philadelphia: United Church Press, 1974), 17–18, 25–26; *Book of Common Worship,* Presbyterian Church (U.S.A.) and Cumberland Presbyterian Church (Louisville: Westminster/John Knox Press, 1993), 795–802, 816–37.

11. *Liturgies of the Western Church,* selected and introduced by Bard Thompson (New York: The World Publishing Co., 1962), 197–98, 269–71, 386–87. John Wesley retained Cranmer's practice in his directions for the worship of Methodists in North America. See *John Wesley's Sunday Service of the Methodists in North America,* with an introduction by James F. White (The United Methodist Publishing House, 1984), 125–27. See also *The Practical Works of Richard Baxter,* vol. 1, 923.

12. *The Book of Common Worship* (1946), 115–18. In the Presbyterian *Book of Common Worship* (1993), 28, 57, the Commandments are one of a number of meditative preparations for worship, and they may also be said following a Declaration of Forgiveness.

13. See Robert Lowry Calhoun, *God and the Day's Work* (New York: Association Press, 1943), 7–16. Richard R. Niebuhr includes an illuminating discus-

sion of faithfulness in his *Experiential Religion* (New York: Harper & Row, 1972), 25, 36–50. Geoffrey Wainwright makes some important remarks about glory and communion with God, as well as the "oscillation between worship and ethics" in *Doxology: The Praise of God in Worship, Doctrine, and Life* (New York: Oxford University Press, 1980), 16–23, 399–434. I especially like the following sentences from p. 10. "I see Christian worship, doctrine, and life as conjoined in a common 'upwards' and 'forwards' direction towards God and the achievement of his purpose, which includes human salvation. They intend God's praise. His glory is that he is already present and within to enable our transformation into his likeness, which means participation in himself and his kingdom."

14. Gustaf Wingren, *Luther on Vocation*, 4–5.

15. John Cotton, "Christian Calling," in *The American Puritans: Their Prose and Poetry*, ed. Perry Miller (Garden City, N.Y.: Doubleday Anchor Books, Doubleday & Company, 1956), 173, 176.

16. "A Treatise of the Vocations or Callings of Men," in *The Works of William Perkins*, introduced and edited by Ian Breward (Appleford, UK: The Sutton Courtenay Press, 1970), 446–47.

17. Ibid., 447–48.

18. *John Calvin: Treatises Against the Anabaptists and Against the Libertines*, ed. and trans. Benjamin W. Farley (Grand Rapids, Mich.: Baker Books, 1988), 278.

19. *The Works of William Perkins*, ed. Ian Breward, 449.

20. John Cotton, "Christian Calling," *The American Puritans*, 174.

21. *The Works of William Perkins*, ed. Ian Breward, 451.

22. Ibid., 451–54.

23. Ibid., 449, 455.

24. Ibid., 456.

25. Ibid.

26. Ibid., 456–57.

27. Ibid., 457.

28. *The Practical Works of Richard Baxter*, vol. 1, pp. 3, 8. Max Weber claimed that Baxter stands out among writers of Puritan ethics and that "his *Christian Directory* is the most complete compendium of Puritan ethics." From *The Protestant Ethic and the Spirit of Capitalism*, trans. Talcott Parsons (New York: Charles Scribner's Sons, 1958), 155–56.

29. Richard Baxter, *A Christian Directory*, 62.

30. Ibid., 1, 394, 547, 737.

31. Ibid., 395, 400.

32. Ibid., 431.

33. Ibid., 431–38.

34. Ibid., 438, 440, 447.

35. Ibid., 449–54. On the authority proper to wives within their households, see pp. 439, 449–57. Amanda Porterfield discusses both the indirect and direct authority of Puritan women in *Female Piety in Puritan New England: The Emergence of Religious Humanism* (New York: Oxford University Press, 1992), 87–95. One of her points is that their indirect authority was sometimes helped by the emotional dependence of Puritan husbands on their wives. Among other things,

this may be a result of the Puritan emphasis on mutuality and companionate relationship that comes through in Baxter's text as well.

36. *The Practical Works of Richard Baxter,* vol. 1, 922–43.

37. Ibid., 547.

38. Ibid., 737–71.

39. Ibid., 771–72.

40. "Whether Soldiers, Too, Can Be Saved," *Luther: Selected Political Writings,* edited and introduced by J. M. Porter (Philadelphia: Fortress Press, 1974), 102.

41. *Account of Our Religion, Doctrine and Faith Given by Peter Rideman of the Brothers Whom Men Call Hutterians* (Rifton, N.Y.: Plough Publishing House, 1970), 107.

42. Richard Baxter, *A Christian Directory,* 740, 743, 775.

43. *Luther: Selected Political Writings,* 117, 119.

44. Baxter, *A Christian Directory,* 776. A stews is a brothel.

45. Ibid., 778.

46. Ibid., 777. Compare this with the following lines of Martin Luther. "To sum up, we must, in thinking about a soldier's office, not concentrate on the killing, burning, striking, hitting, seizing, etc. This is what children with their limited and restricted vision see when they regard a doctor as a sawbones who amputates, but do not see that he does this only to save the whole body." *Luther: Selected Political Writings,* 103.

47. Baxter, *A Christian Directory,* 778.

48. See, for example, Eric Mount, Jr.'s book *Professional Ethics in Context: Institutions, Images and Empathy* (Louisville: Westminster/John Knox Press, 1990).

49. See Patricia Voydanoff, "Work and Family Relationships," *Family Relations: Challenges for the Future,* ed. Timothy H. Brubaker (Newbury Park, Calif.: Sage Publications, 1993), 98–111.

50. Wade Clark Roof, *A Generation of Seekers: The Spiritual Journeys of the Baby Boom Generation* (San Francisco: HarperSan Francisco, 1993), 200.

51. Philip Culbertson, "Explaining Men," *Sexuality and the Sacred: Sources for Theological Reflection,* ed. James B. Nelson and Sandra P. Longfellow (Louisville: Westminster/John Knox Press, 1994), 184, 192. Culbertson also writes of changing "how men's traditional sex-stereotyping heritage imprisons them." Others write of the burdens that boys carry with them as a result of their experiences of "their fathers as rejecting, incompetent, or absent." See Samuel Osherson, *Finding Our Fathers: The Unfinished Business of Manhood* (New York: Free Press, 1986), 3.

52. See, for example, Jack O. Balswick and Judith K. Balswick, *The Family: A Christian Perspective on the Contemporary Home* (Grand Rapids, Mich.: Baker Book House, 1989), 11, 168. The Balswicks, who by most measures are theologically rather conservative, intend to present "an integrated view of contemporary family life which is based upon social-science research, clinical insights, and biblical truths." Nonetheless, they also write as follows: "The current clash between the traditional and modern definitions of gender roles confuses women and men alike. The anxiety produced tempts many Christians to react defensively against the current redefinition. But the present situation should be viewed as an opportunity—an opportunity for both females and males to become more fully

developed human beings as God intended. Such change will benefit children, families, society, and the individual men and women themselves." See also Patricia Voydanoff, "Work and Family Relationships," in *Family Relations: Challenges for the Future,* 111.

53. This last question, which has become increasingly important for the churches, is one that the Balswicks also mention, and without the expected rush to judgment. See their book, *The Family: A Christian Perspective on the Contemporary Home,* 187–89.

54. There is agreement on just about all sides that any discussion of family issues needs to start with some definition of what a family consists of. See, for example, "The Family Man: An Interview by Kim A. Lawton of Gary Bauer," *Christianity Today* 36, no. 27 (9 November 1992): 27. Bauer is president of the conservative Family Research Council.

55. For example, a paper for the Ford Foundation claims that current trends in women's roles and employment "present a great challenge to government policy makers, employers, social service providers, educators, and the families themselves, especially at the lower end of the income spectrum." It also states that "to help define and address this challenge the Ford Foundation is embarking on two related efforts—one directed at creating more choices for families trying to balance work and family responsibilities, and the other addressing the growing need for early childhood services." *Work and Family Responsibilities: Achieving a Balance,* A Program Paper of the Ford Foundation (New York: Ford Foundation, 1989), v.

56. See, for example, Pamela D. Couture, *Blessed Are the Poor? Women's Poverty, Family Policy, and Practical Theology* (Nashville: Abingdon Press, 1991), 159–84.

57. At this point and others in this chapter, I have benefited from Douglas J. Schuurman's very important discussion in "Protestant Vocation Under Assault: Can It Be Salvaged?" *The Annual of the Society of Christian Ethics (1994),* ed. Harlan Beckley (Boston: The Society of Christian Ethics, 1994), 23–52.

58. Karen Lebacqz, "Love Your Enemy: Sex, Power, and Christian Ethics," *The Annual of the Society of Christian Ethics (1990),* 5, 9.

59. Marie M. Fortune, "Violence Against Women: The Way Things Are Is Not the Way They Have To Be," *Sexuality and the Sacred: Sources for Theological Reflection,* ed. James B. Nelson and Sandra P. Longfellow, 326.

60. Lebacqz, "Love Your Enemy," 7.

61. See Alisdair I. McFadyen, *The Call to Personhood: A Christian Theory of the Individual in Social Relationships* (Cambridge, Mass.: Cambridge University Press, 1990), 232–35.

62. M. Scott Peck, M.D. *The Road Less Traveled: A New Psychology of Love, Traditional Values and Spiritual Growth* (New York: Simon & Schuster, 1978), 168; *Spirit Centered Wholeness: Beyond the Psychology of Self,* ed. H. Newton Malony, Michele Papen-Daniels, and Howard Clinebell (Lewiston, Maine: The Edwin Mellen Press, 1988), 15–16. See also Howard Clinebell, *Growth Counseling: Hope-Centered Methods of Actualizing Human Wholeness* (Nashville: Abingdon Press, 1979), 32–36.

63. See James Luther Adams, *Voluntary Associations: Socio-cultural Analyses and*

Theological Interpretation, ed. J. Ronald Engel (Chicago: Exploration Press, 1986), 179.

64. James Luther Adams, *The Prophethood of All Believers,* ed. George K. Beach (Boston: Beacon Press, 1986), 262.

65. Christopher Lasch, *Culture of Narcissism: American Life in an Age of Diminishing Expectations* (New York: Warner Books, 1979), 27–70, 103.

66. See Paul Ramsey, *Basic Christian Ethics* (Louisville: Westminster/John Knox Press, 1993), 160–63.

67. See Emil Brunner's complaints about "the reduction of the human person to a cog in the social machine." Emil Brunner, "And Now?" in *Man's Disorder and God's Design,* The Amsterdam Assembly Series, book 3, *The Church and the Disorder of Society* (New York: Harper & Row, n.d.), 176.

68. See, for example, R. C. Sproul, *Following Christ* (Wheaton, Ill.: Tyndale House Publishers, 1991), 253–72. Sproul writes of "a holy summons to fulfill a task or a responsibility that God has laid upon us." He is also concerned that as persons attempt to discern their particular callings they ask how their gifts, talents, and aspirations (their "motivated abilities") fit with organizational working structures. But aside from a clear rejection of things like prostitution and bank robbing, there is not much of a critical dimension. Sproul's chief concern is that we strive "to be the most honest, patient, hardworking, and committed workers we can be." Similarly, Chuck Colson and Jack Eckerd repeatedly mention that the Protestant notion of vocation means that the individual should use his or her gifts to serve God in the world. But the chief focus reduces to a strong work ethic. Compared to Baxter, the critical dimension is Polyannaish. See Chuck Colson and Jack Eckerd, *Why America Doesn't Work* (Dallas: Word Publishing, 1991), 36–40, 93–94, 129–30.

69. According to Robertson, the "new world order," of which George Bush spoke at the end of the Gulf War and again after the failed coup of August 1991 in the Soviet Union, is an attempt to eliminate national sovereignty and to have the United States turn its defense over to the United Nations. See Pat Robertson, *The New World Order* (Dallas: Word Publishing, 1991), 7, 176–77; idem, *The Turning Tide: The Fall of Liberalism and the Rise of Common Sense* (Dallas: Word Publishing, 1993), 144–45.

70. Robertson, *The New World Order,* 263; idem, *The Turning Tide,* 291.

71. Robertson, *The Turning Tide,* 301. The words in brackets are my own.

72. Robertson, *The New World Order,* 261; idem, *The Turning Tide,* 301–302. As I write, these now have come to include the election of Oliver North to the United States Senate. See *The Richmond Times Dispatch* (10 June 1994), A1.

73. Robertson, *The Turning Point,* 164, 291. Robertson's decision to go to Deuteronomy, Kings, and Chronicles for his understanding of God's blessings and judgments is an interesting one. Among other things, it does not engage psalms from around the time of the collapse of Jerusalem, the Temple, and the dynasty. Israel's political demise here calls into question "the old theories (Deuteronomic and sapiential) that good people prosper and evil people suffer." See Walter Brueggemann, *The Message of the Psalms: A Theological Commentary* (Minneapolis: Augsburg Publishing House, 1984), 169. I would also argue that

Robertson's covenantal utilitarianism is severely undercut by any adequate theology of the cross.

74. Robertson, *The Turning Tide,* 293–94, 300.

75. Ibid., 303. This is also the basic theme at the close of Robertson's *America's Dates with Destiny* (Nashville: Thomas Nelson Publishers, 1986), 297.

76. See his characteristic claim that "the most important social task of Christians is to be nothing less than a community capable of forming people with virtues sufficient to witness to God's truth in the world." Stanley Hauerwas, *A Community of Character: Toward a Constructive Christian Social Ethic* (Notre Dame, Ind.: University of Notre Dame Press, 1981), 3. See also idem, *After Christendom: How the Church Is to Behave if Freedom, Justice, and a Christian Nation Are Bad Ideas* (Nashville: Abingdon Press, 1991), 133–52.

77. Hauerwas, *A Community of Character,* 173; idem, *Naming the Silences: God, Medicine, and the Problem of Suffering* (Grand Rapids, Mich.: William B. Eerdmans Publishing Co., 1990), 118; idem, *Suffering Presence: Theological Reflections on Medicine, the Mentally Handicapped, and the Church* (Notre Dame, Ind.: University of Notre Dame Press, 1986), 39–47, 81–82.

78. Stanley Hauerwas, "Work as Co-Creation: A Critique of a Remarkably Bad Idea," *Co-Creation and Capitalism: John Paul II's Laborem Exercens,* ed. John W. Houck and Oliver F. Williams, C.S.C. (Lanham, Md.: University Press of America, 1983), 48.

79. John Howard Yoder, *The Priestly Kingdom: Social Ethics as Gospel* (Notre Dame, Ind.: University of Notre Dame Press, 1984), 83, 210.

80. Douglas J. Schuurman, "Protestant Vocation Under Assault: Can It Be Salvaged?" *The Annual of the Society of Christian Ethics (1994),* 33.

81. Stanley Hauerwas and William H. Willimon, *Resident Aliens: Life in the Christian Colony* (Nashville: Abingdon Press, 1989), 12, 44–47. It is also part of what lies behind Yoder's complaints about a "Constantinian" Protestant ethic of vocation, "whereby what it means to do the proper thing in one's given social setting is determined by the inherent quasi-autonomous law of that setting, whose demands can be both known and fulfilled independently of any particular rootage of Christian faith." Yoder, *The Priestly Kingdom,* 83.

Index of Authors

173

CPSIA information can be obtained
at www.ICGtesting.com
Printed in the USA
LVHW091746030222
709971LV00006BA/875